To Irene
Pat, John, Linda, Terry and
Jim and families,
Thankyou for enriching my
life, for including me in your
beautiful family, and for
believing in and loving me.

A GIRL CALLED TIM Your
Aussie
daughter
and sister,
June
(2011)

A GIRL CALLED TIM

ESCAPE FROM AN EATING DISORDER HELL

JUNE ALEXANDER

NEW HOLLAND

To George and our children: Shane,
Rohan, Benjamin and Amanda

FOREWORD

In 35 years of knowing June I have come to respect her writing talent and her ability to describe what has happened in her life. She recognises that mental illnesses existing in our community are frequently misunderstood, often misdiagnosed and therefore go untreated. I believe her story will benefit many sufferers of mental illness, together with their families and friends, and provide helpful insights for mental health professionals.

Each story, of course, is personal and this is June's story. As all good clinicians know, it is important for people who are 'suffering'—as a result of life events, which have had major influences—to discuss and deal with their distress. Overcoming anxiety, such as a real or perceived fear of rejection, can be liberating and uplifting.

At times in June's journey, she candidly describes crossing the fine line between being 'well' and 'unwell' mentally—that is, losing all sense of self in an environment where awareness and acknowledgement of mental illness are minimal.

Her story illustrates the importance of early intervention when a child or adolescent develops a mental illness. In June's case, anorexia nervosa. Apart from putting mental, emotional and physical health at risk, the illness can have a severe and long-term impact on relationships.

Psychotherapies, of which there are many kinds, are quite complex. They must be individualised. June appears to have benefited greatly from what has happened to her and has a clear understanding of what has been important to her wellbeing. Perceptions are not necessarily facts, but they are important in the way they influence the sufferer. Discussing things openly and trying to understand them with support is usually very helpful.

The role of psychotherapy and/or medication is at times controversial. Many people with mental illness, and their families, are reluctant to try the addition of pharmacological approaches, but in June's case, it was of great benefit. She freely acknowledges that she needed medication. I recognise that many people are opposed to medication but it is a great aid to many, especially when anxiety levels become too high.

June has researched her subject thoroughly and has spoken to many sufferers, care givers, clinicians and academics. She has recognised that there are many women (usually) aged in their twenties, thirties, forties and beyond, whose lives are inhibited because childhood experiences have gone undetected, untreated or ignored. She is of the opinion that discussing such experiences with an appropriate therapist is beneficial and should be encouraged. Her story illustrates that a trusting relationship, no matter what is going on, is extremely important and that with the right guidance, support and care, quality of life can be enhanced at any age.

The same person cannot help us all and it is important for sufferers to persist until they find the right therapist. As June explains, she tried others before she found what she believed to be the right one, and wants others to take this approach. Do not give up. The hard work and perseverance brings rewards.

Readers will find inspiration in the pages to follow and I wish you well in continuing your own journey.

Graham D. Burrows, AO, KCSJ
BSc, MB, ChB, DPM, MD, DipMHlthSc(Clinical Hypnosis)
DSc, FRANZCP, FRCPsych, MRACMA, FAChAM
Professor of Psychiatry
President of the Mental Health Foundation of Australia

CONTENTS

MY MANY MOVES AROUND
VICTORIA, AUSTRALIA

Stanhope

S

Bendigo

Ballarat

MELBOURN

Geelong

Clifton Springs

Colac

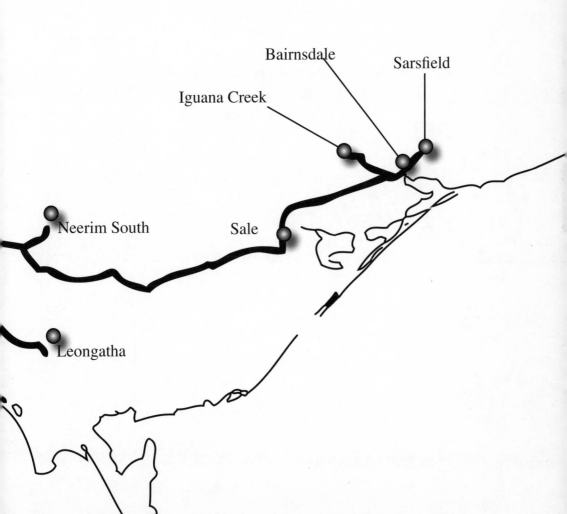

Wangaratta

on

Bairnsdale

Sarsfield

Iguana Creek

Neerim South

Sale

Leongatha

Forgiveness is the fragrance the violet sheds on
the heel that has crushed it.
— Mark Twain

INTRODUCTION

This memoir is about a journey of more than 40 years with two eating disorders.

I was 11 years old, in Grade Six at primary school, when I developed a mental illness called anorexia nervosa. It starved my body and I became emaciated. Eventually I gained weight and everyone, including me, thought I was well again. But anorexia hid inside my brain, and continued to sabotage my mental and emotional health.

My memoir is written almost entirely from my diaries, which I began writing at the age of 12. The process of diary writing was important for, although not aware of this at the time, it helped me stay alive. Many years on, when I summoned the courage to read my journals, I was rewarded with a heightened understanding of self, of the influences and environment that shaped my childhood. This was liberating in moving forward with my present. For decades my life had seemed like a jigsaw puzzle – there were pieces missing. I had gaping holes within. My diary contained clues to help heal and fill those gaps.

Isolated by my illness, my diary was frequently my only friend, my only link with a tiny thread of self. Often, tears soaked the page as I off-loaded loneliness, despair, alienation and rejection. Other times, my writing ran crookedly over the page, thoughts spilling haphazardly out of a mind numb from bingeing or heavily dosed with prescription drugs.

My love of the written word began when I was three. My earliest memory is of sitting cross-legged on the linoleum-covered kitchen floor, turning the pages of the daily newspaper and thinking: 'When I grow up I will read every word on every page'. Even the tiny print in the Birth and Death columns. Words were fascinating. They were full of promise and possibilities. They could describe and express, reveal and reflect.

Their shape, their look, big words, little words, the way they could mix and match to mean and convey different things – was mesmerising. They were friendly. Above all, they were an escape from the outside world. They connected with me and when *I wrote them, they belonged to me.*

When given a small, soft, covered diary for my 12th birthday, the little book quickly became my best friend.

Initially, entries were mostly matter-of-fact observations. I went to school at this time and came home at that time. Expressions of emotion—happy or sad—were rare. As our relationship grew, I began to share my heart and soul. Some entries were cryptic due to concern that my mother read my entries while I was at school and for several months, I resorted to writing entries in shorthand, to defy her curiosity.

Reading my diaries, from age 12 to 55, was cathartic and often scary.

I felt I was tumbling back in time, re-living an arduous journey to regain my life and be 'normal'. I felt I was climbing my mountain all over again.

Almost a year had passed since I developed anorexia when I wrote my first diary entry on January 1,Tuesday, 1963:

Woke up at 5 o'clock. Had breakfast at ¼ past 7. I had 1 round of toast + 3 bits of meat ....

Note: Most names in this book are real. Pseudonyms protect privacy in several instances.

1. SCHOOL DOCTOR VISIT

I loved sleeping in my camp bed on the wooden verandah. Except for the bloody flies. As soon as the summer sun peeped over the hill and into our river valley, the dopey things woke up and started buzzing around my head.

This particular January morning I tried to swat one that landed on my face. The sudden movement caused my narrow bed to wobble on its shaky legs, their rusty hinges creaking loudly. Oh well, the flies were a sign it was time to get up anyway. I had big plans for the day.

School holidays were always fun on our family dairy farm, and the 1962 summer holidays held much promise. My days were full of helping my dad milk the cows, feeding the calves, shifting spray irrigation pipes, playing cricket with my cousins and swimming in the river. At 11 years old, I was a tomboy through and through, and proud of it.

As I stirred in my bed, so did Topsy, my tortoiseshell cat. She burrowed under the covers and kept my feet warm during the chill of the night, but now she knew it was time to rise. I lay still for a moment and listened, beyond the buzz of the flies and Topsy's purr, to the gentle rumbling of rapids as the clear waters of the Mitchell River trundled over a stretch of rocks, 500 metres down the hill from our farmhouse. The roosters were crowing, Rip the dog was barking, the cows were mooing and the milking machine engine was putt-putting away.

Our farm was nestled at the head of the fertile Lindenow Valley, through which the river wended towards Bass Strait via Bairnsdale and the Gippsland Lakes, about 30 kilometres away.

People entering the valley floor along Findlay-Alexander Road would round a corner and see our Federation-style house a mile straight ahead, its red roof peeping over the hedge of mauve-flowering bougainvillea like a welcoming beacon. Smoke rising from a tall red-brick chimney was a sure sign someone was at home. The narrow gravel lane petered out to a dirt track at our farm's big entrance gate, and hardly a day went by without someone calling in for a cuppa. A smaller, period-style garden gate led from the house paddock into the house yard where, sheltered by the bougainvillea, a large and colourful cottage garden prospered.

A circular concrete footpath arched uphill through the garden to a grand, leadlight front door on the left. Only strangers knocked on that door—usually peddlers, evangelists or people who had lost their way. Everybody else followed the path to the right, leading to the back door. In constant need of new fly-wire, this door opened into a small porch where we hung our coats and hats. The washhouse was to the right, the kitchen was directly ahead and the passage was to the left. The passage, about as long and wide as a cricket pitch, led straight to the front door. Along the passage, doors on the right opened to the pantry, the bedroom I shared with my sister, Joy, who would soon be 14, and the sitting room; doors on the left opened to the bathroom, my parents' bedroom and the top room, or guests' bedroom.

The front door opened onto the L-shaped wooden verandah. From there, views extended over flowerbeds, lawns dotted with cypresses shaped like giant high tin loaves and a garden border of sprawling, mauve-coloured bougainvilleas, to the lush valley beyond. The verandah was the adults' favourite place to sit and chat—especially in the morning sunshine, and again in the afternoon and evening, when the hot sun had sunk behind the house. They sat on a wooden bench and also on my camp bed—no wonder it was creaking! The verandah was also perfect to spot people 'coming up the road'.

One of the first things we explained to newcomers was that the toilet—its white weatherboards and pitched, red corrugated iron roof matching our house—was out the back gate in the house paddock. When nobody was around you could leave the toilet door open and gaze over the gully and hills. The view was enough to help the most constipated person relax. Besides the outhouse, the six-acre house paddock was home to the hen house, wood heap, orchard, car shed, tractor shed and stable.

My paternal grandfather, Duncan Alexander, built the house shortly after purchasing what was then a 52.6 hectare property in the early 1900s.

A small, spritely man who played golf in his younger days and had a lifetime passion for fishing Gippsland rivers, Duncan grew up in the tiny township of Walpa, near Lindenow, about 13 kilometres from the farm. Walpa had developed during the late 1800s and early 1900s when land was opened up to pastoralists and selectors.

Duncan married Alvina Whitbourne, an accomplished horsewoman who was raised on a property beside the Mitchell River at Wuk Wuk, a settlement between our farm and Lindenow. Alvina was a descendant of the pioneering Scott family who had travelled with a horse and dray across the Great Dividing Range from the Monaro High Plains in New South Wales to settle at Delvine Park, near Bairnsdale, in 1845.

My paternal grandparents had two children—Carlie, born in 1920, and my father, Lindsay, born two years later. Carlie married young and moved to Melbourne while Lindsay insisted on leaving school at 14 to be a farmer. In 1947 he married my mother, Anne Sands, one of eight children born to Neville and Elizabeth Sands. Elizabeth was the daughter of a miner and Neville was a miner too. Early in their marriage, Neville worked in the black coal mine at Wonthaggi, in South Gippsland. Suffering health problems, including the loss of a lung, he and his young family moved east to Bairnsdale, where he worked in orchards before settling a little further east, at Buchan South. My mother was born there, at home, in 1925. My grandfather Neville worked in a nearby quarry, extracting black marble. Some of this marble was used to create 16 Ionic columns for Melbourne's Shrine of Remembrance, which opened in 1934, and some was shipped to London for inclusion in Australia House.

Around 1940, the Sands family moved 100 kilometres southwest to Woodglen in the Lindenow Valley to work on a dairy farm. My mother, 15 by this time, and her sisters, Margaret and Gladys, worked with their father in the milking shed. My mother couldn't remember a defining moment when she met my father, but as they lived only four kilometres apart, they possibly met at a dance in the nearby Glenaladale Hall, at a local cricket match or tennis tournament. They wed a few weeks after my mother's 21st birthday and lived in the same house as my grandparents. My sister, Joy, was born in 1948 and I followed on December 27, 1950.

When I was five years old, my grandparents moved into a house in East Bairnsdale, 28 kilometres away. Joy and I sometimes stayed with them.

This experience of 'town life' included a playground and milk bar in the same street, friendships with children across the road, and an occasional outing to the picture theatre. Mostly I was desperately shy and sought shelter behind my sister.

Grandpa Sands was the first of my grandparents to die, when I was seven. In my favourite memory, he sits on a small wooden bench on the verandah of his rented fibro-cement farmhouse at Woodglen, playing his button accordion. Grandma Alexander died when I was 10. I was not taken to either funeral. I missed my grandmother especially. She had patiently taught me, a left-hander, how to knit and crochet. I talked to her in my prayers every night. When she and Grandpa Alexander lived on the farm, I occasionally awoke in their bed, always feeling safe and snug with a grandparent either side of me. My parents placed me there when my bed was needed for visitors. Grandma would scratch my back, let me help undo and do-up her tight-fitting corsets, and brush her beautiful, long, silvery-white hair that she pinned into a neat bun during the day.

When Grandma died, she left a small Vegemite jar with a hand-written piece of paper taped on top, stating: *'This is June's'*. The jar contained pennies, halfpennies, threepences and sixpences. I treasured that little jar, more for its message than its contents. In years to come, those three words, penned in my grandmother's hand, would give me strength.

After my grandparents moved to Bairnsdale, their bedroom became known as the 'top bedroom' for guests. From the age of five to 10, when my bed was required for visitor over-flow, I slept on an inflatable rubber mattress on the floor of my parents' bedroom. By summer 1962, I was sleeping on the camp bed on the verandah. Visitors at this time of the year were mostly city cousins, and their parents, my Aunty Carlie and Uncle Roy.

My cousins were allowed to sleep in, but I knew that when my mother came briskly out the back door, like now, I had two minutes in which to get up. That's how long she took to go out the back gate to the toilet to empty her chamber pot, rinse it under the garden tap and return it inside to its seclusion under her bed. I needed to jump out of bed before she came out the back door again, this time to briskly sweep the concreted garden path. Otherwise, she would wave the broom to remind me that Dad was expecting his tea and toast. Besides, if I didn't get up right then, the flies would drive me crazy.

I threw off the thin grey woollen blankets and swung out of bed, pulled on my shorts, T-shirt and gumboots, headed for the back door and yelled: 'Mum, I'm ready to go to the dairy—is Dad's tea and toast ready?'

She loaded me up with a chipped enamel plate carrying several thick slices of high tin bread. The bread had been toasted on a homemade wire fork over embers in the firebox of our small, shiny, black wood stove, and soaked with butter. An old saucepan lid was placed on top to keep the flies off. With this in one hand, I took the handle of the shining clean billy, half-filled with well-sugared black tea, in the other, and plodded in my boots down the garden path, out the front gate and down the gravelled track to the unpainted weatherboard dairy as fast as I could without slopping the tea or dropping the toast.

While I walked, I thought about what the day would bring. My cousins and I had made plans the previous night for a maize cob fight in the stable after breakfast, followed by a swim in the river before lunch. My favourite 'swimmy hole' was by the willows and windmill downstream from the rapids. There, depending on water flow, the river was about 50 metres wide and was bordered with a small sandy beach on the far side.

I took over milking our cows while Dad stood in the dairy's wash-up room and ate his toast, washing it down with a pannikin of tea poured from the billy. Our dairy herd of about 45 cows was milked four at a time with machines powered by a diesel motor. By the age of 11 I knew pretty much how everything worked, as I'd been going to the dairy since I could walk. At first, my parents sold cream in cans that were collected by a lorry and taken to a butter factory in Bairnsdale. The leftover milk was fed to our pigs. Then we progressed to selling water-cooled milk. The milk, always deliciously warm, frothy and sweet, fresh off the cows, was cooled as it ran over small stainless steel bars filled with water from an underground tank. After cooling it was stored in a big stainless steel vat until the milk tanker came, once or twice daily, to collect it.

I managed to milk a few cows before Dad returned to the yard and then I fed the calves. First I went to the wash-up room, which was more modern than our house because a briquette hot water service provided running hot water. I used a well-worn broken axe handle to mix powdered milk with water in two big stainless steel buckets. To prevent lumps forming and floating on top, I mixed the milk with first cold and then hot water. For extra nourishment I added fresh milk from the big vat, and heaved the buckets, swinging one and then the other, trying not to let milk slosh into my gumboots, to the wooden calf pens behind the dairy.

I poured the milk into tins, made by Dad from five-gallon (19 litre) oil drums, and fed the calves, which were bellowing for their tucker. Knowing the greedier calves would drink fast and headbutt for more, I held onto the tins' wire handles and used a stick to ensure the little ones got their share. Minutes later, tummies full and tails swinging, the calves pranced and kicked up their hooves as I shooed them out of their pen into the calf paddock. Checking that their trough, which had been carved from a log, was filled with fresh water, I returned to the wash-up room to scrub the buckets. I washed Dad's tea billy too, and filled it with fresh milk to carry up the hill for Mum to serve at breakfast.

My lazy cousins were still in bed. Wondering where Mum was, I heard her call from up the hallway. I found her in her bedroom. Bother! What did she want?

Mum closed her door. This seemed serious.

'Tim, I have something to tell you.'

What had I done?

'Did you notice anything when you got up this morning?'

Notice anything? What?

I hadn't made my bed but Mum usually made that for me while I was out helping Dad with the farm jobs.

'No,' I said.

'Did you notice your pyjamas, or look at your sheets?' she asked.

What had I done? Had my cat made a mess? Couldn't have been me.

'No,' I said.

'I found some blood,' Mum said.

'Blood? What blood?'

Then Mum was talking. I could hear her but absorbed only snatches of what she said.

After talking about 'periods' and 'bleeding every month', she withdrew a small book from her dressing table drawer and told me to read it. The book's title was something like *Mothers and Daughters*. I thought I'd read every book in the house long ago, but I hadn't seen this one before.

Then Mum pulled something from another of her dressing-table drawers. It was a thin, circular, elasticised belt with two dangly bits. From a bag in the depths of her wardrobe she pulled a white flannelette nappy. I watched, numbed and horrified.

Spreading the nappy on the blue eiderdown of her freshly made bed, she folded it several times into a thick, narrow shape. Next, using two large safety pins from a little box on her dressing table, she attached the ends of the nappy to the two dangly bits. Mum held her work of art out towards me and said, 'Wear this pad.'

I took it, speechless. My mother walked from the room, closing the door behind her. But not before pausing to add: 'And no swimming today or tomorrow; not until you finish bleeding.'

I didn't want to hear any more. I felt disgusted. Me, wear a nappy, a baby's thing?

Left alone, I slowly lowered my shorts and my pants. There was a little red patch. I took my pants off and pulled the bulky pad on.

I felt a great need to escape that bedroom, and the house. I shoved the book under my camp bed pillow on the verandah, pulled on my gumboots and headed back to the dairy to help Dad wash the yards and clean up after the milking. As I walked down the track, kicking pebbles with my boots, I stopped. My mother's words hit hard, like a lightning strike. My world had changed forever. For a week every month I would have that bleeding—because I was a girl. I didn't want to be a girl; I liked being Tim. This was what Mum called me when she was happy with me. When she was annoyed, she called me Toby.

I'd wanted to be a boy for as long as I could remember. My boy cousins had shown me their 'willies' and I wanted one, too. My 'fanny' was a huge disappointment. At the age of six or seven I had lined up beside several boy cousins in the grassy calf paddock. Together we had lowered our shorts and faced the timber wall of an old storage shed. We'd stood two metres out from the shed and our goal was to see who could 'pee the highest' up the wall. 'Ready, set, go!'

The boys' wee reached almost as high as the shed roof. I leaned back and pushed as hard as I could but mine didn't go beyond the toe of my gumboots. Most of the warm yellow liquid fell directly south into my boots, soaking my socks and making my feet squelch and smell. Not having a willie was frustrating, but to learn that my fanny would bleed once a month was devastating.

I shook myself and trudged on to the dairy. I was sure I was as handy as a boy in all other ways. I preferred farm work to house jobs. Besides feeding the calves twice a day and helping with the cows, I set rabbit traps, drove the tractor and helped to shift the irrigation pipes.

Would Dad notice I was different? He said nothing as I entered the dairy to sweep and hose the yards and help put water through the pipes to clean the machines now the last cow had been milked. But that stupid nappy was chaffing my inner legs. I hoped it wasn't bulging through my shorts. By now it was nine o'clock. I walked back up the hill for breakfast.

My sleepy cousins were starting to appear.

They said nothing. Just as well they didn't know about this sudden complication in my life. They would laugh if they knew I was wearing a nappy. After breakfast, in the stable downhill from the house, we drew an imaginary battle line and prepared for the maize cob fight. We gathered old, shelled cobs off the dusty dirt floor for ammunition, hid among the bales of hay, old machinery and hessian bags brimming with full cobs, and the war started. Mum growled if we threw full cobs, as they were food for the chooks, but in the heat of battle we threw them anyway. That day we decided the Allies were invading Germany. The cobs, especially if unshelled, hurt if they struck bare skin, and that was our aim. We had to draw blood on the enemy, usually on their face or arms, to claim a victory.

Waging war helped me to momentarily forget my other bloody problem, but I had to mumble, 'Mum wants me to do a job in the house' when my cousins asked why I wasn't going for a swim.

'Chicken,' they said.

The next few days seemed like years, but then I was free to go swimming again, between helping Dad with the cows and shifting the irrigation pipes on our 24 hectares of river flats.

My happiness was short-lived. In the first week of February, I pedalled my bike out of the valley to attend the local state school, Woodglen Primary, Number 3352, five kilometres away. Surrounded by farmland and flanked on three sides by tall pine trees, the school comprised one classroom, a porch where we hung our bags and where the little children listened to 'Kindergarten of the Air', and a tiny storeroom for our sport equipment. I was in Grade Six, my final year of primary school, and my cousin Daryl was the teacher. Daryl, who had been my teacher since Grade Four, had grown up in Melbourne but I knew him well as, along with many other cousins and family friends, he often stayed at my parents' house.

There were five girls and three boys in Grade Six. Our grade was the biggest in the school, which had a total enrolment of 24 children. Most of our parents were dairy farmers. Some, like my parents, owned their property; others, including a recently arrived Dutch family with 13 children, share-farmed on a larger property.

I enjoyed learning, but something about Daryl made me uneasy.

Every morning we stood beside our wooden desks and he said: 'Good morning, boys and girls' and we'd chorus: 'Good morning, Mr Orgill' before sitting down to work. Except I refused to say 'Mr Orgill'. He was my cousin, after all, and only 12 years older; he wouldn't let me call him 'Daryl' at school, so I called him nothing. This meant I rarely put my hand up to volunteer a 'morning talk', even if I had some world-breaking news, because we had to open our show-and-tell with 'Good morning, Mr Orgill, girls and boys.'

But one day he announced that everybody in the school had to take a turn at presenting a morning talk. I don't remember what I spoke about, but I do remember weeks of anxiety, worrying about how I was going to get the courage to say 'Mr Orgill'.

My mother and sister, Joy, called me 'stubborn' and 'pig-headed'. I couldn't help it. Something about Daryl had me on edge.

Every Monday morning we lined up by the weatherboard shelter shed for a flag-raising ceremony and sang *God Save the Queen*. Standing at attention with my hand over my heart one morning several weeks into Term One, I glanced along the line and my heart went thump as I realised I was the only girl with breasts.

When I ran, my breasts bounced up and down and hurt. If I held them they didn't hurt, but I couldn't do that when playing with the boys or within sight of Daryl.

In March, 'Mr Orgill' announced that the school doctor, who visited our school every three or four years, would come in June. He gave us forms for our parents to fill in and sign.

I gave my form to Mum, saying I didn't want to see the doctor, but she said: 'Don't be silly, you have nothing to worry about, Tim. It will be over in a flash, you'll see'.

Her words provided no comfort. I would have to undress to my panties and singlet. Maybe I would have to take off my singlet as well. I'd be in the classroom, which had large multi-paned windows on two sides, and no curtains. For a reason I could not explain, I was extremely fearful of Daryl seeing me undressed.

My sister, Joy, brushed my concerns aside. Daryl hadn't been her teacher, since she'd started high school at Bairnsdale the year he came to Woodglen, three years ago now. Joy and I shared the same bedroom and Daryl gave her the creeps too, but when I said I didn't want to see the doctor, she said: 'All the other girls will be undressing; you won't be the only one.'

But I would be the only one with sissy breasts. This was definitely something I couldn't talk to Dad about. I had nobody else to turn to.

The doctor's visit was only three months away and my breasts were growing bigger. Soon I would need to wear a bra. This was a big worry.

Sitting on the grassy school ground in the shade of the pine trees during playtime one Friday afternoon, there seemed no way to avoid the doctor's visit. Suddenly, however, I knew what to do.

It was as though my brain was zapped from outer space. Ping!

Anorexia nervosa was developing and starting to manipulate my mind. Oblivious of this, I only knew I felt less anxious.

Classmates were calling me to come and play; they could not see my special new 'thought-friend'.

That afternoon, when classes resumed, a health lesson serendipitously provided encouragement. With other pupils I sat cross-legged on a carpet square with my health booklet to listen to the voice booming from our big wireless. It described a new word: c-a-l-o-r-i-e. A day earlier the word would have held no interest but now my mind clung to it like a magnet.

The lesson was about food values and burning energy. My booklet listed the calorie content of several foods and the number of calories absorbed in 30 minutes of walking, swimming, running and bike riding. My mind recorded the entire lesson word for word and I immediately began to eat less and exercise more.

When tempted to eat, I pushed my hunger pangs aside. The more hungry I was, the better I felt. If I was feeling weak, I brushed my teeth, which helped me think I had eaten a meal, though I'd eaten nothing.

I had no idea of my weight. The only scales I had seen were those belonging to the school doctor, or those with a penny slot outside chemist shops in Bairnsdale's Main Street. I went to town three or four times a year and was too shy to weigh myself in view of passers-by. All I knew was that I wanted to lose my breasts before the school doctor's visit.

Until now, I had been pleased when my clothes became tight, because this showed I was growing, and I wanted to be tall and strong, like Dad. But now I didn't want to grow. I could not be like my dad, and didn't want to be a girl, either.

I continued to feed the calves before riding my bike to school, but did my jobs faster so I could work out on the playground equipment before lessons started.

I swung across the monkey bar and, like a monkey after a coconut, shinned up the pole; I reached for the clouds on the swing, did chin-ups, climbed the ladder, zipped down the slide, and turned myself inside out on the jungle gym. I worked out again at playtime and lunchtime, counting and always increasing the number of turns on each piece of equipment. My friends could not keep up with me.

At home I chopped more wood, looked after the chooks and fetched the cows for milking, running from job to job.

Mum and Dad thought I was wonderful. Mum was calling me 'Tim' all the time, I was so helpful, and I almost burst with pride when Dad told an uncle that I was a left-hander at writing but was his 'right-hand man on the land'.

Exercise was easy but eating less was more complicated as Mum was in charge of the kitchen.

Breakfast was straightforward. Mum was usually helping Dad in the dairy when I was in the house changing out of my cow yard gear into my school clothes. She would leave the table set with Weet-Bix on a plate or porridge keeping warm in the saucepan on the side of the stove, thick slices of bread on a plate to toast and tea in the pot. Joy left an hour earlier to catch the bus to high school and any visitors would still be in bed.

The cats loved the porridge and Weet-Bix. Besides Topsy, we had about 12 cats. Some were part feral, having been dumped by uncaring owners in the bush land adjacent to our property. Timid, they lived in the stable and haystack where they caught mice; some bravely hung around the back door of the house in the mornings and evenings, hoping for a dish of stale milk, or scraps from the kitchen.

They purred as I fed them my cereal, urging them to eat it all before Mum returned from the dairy. Next I took a thick slice of high tin loaf outside, through the back gate, throwing chunks to the chooks, who snapped the bread up in their beaks and dashed about, clucking madly and throwing their heads back as they gulped their treat down. Then I ran back inside, cut a paper-thin slice of bread to toast on the open fire, spread some Vegemite and washed it down with a cup of black, sugarless tea. From the age of five I'd been drinking tea from a favourite cup that Mum half-filled with milk, and sweetened with several teaspoons of white sugar. Not any more. Every day I found new ways to reduce my calorie intake.

Lunch on school days was easy, too. Mum cut two big rounds of sandwiches, wrapping them in waxed paper and placing them in my blue lunch tin, the lid kept on with an old Fowlers Vacola preserving jar ring. I asked for only one round but she wouldn't listen and when I came home from school with one sandwich untouched, she was upset.

'You need two rounds; you're a growing girl. And besides, this is wasteful,' Mum scolded.

I thought of another solution. The next day I took an empty tin home.

'That's better,' Mum said.

Some children at school came from poor families who sometimes had no bread for making lunches, so I offered my sandwiches to these children. I gave them the cheese, jam, meat and peanut butter sandwiches, keeping a Vegemite, fish paste or tomato one for myself. My classmates also enjoyed my play snacks of lamingtons, jam drops, Madeira cake, chocolate slice and Anzac biscuits. I smiled as they ate while I went hungry; I enjoyed watching them eat.

The evening meal was the one daily meal shared by my family. Mum served the food on our plates and set them on the oval-shaped, oak dining table that stood in the middle of our kitchen. I dreaded casseroles, stews and gravy. Desserts were particularly messy.

I became resourceful and devious. By sitting down first, when Mum's back was turned at the sink and others were combing their hair before coming to the table, I had time to move food from my plate to the next plate, which belonged to whoever was visiting. This was a relief. If Mum left the kitchen for a moment, I risked reaching across the table and placing my meat on Dad's plate. Sometimes I gave his plate a roast potato as well. These were his favourite foods and together with Grandma, Dad was my favourite person in all the world.

When everyone was seated and busy eating or talking, I grabbed fistfuls of food left on my plate, whipped it under the tablecloth and slid it in my pockets. This was why I didn't like sloppy foods, like mashed potato and meat covered in gravy. I ate a small amount of cabbage or carrot, and pretended it was a lot, chewing it over and over, finishing my meal at about the same time as everyone else. Or I pretended to chew and swallow nothing.

Main courses were a trial but desserts were worse. They were sticky or soft and hopeless for slipping in pockets.

Mum made chocolate sauce puddings, apple crumbles, apple puddings, golden syrup dumplings, jam tarts, sago puddings and custards, usually served with stewed or preserved fruit. Made with full-cream milk and butter, the desserts also contained sugar, available by the cupful from a big hessian bag in our pantry.

My heart sank when Mum insisted on pouring custard sauce or cream over the top of a steamed pudding. About the only dessert I could slip safely in my pocket was cinnamon apple cake, and even that was messy.

I tried to tell Mum, 'I'm full. I don't want dessert, thank you,' but she would reply, 'What's wrong with you? I thought you wanted to be tall and strong like your Dad.'

Nothing but a cleaned-up plate satisfied my mother. She would remind me how as a child she ate 'bread and dripping through the week and bread and jam on Sunday,' and for good measure would add: 'Think about those poor starving children in India, be grateful and eat up.'

I couldn't see how the eating of my dessert would ease the plight of children in India. I wanted to lose my breasts. I couldn't tell Mum that, so I waited for everyone to leave the table and for her to leave the kitchen, even for a moment. Then I'd jump up and toss the food off my plate into the scrap bowl and run it outside in the dark to Rip the dog, whose turn it was for a meal at the end of the day. Rip developed a real sweet tooth.

Summer passed into autumn, and autumn was nearing winter. My periods were on time every month. At school, I remained the only girl with breasts but they were shrinking and I hid them by wearing more clothing as the weather turned cooler.

However, Mum was starting to question my behaviour. I was quieter and on weekends, I liked to disappear into the bushland adjacent to our property, my thoughts as my companion. My mother and sister called me 'stuck up' and 'rude' when I didn't want to join them in visiting our neighbours, who put the kettle on for a cuppa, whatever the time of day, and served sugar-laden cakes and biscuits.

I had friends on neighbouring farms but preferred to be alone or doing outdoor jobs. Luckily Mum liked me to help Dad and I was with him every possible moment. She worked hard, helping on the farm when I was at school, and she kept our house spotless and our large cottage garden beautiful.

Some local families had electric power, but it hadn't entered our valley yet, so Mum did her housework manually: polishing the linoleum floors on her hands and knees, beating her cake mixtures with a wooden spatula, and washing our clothes in a wood-fired copper. She prodded the clothes with a broken axe handle before heaving them into a concrete trough to rinse in cold water, and wrung them by hand before pegging them on the outside line. The steel-bladed Southern Cross windmill by the river provided our water supply, pumping water to a tank 100 metres uphill from the house to gain sufficient pressure. Careful usage was essential because otherwise, when the wind didn't blow, the tank ran dry.

One night, lost in thought over how to avoid the shepherd's pie that Mum was baking for tea, I forgot to turn off the tap into the calves' trough. Next morning, Dad gently asked, 'Did you forget to do something last night?' The tank had run dry. I blushed and hung my head. I would not forget again.

The following week the doctor came to school. My chest was almost flat. As far as I could tell, Daryl stayed out of sight. Nobody laughed as I lined up with the other girls in panties and singlets. The doctor chatted, probed and listened to each of us in turn before passing us on to the nurse who weighed us. At 6st 12lbs (43.5 kilograms), neither the doctor nor nurse noted my weight loss because they hadn't seen me for four years.

My report was good on every count. While dressing I looked sideways and was pleased to notice other Grade Six girls were growing breasts too.

I had worked hard for three months, preparing for the doctor's visit. Now it was over. That afternoon, pushing my bike through the school gate to pedal home, I felt relieved I would not have to risk making Mum cross at mealtimes any more.

2. MY ILLNESS DEEPENS

Globules of fat on the meat chunks peered out of the lamb stew, daring me to eat them. It didn't help that the stew's rich brown gravy had merged with its companion—a large blob of white-as-snow potato mashed with generous lashings of creamy milk and butter. For the first time in months I had looked forward to sitting down to tea. Tonight Mum wouldn't have cause to growl. But, confronted by the lamb stew and potato, guilt set in.

I loaded my fork, and could go no further. The fatty globs glared at me. I skirted them, eating the boiled carrot and cabbage, carefully avoiding the bits that touched the stew and mashed potato.

Mum grumbled. 'Wasteful,' she muttered, taking my plate away. Then she served steamed apple pudding with a rich custard sauce poured over top. This dessert, once my favourite, now sparked terror.

'For goodness sake, eat!' Mum begged. The pudding was one of Grandma Alexander's recipes. I loved Grandma, but I couldn't eat her pudding; I wanted to run from the kitchen and hide.

Everyone else finished the meal and I sat alone with my pudding, now cold and soggy. An hour later, Mum snatched my bowl and furiously scraped the contents into the slop dish. Wanting to please her by eating something, I decided on two dry biscuits. I knew exactly how many calories they contained and could eat them without feeling guilty.

Getting the biscuits out of the jar in the pantry cupboard, I nibbled them slowly, trying to make two seem like 12 to show Mum, 'Look, I am eating, I am eating'. But Mum erupted. 'Why eat those, and not what I cook?' she snapped. 'Isn't my cooking good enough for you?'

'Of course it's good enough, Mum. Everyone loves your cooking,' I wanted to say. But I didn't know how many calories were in the rich pudding.

My life had become complicated since my periods arrived. I wished they would go away. I was achieving top marks at school, and was helping with jobs on the farm, but was always thinking about food—what I would eat, and how much exercise I would have to do to burn the calories I ate. Mostly such thoughts were a comfort. They helped me feel I could cope, no matter what was going wrong in the family or on the farm.

Occasionally, Mum caught me out: washing my clothes, she would find dried egg yolk, cake crumbs and gravy in the pockets. She would growl but I could not do anything about it. (Neither of us knew that anorexia nervosa was taking over my mind.)

'I can't eat,' I wanted to shout. She made me sit at the dinner table for hours, while she dashed about, doing jobs, but failed to weaken my resolve. She tried to coax, calling me Tim, and tried to threaten, calling me Toby, but the thoughts of my illness were stronger than both of us.

A new challenge arose when Dad announced he would take Joy and me to old-time dancing classes in a Bairnsdale church hall every second Thursday evening. This was in preparation for waltzing and foxtrotting our way into the social life of our local district. Saturday-night dances were held at community halls in our home district of Glenaladale, and nearby Fernbank and Flaggy Creek. I was still wearing bobby socks, but Mum decided the time had come for me to wear a bra. This was wishful thinking on her part because by now I hardly needed one.

She handed the bra to me when I was about to bathe and dress for my first dancing lesson. I shut myself in the bathroom. Probably a hand-me-down from my sister, the white cotton contraption with its multitude of hooks made me cry with frustration as I tried to fasten them. Fearful of being seen, I refused to call for assistance. Finally I solved the problem by doing the hooks up at the front and pulling the bra around my chest until everything was in place. I didn't want breasts or a bra, but at least the dancing would be good exercise.

After each dance session Dad broke open an 8oz. (220g) block of Cadbury's plain chocolate to share on the half-hour drive home. At first, having danced for more than an hour, I allowed myself to suck on three small squares, but as the weeks went by, I reduced this to two small squares, then one and then none. I believed that I did not deserve any chocolate. I was happy for Joy, and the neighbours' children who travelled with us, to eat my share. With each weekly dancing lesson, my clothes hung more loosely.

Home life was changing too. Dad bought a lighting plant. This accumulation of batteries replaced the old diesel motor in the engine room at our dairy, and powered the milking machines. Instead of striking a match to light kerosene-filled Tilley lanterns in the shed in the early morning and at night, Dad now flicked a switch. Linked to our house, electric lights replaced our kerosene lamps, candles and torches. We were becoming modern.

The new power source meant Mum could purchase her first electrical appliances. She especially loved the electric cake mixer, because she could leave it to do the beating while she did other jobs. Dad said the sponge cakes didn't taste as good as when Mum beat the butter and sugar mixture by hand with a wooden spatula. But there was no going back. Sometimes, while Mum went out to the clothesline or down to the chook yard, I had taken a turn at the hand beating and my arms ached within seconds.

Besides labour-saving devices, Dad bought something for us to relax with: a television set. This box on four legs was given pride of place in a corner of our sitting room. Even with a tall aerial attached to the sitting room chimney, the reception was poor. It bounced off one side of the valley onto the other and we saw two images instead of one. The images were more ghostly grey than black or white, but we could discern a picture. There was no squabbling over what channel to watch because there was only one: the Australian Broadcasting Corporation (ABC). We watched television only at night. There was a strict rule about not using electricity until Dad started the afternoon milking about 5pm; this was because switching the power on and off reduced the life of the lighting plant batteries. So each night after tea our family, plus any visitors, proceeded from the kitchen to the sitting room, sat in front of the television set and switched on to the world outside our valley.

At first I was excited, but to watch television I had to sit down. I tried but could not sit still and was pleased when Mum said: 'You should be outside helping your father. You know how tired he is.' She was always telling me how tired Dad was. So I pleased her by staying outside, helping Dad, often until after dark. This was preferable to doing sissy indoor jobs, like cleaning the bath with White Lily, polishing the cutlery with Brasso or shining brass doorknobs.

I continued to feed the calves before and after school and the chooks looked forward to their late-afternoon feed of wheat, pellets, and maize. On weekends I helped Dad feed our cows with small, rectangular bales of grass, oats or lucerne; also freshly cut saccaline, which looked like sugar cane, and sometimes silage, a compressed grass that was dark green and smelly but that the cows loved. I sat on top of the loaded trailer and, while Dad drove the tractor around the paddocks on both the flats and the hills, I tossed the fodder to the cows. I always felt happy, working with Dad.

With spring coming, I helped to herd the cows about to calve down from the hills to the lush house paddock, which doubled as a nursery. From there the cows would proceed to the dairy. Separating the newly born calves or poddies from their mothers at about one week, Dad gave them a few lessons at drinking milk from a bucket. I learnt to do this too, putting my fingers in a poddy's mouth so it would suck, and dipping its nose in the bucket. The poddies soon caught on. I looked after them until they were about three months old and ready to be weaned on to solids like grass and hay. Most of the boy 'bobby' calves were sent to the calf sale at one or two weeks of age. The girl calves were lucky—they could look forward to growing into heifers and joining the dairy herd.

Each May and September school holidays, for as long as I could remember, I set traps to catch rabbits, which were a pest. In the past year, Dad had shown me how to set snares on boundary fences for kangaroos and wombats as well.

My latest rabbit catch became a stew. Mum knew I loved the tender, fresh meat, more so because I'd hunted and gathered it myself, but now I refused to eat it.

She was angry. 'Why won't you eat, who do you think you are?' Then, with Dad in the washhouse, scrubbing his hands and combing his wavy hair as he always did before coming to the table, she said, 'If you don't eat, I'll tell your father, and you know he has enough worries already.'

Besides telling me that Dad was tired, Mum was forever providing updates on his worries. We had too much rain, not enough rain; too much wind, not enough wind; butterfat prices were falling, superphosphate prices were rising; in autumn the cows' milk was drying off too early, in spring the cows were blowing up with milk fever; all year round, machinery was breaking down. I felt the burden of my parents' worries, but couldn't eat the rabbit. The guilt caused me to run for miles along the rocky river track, and eat only a dry crust of bread and half a tomato the next day.

At the end of September I began my final term at primary school and was exercising three hours a day. With my thinness more apparent, my mother tried to persuade me to swallow a vitamin mixture. I refused. I hated the smell and feared the calories.

Sometimes she became very upset.

One afternoon after school she insisted I accompany her to visit an old friend, Mrs Banks, a widow, several kilometres around the corner of our valley. Anyone who lived just outside our valley was referred to as being 'around the corner'. I didn't want to go, my thoughts were screaming at me not to go, but Mum promised, 'We'll take a bunch of flowers and stay only a few minutes'. In the car on our way there, she revealed we were invited for afternoon tea. Dismayed, I said, 'But I need to be home to do my jobs.'

'Don't be impatient, and don't be rude,' she warned as she pulled up beside Mrs Banks' wooden picket fence. Mrs Banks was waiting at her front gate to greet us. The flowers were presented and admired, and we wandered as slow as snails around Mrs Banks' pretty garden on our way into her cottage. I tried to suppress the urge to run.

Then came the dreaded, 'Come inside and have a cup of tea.' In we went, and I sat on a chair beside Mum at the small kitchen table, struggling to keep still while the two women chatted. Wood was fetched, and the fire stoked, to help the kettle boil. It took forever.

I politely declined the offer of a glass of milk or a glass of sugared cordial. Mum glared.

'I'd like a glass of water, please.' Things deteriorated fast. Mrs Banks offered a plate of homemade biscuits and cake. I wanted to escape. I could feel my cheeks going beetroot red under my snowy hair as I said, 'No thank you, Mrs Banks.'

Seething at my poor manners, Mum accepted a biscuit with her cup of tea. The chat continued. *'Mum's angry but I can't stay here,'* I thought. She was about to get angrier because suddenly my hands, on which I'd been sitting, broke loose and I began squirming on my chair, swinging my legs and folding and unfolding my arms. I nudged Mum while Mrs Banks refilled the kettle.

'I want to go home,' my eyes begged.

'Sit still,' she flashed back. Mrs Banks returned and conversation continued.

Suddenly my anorexic thoughts took over. I stood and blurted, 'I want to go home to help Dad in the dairy.'

'Just a few more minutes,' Mum smiled sweetly. Veiling her annoyance, she said the biscuits were so crisp and crunchy she would eat another one. Pleased with the praise, Mrs Banks offered to write out the recipe. Mum and her neighbours were always swapping recipes.

'Thank you, Alice, I'm sure Lindsay will like them,' Mum said.

'You stay for your recipe and I'll walk home,' I chipped in, thinking this was a good time to make a break and the four kilometre walk would compensate for the time I was seated. But Mum stood too, smiled and said to Mrs Banks: 'I'll get the recipe another time. We'd better go home now.'

The truth was, Mum couldn't bear the thought of me walking home along the road. She'd worry a neighbour might drive by and see me not walking, but running. I was an embarrassment.

I raced out of the house to the car. I stood beside the passenger door and hopped from one foot to the other while Mum and Mrs Banks dawdled, with Mum choosing a few plant cuttings to strike for her garden. The farewell at the front gate took an eternity. At last Mum opened the car door and sat behind the wheel of our black FJ Holden.

She was angry. 'How dare you?' she raved as she drove us home. 'You can't sit still for half an hour. What's got into you?'

She didn't know I had anorexia. She didn't wait for an answer before continuing, 'You were good. Now you are rude. Everyone will be talking about you and your bad manners. You always want your own way. Why don't you think of others?'

On and on she went. I said nothing. She would not believe I did not want to be difficult, that my mind was being overtaken by thoughts that were not really me. I wanted to get home and run, run, run to make up for all that horrid sitting down.

One Sunday, a few weeks later, I was invited to play with a school friend, Louise, at one of the grandest farmhouses around the corner. The invitation included Sunday dinner. I didn't want to go and said I preferred to wander in the bush and look for wombats sunning themselves on their mounds, or watch lyrebirds doing their dance.

'You have to go.' Mum was distraught. She didn't know what was worse: declining the invitation or making me go and risking further embarrassment.

'You must go,' she said, exasperated. Joy upset her, and now I was upsetting her, too. It was impolite to turn down invitations.

'I'll run away if you don't go,' she threatened. Sometimes when my sister was rude, Mum ran out the back gate, slipped through the house paddock's wire fence and disappeared up the gully. She always returned after a few hours, but I worried and silently resented my sister for being horrid. My sister back-answered, shouted, swore and poked her tongue at Mum. I didn't understand why, preferring to avoid the house so I didn't have to listen to the noise. I tried to be good so as not to cause sadness. But now Mum was threatening to run away because I didn't want to go out for lunch.

Somehow finding the courage to override the urge to stay at home, I said: 'Yes, I'll play with Louise and stay for dinner.'

I rode my bike the three kilometres to Louise's house, the last 400 metres comprising a dirt laneway bordered by a cypress hedge. We had time for a play before lunch so we climbed the hedge, trying to get all the way through, from branch to branch, without putting our feet on the ground. By the time the lunch gong sounded, we looked and smelt like little cypress trees ourselves, with sticky green bits in our hair, inside our blouses and over our woollen jumpers. Exercise was good, but my day was about to deteriorate fast.

The Morrison family, one of the region's earliest settlers, had a big dairy farm and employed a share-farmer to help milk their cows. Louise and her two older sisters and parents lived in a big cream-brick house surrounded by a rambling cottage garden.

Every child in the district loved going to birthday parties at Louise's house. We played games like 'Pin the Tail on the Donkey' and 'Drop the Hanky' before sitting down to a brightly decorated table laden with party food. There would be jelly set in orange quarters, macaroons so light they almost floated away, hundreds and thousands sprinkled on quarters of buttered bread, dainty squares of hedgehog, marshmallow in ice-cream cones and hot sausage rolls. All were homemade.

Until now I'd felt special, being invited to birthday parties and Sunday dinners as well. That was before anorexia developed in my mind. Now, I was filled with dread. Sunday dinner loomed like a heavy black cloud and there was nowhere to take cover.

Louise's mother was a great cook but to me appeared a stout and scary, no-nonsense woman. Louise had confided several times how she'd had her mouth washed out with something that tasted horrible for telling fibs. Now I sat at the kitchen table with the family, a plate loaded with slices of roast beef, baked potatoes and pumpkin and boiled peas, drenched with rich gravy, before me. I felt I was before the firing line.

Fearful as I was of Mrs Morrison, I could eat only the peas; terrified, I ate them slowly, one at a time, trying to avoid the gravy. There was no opportunity to shift food into my pocket. So I shifted it around on my plate, and pretended to eat, but I was fooling nobody. Looking downward, sensing everyone was staring at me, my face turned bright red. I wanted to disappear under the table.

'This is the worst meal in my life,' I thought. 'Everyone has finished eating and is waiting for me.' At last Louise's mother removed my plate. 'What a wasteful child,' I knew she was thinking.

Without a word, she served dessert. Big bowls of jelly, custard and preserved peaches, topped with a blob of thick cream fresh from the dairy, were passed around the table. Normally I would love this but now studied my bowl with a sinking heart. The jelly and custard had been sweetened. The peaches were submerged in syrup. Louise's dad and her big sister cleaned their bowls and left the table. Her mother was clearing the table and washing the dishes.

I sat, too scared to move, apart from my swinging legs, out of sight under the tablecloth. Louise sat loyally beside me. At last we were shooed outside. Relieved, I didn't want to stay a moment longer and said I had to pedal home.

'Got to help Dad with the cows and calves,' I said.

I feared that Louise's mother would telephone Mum and tattle. Sure enough, as soon as I entered our back door Mum lectured me on my pig-headedness and poor manners. *'Blow Louise's mother,'* I thought. She had phoned to ask if I was sick, but I'm sure both mothers considered my behaviour just plain rude. I couldn't wait to get outside to start my jobs and to be alone with the bossy thoughts in my head. Mum did not make me go for meals at anyone's house again.

There was one social event I could not avoid. One evening during the week before Christmas, everyone in the Glenaladale, Woodglen and Iguana Creek district gathered for our primary school's annual concert in the 'Glen' Hall. Gum tips, colourful paper streamers and bunches of balloons camouflaged the unlined timber walls. The Christmas tree was a big cypress branch, standing in a 44-gallon drum covered in red and green crepe paper. Our mothers helped us to decorate the foliage with balloons and paper chains, angels and Chinese lanterns that we had made with small squares of coloured paper at school. Set in the corner beside our little performance area, the tree evoked much excitement as the mothers' club members placed gifts around its base. 'Which one is mine?' the children looked at each other and giggled. Anticipation mounted as we presented our carols, skits and nativity play. Our parents laughed and clapped.

Normally I would be as excited as everyone else, but tonight I stood in the back row, trying to hide in the shadows of the tree. The concert over, a bell clanged and the children clambered to sit on the front wooden bench, as big, jolly Santa entered the hall door, waving his bell and singing 'Ho, ho, ho'. He called to us, one by one, asked us what we wanted for Christmas and gave us our gift from the tree. Over the years I had asked for a pony, a gun, and a cowgirl suit. I didn't know what to ask for this year and didn't care. I could not laugh or smile. Santa gave me a pen, commemorating completion of Grade Six, and I hurried back to my seat. I wanted to go home. I felt removed from my friends and sensed their parents were looking at me.

My chest was flat and my periods were sporadic; my mind was full of thoughts of food and exercise. Anorexia had dominated my final year of primary school.

Christmas Day was not happy for my family that year. My city cousins, who gave me an excuse to sleep on the verandah, didn't visit because they had moved from Melbourne to Portland, on the western side of Victoria, too far to travel to our farm.

So there was just Mum and Dad, Joy, me, Grandpa and a few old family friends for Christmas dinner. For a gift, my parents gave me a beautiful, solid timber, locally made desk. Complete with pencil tray and drawers, it was an encouraging acknowledgement of my budding writing passion. I'd won my first essay competition at the age of nine; I wrote about rice and the prize was a fountain pen. More recently I had been writing adventure stories, sometimes reading them at school, and some were published in the *Australian Children's Newspaper*.

For Christmas dinner I tried to impress Mum by eating a boiled chicken leg, my first meat in months, and a big serve of boiled cabbage. Lately I'd been eating a tomato for dinner so this was a feast. By now Mum had accepted that putting food on my plate was a waste if I said I would not eat it. There was no point giving me roast beef, lamb or pork, roast potato, pumpkin, and thick, brown gravy, or any of the plum pudding, served with warm custard sauce and cream. Mum did not need to hide any threepences or sixpences in a pudding serve for me that year.

She was pleased I ate the chicken but afterwards I ran up the hill behind our house, to work that chicken leg off while bringing the cows home to be milked. We were in a drought, and the cows had to walk a long way from the dairy to feed on pasture between milkings. Now that I was on holiday, I happily herded the cows to the far paddock in the morning, and collected them in the afternoon. I also set more rabbit traps.

Nature had a strange effect in a drought. Rabbits were plentiful and I caught some without disguising the traps with the usual square piece of newspaper under a layer of soft, powdered dirt, at the entrance to their burrows. Grey, white, ginger and black—I'd not seen such colourful little bunnies before. They were emaciated like me. I could not eat because my anorexia was dominating my mind. The bunnies could not eat because there was no food. I put them out of their misery, breaking their necks, not bothering to take them home to skin.

Two days after Christmas Day, Mum baked a big sponge cake, filled the halves with whipped cream, iced the top in pink and decorated it with sprinkles for my 12th birthday. A year ago I was full of fun and vigour. Now, almost a skeleton, I tried to appear excited when unwrapping my parents' gift to find my first wristwatch, but could not eat one crumb of the beautiful birthday cake.

3. PATTY CAKE BREAKTHROUGH

'A holiday will bring back your appetite, make you well in time to start high school,' Mum said, coaxingly.

I was to stay two weeks of the summer holidays with my Aunt Marion and Uncle Alf in Blackburn, an eastern suburb of Melbourne. Immediately I began to worry about how to avoid the delicious meals my sweet aunt was sure to serve. But I agreed to the holiday because Uncle Alf was promising to take me to the cricket.

Not just any cricket, but the Test Cricket: a five-day match between Australia and England, at the Melbourne Cricket Ground. On December 28, 1962, the day after my 12th birthday, Mum drove me to Bairnsdale to catch the train called the *Gippslander* for the five-hour journey to Melbourne. In my small blue suitcase, safe among the clothes that Mum had neatly packed, was my box brownie camera, my new pen from Santa and a Christmas gift from Daryl—a small, soft-covered, green diary. I treasured Daryl's gift. I had not seen a real diary before, with a calendar and a page for every day, and now I had one of my very own. I felt grateful to my cousin. He knew I was not well and that I loved writing.

There was also a jar of vitamin tablets. Oval-shaped sores had broken out on my fingers and wouldn't heal. On hot days my ankles swelled like balloons and my feet were heavy to lift up, put down, lift up and put down as I worked through my daily exercise routine. Puffy veins ran like blue streams down my arms and over my hands. I felt removed from my limbs, as though they were not part of me. I felt removed from my self. I did not understand what was happening.

Mum took me to a doctor before I boarded the train. She was pleased I sat still in the waiting room. She did not know I had walked for five hours the day before and two hours early that morning. The doctor insisted the only way to ease the swellings around my ankles, and to heal the sores on my fingers was to take two vitamin tablets daily. I hated their smell. 'Must be calories,' I thought. I would have to walk more as payback for swallowing them.

'Your ankles will swell and the veins will stand out on your arms until you gain weight,' the doctor warned. My thin arms, covered in soft, fine hairs like on a newborn baby's head, embarrassed Mum, so I wore a cardigan on hot days, when my veins were puffiest.

Mum waved goodbye until the train left the railway station. As soon as I sat down I opened the latches on my suitcase and withdrew Daryl's gift, the small diary. I'd made occasional notes in exercise books before but this was my first real journal, and I looked forward to sharing my life with it. We would be best friends. I tried but could not wait for the New Year; I began writing immediately, December 29, 1962, on a spare page at the back of the book. I recorded my daily exercise, amount of food consumed and, starting the next day, the cricket scores.

At my aunt and uncle's place, without outdoor jobs to burn energy, I walked around the suburban streets for more than an hour each morning and evening, before and after attending the cricket. An icy pole or a soft drink required an extra hour's walk.

I attended the cricket for three days, but did not go on the last day when England was set to win the match, the second in the Test series.

My aunt and uncle, who had two children younger than me, did not scold me for not eating. One evening I tried really hard and ate a lettuce leaf, two pieces of tomato, one piece of meat and half a potato for the evening meal, which they called 'dinner'. Another evening, my aunt and uncle took my cousins and me to Luna Park, an amusement venue at St Kilda, on the foreshore of Port Phillip Bay. A ride on the roller coaster, called the Big Dipper, enabled me to forget my bossy thoughts for a moment and smile. Nothing in the city, however, could match my longing for the farm, the bushland and the Mitchell River, and I was glad to catch the train home on January 14. Mum had been hoping my holiday would encourage me to eat more food, but my weight had dropped from 39kg to 38kg.

In Blackburn, I had weighed myself on scales at the local chemist shop. I had wandered into newsagents and bookshops, looking for magazines and books featuring diets and exercise, sneaking a look and memorising lists of calories.

The holiday had backfired. My illness had acquired new tricks to increase its hold.

Two weeks later, Mum and Dad took me to a doctor in Sale, a town on the Princes Highway, about an hour's drive from our farm. I was vaguely aware that my parents were worrying about me but I was tired and unable to respond.

Blood tests revealed no abnormality.

Since my holiday I had become fixated on meat pies and peanuts. With no freezer, and being frugal, Mum did not buy pies; she made them. As one of a large family growing up in the Great Depression, she steadfastly refused to buy anything she could make herself.

I was fussy. The pie had to be exactly like the Four 'n Twenty meat pies sold at the MCG. I was obsessed with this brand of pie because one of my aunt's women's magazines had listed its calorie content. I could eat one pie a day but first I had to walk or run the equivalent of that many calories. Every moment of every day was focused on controlling the calories to avoid feeling a huge and frightening emptiness.

Flabbergasted and annoyed, because I refused to eat anything else, Mum banged away with her rolling pin in the hot pantry, making pastry with flour and butter, lining special little pie tins, cooking the mince over the hot wood stove, covering the pies and baking them in the hot oven, fair in the middle of a scorching summer.

Mum could not understand why, if I would eat a pie, I wouldn't eat food she cooked for the rest of the family. She made the pies against her will, and she had to make them carefully. I watched her make them and wouldn't eat them if the pastry was too thick, or the meat too fatty.

'They have to be exactly like the bought ones,' I stubbornly said. They had to have the same weight, the same amount of meat, pastry and calories. The possibility of one extra calorie caused me great anxiety. The only way to appease this fear was to exercise more, just in case. I appeared difficult and selfish but couldn't help it.

Mum didn't know that I struggled to convince myself that I should eat anything at all.

The salted peanuts were easier to control. I counted them and allowed myself up to 60g some days. As with the pies, first I had to burn the equivalent number of calories, and make myself wait until late in the afternoon, when I would eat each one slowly, sucking the salt off first, and letting each half nut almost melt in my mouth before starting to chew it.

Reading was a luxury. If I had completed all my exercise routines and jobs for the day, I allowed myself to read a book while eating my peanuts, but I had to avoid Mum. If she found me she would scold: 'If you can eat peanuts why can't you eat one of my biscuits?'

Food created an endless stream of obstacles. One afternoon towards the end of January we drove to Bairnsdale so a childhood friend, Ken, could catch the train home to Morwell, a town about halfway to Melbourne, after a holiday on our farm. Ken and I had grown up having fun together during the school holidays: kicking the footy, setting traps for rabbits and wombats, playing table tennis, hookey, and board games such as draughts, but my illness denied me the freedom to have fun with Ken any more.

We arrived in town early enough for Mum to buy some fruit and vegetables at the greengrocer's before going to the railway station. I tagged along behind her. Ken, spotting a Dairy Queen soft-serve ice-cream sign at the milk bar next door, was off like a shot. He returned at the same time as Mum completed her purchases, and was beaming from ear to ear, juggling three cones filled with swirls of the soft white confection. This was his way of saying 'thank you' for his holiday. His kind gesture must have used all his pocket money. He held a cone out to me. I wanted to reach for it, and say 'thank you', but instead mumbled, 'I don't want it,' my arms hanging limp at my sides. Mum accepted her cone with grace and glared at me. I wanted to sink through the concrete footpath of Bairnsdale's Main Street. For once the pull of my Mum, coupled with my desire not to hurt Ken's feelings, enabled me to respond. I reached out and accepted my cone.

Ken was happy, my mother relieved. We crossed the street to the car. As we left the kerb I lagged behind and dropped my cone in the gutter. Opening the car door, Mum turned to see my empty hands. Ken looked too; he looked hurt, bewildered.

'I can't help it, I was made to do it,' I wanted to scream, but could manage only: 'Sorry, I dropped it.'

After Ken departed on the train, Mum, angry and upset, took me to Foards, Bairnsdale's main clothing store, to buy my new summer uniform—a grey dress and maroon blazer—for secondary school. The school year would start the following week and Mum had delayed fitting me out, hoping I would gain weight first. Now, the store had no uniforms left in stock. *'This is my punishment,'* I thought, *'for not eating the ice-cream'.* I went home with the only items that were available: black shoes, grey socks and sandshoes.

I was up at 6.30am for my first day at secondary school. There were 38 children in my class, 20 boys and 18 girls.

My anxiety at being out of uniform gave me nightmares. Of 150 Year Seven students, I was one of five girls without the correct dress.

When told the store had sold out of uniforms, Mum, against her will, because she hated buying anything to fit my skeletal frame, bought me a new dress to wear to school until the uniform arrived. I hated this sissy dress, which I wore with my new black shoes and grey socks. Made of fawn-coloured gingham with a white lacy collar and short puffed sleeves, it was lined with a stiff net petticoat that prickled my legs when I sat down.

I wanted to sink through the asphalt of the quadrangle when the girls' senior mistress called a school assembly and drew attention to students out of uniform. Two weeks passed before my school dress and blazer arrived in the mail.

Sitting alone on a wooden garden seat at school lunchtimes, I pretended to eat the sandwiches Mum packed for me and then, checking no one was looking, would drop them in a bin. None of my primary school classmates were in my class and I didn't know or care where they were in the big school grounds. Joy was at a senior campus on the other side of town and had her own friends.

Going to high school meant I was away from home from 7.30am until 5pm. On my first school night Mum made a special effort and had tea ready early. I ate a tomato. Eating less was necessary to compensate for exercising less. I sat for hours on the school bus, and in class, and now didn't have time to feed the calves before and after school.

The challenge of schoolwork was a diversion, but fresh problems were brewing. Almost a year to the day my periods had started, they stopped completely. When I was two weeks overdue, Mum took me to a doctor in Maffra, a town about 50km from home. The doctor, trying to find a reason why I wasn't eating, told Mum I didn't want to grow up, that I wanted to be a boy. My weight had dropped to 37kg. I saw another doctor the following week, so weak I no longer cared what happened to me.

Saturday, March 9, Joy's 15th birthday, dawned hot. I mustered the strength to go swimming in the river and saw a big black snake slither into the water from the grassy bank. As with the red-backed spiders that spun webs in the stable, I treated snakes with guarded respect. This latest one was a whopper and I would tell Mum about it. My family had enough snake stories to fill a book. One brown snake had wrapped itself around Mum's ankle as she carried a big basket of washing under the bougainvillea arch and through the back gate to the clothesline; another day, when our parents were milking the cows, Joy had shot a black snake on our front lawn, using the .22 rifle that was kept in our washhouse. One bullet and the snake was dead. I was impressed. Dad said a snake did not die until after sundown so we did not worry when it continued to writhe and wiggle.

Back at the house after my swim, I found Mum standing at her pantry workbench, preparing cake mixtures to bake for the birthday celebration.

She paused to wipe sweat from her brow while beating the sugar and butter with the wooden spatula. Dad hadn't started to milk the cows yet so there was no power for her electric mixer. I stood at the end of the bench watching her fold in the eggs and flour, and wished she wasn't so tired.

Dusting her hands on her apron, Mum poured the smooth mixture into two round sponge cake tins and carried them through to the little stove in the kitchen. With a potholder she opened the oven door, lifted out two trays of patty cakes and put the sponge mixture in. There was no temperature control on our stove. Mum managed the heat by monitoring the wood placed in the firebox, and adjusting the flue.

She checked the time for the sponges and carried the trays of patty cakes into the pantry. 'Oh no,' she cried. The patty cakes, nothing like Mum's usual little peaked mountains of perfection, had shrunk into flat, rubbery pan-cake shapes.

'I'll have to throw these out to the dog and the chooks, no-one will want to eat them,' she said wearily. She had no time to bake more patty cakes before helping with the afternoon milking and was about to cry. My heart went out to her.

'Don't worry, Mum, I'll eat them,' I suddenly said. My words popped out, just like that. For more than a year anorexia had imprisoned my thoughts and now suddenly released them.

Mum was thrilled. Her flop had turned out a winner. I ate the entire batch of 12 rubbery cakes before the day was out.

I was pleased Mum and Dad were happy but I felt strange. Soon I was eating more than rubbery cakes. I was eating my meals, and the urge to hide food and to constantly exercise ebbed away.

Because I was eating and gaining weight, my parents cancelled further medical appointments and Mum celebrated by taking me shopping for my first pair of stockings, complete with suspender belt and a small corset called step-ins. The step-ins held my stockings up and my tummy in. I didn't have much tummy to hold in – in fact there was a lake between my bony hips—but felt I was starting to grow up. We were about to have a rare weekend away from the farm, to attend a cousin's wedding near the central Victorian city of Bendigo. We went shopping again while we were in Bendigo and noticed scales outside a chemist shop. I'd gained half a kilogram but remained thin, weighing 14kg less than my mother, who was always slim and ate like a bird. My sister, who loved vanilla slices, chocolate and fresh bread, was 28kg heavier than me.

Each week I gained weight and, without anorexia dominating my thoughts with food, food, food, began to notice life around me. I noted in my diary that the United States sent a man into space. His name was Cooper and he orbited 23 times before returning safely to Earth.

My city cousins came to stay for the May holidays. The weather being too wintry to sleep on the verandah, I was back sleeping on Mum and Dad's bedroom floor while my cousins took over my room. Luckily I had a water bag, filled from the kettle on top of the stove, to keep me warm for at least the first part of the night.

I set my traps again and fed the calves while my cousins, as usual, slept in. One morning I was busy in the yards with the calves when Alicia, one of my girl cousins, bounded down the hill to the dairy, calling my name.

'I'm over here in the calf pen, look where you put your feet,' I yelled back.

Some of the calves developed scours from upset tummies while adjusting from their mother's milk to my powdered brew and they squirted smelly yellow 'custard' all over the place.

I had been treating the worst-affected poddies, holding them in a corner of the dusty yard, opening their mouths and stuffing pink scour tablets inside. This was a messy job and I was not in a good mood.

'Ade's reading your diary,' Alicia said, with telltale glee.

I saw red. I opened the pen gate, shooed the calves out and raced up the gravel track towards the house. Ade was coming down to the dairy. Younger than me, but a good 15kg heavier, he was laughing but not for long. I met him halfway.

'Have you been reading my diary?'

Ade thought this was a joke. 'Yes,' he grinned.

I sprung and pounded his tubby chest with my fists. He fell backwards into the grass on the side of the track. I rode him to the ground, sat on him, pressed his hands above his head with my feet and continued to pummel him. He was crying now.

'Don't-you-ever-tell-anyone-what-you-read, and don't-read-my-diary-again,' I said, punching home every word.

Alicia, who witnessed these proceedings, was crying too.

'Ade's not moving,' she wailed.

I paused in my pounding.

She was right. I'd winded him. Now I'd be in trouble.

I patted his face.

'Ade, Ade, come on Ade.'

Ade stirred and I heaved him into a sitting position.

We reached agreement: I wouldn't punch him any more in return for him forgetting what he read in my diary, and not telling anyone I'd whacked him. We were quickly best of friends again.

I gained 7kgs in three months and was doing well at school, becoming more outgoing and making new friends. Both classmates and teachers said, 'June, you are coming out of your shell'.

Following the subsidence of my anorexia, I had emerged from being the quietest to one of the most bubbly students in the class.

Unaware that this was the calm before a storm, I was enjoying the freedom of being me.

On Saturday, November 23, the USA was in the news again. I was helping Dad clean up in the dairy after the morning milking when we stopped to listen as the news crackled over our shed wireless.

I had not heard the word 'assassinated' before but wrote in my diary as best I could:

Very history-making day.
PRESIDENT KENNEDY OF AMERICA WAS SACINATED IN DALLAS IN TEXAS. VERY SAD! TERRIBLE.
Everyone is sad, as Mr Kennedy has done a great good many things to the world. He was only 46. He was shot in the head, died 35 minutes later.

As I trudged up to the farmhouse a short time later, carrying a billy of milk for breakfast, I wondered why some people were cruel.

One month later, I celebrated my 13th birthday with a big slice of birthday cake. I weighed 55kg, almost 18kg more than 12 months before, and was 160cm tall. Almost free of food thoughts, I embraced my summer holidays. Straight after Christmas, Aunty Carlie and Uncle Roy took me to Adelaide, South Australia, a 15-hour drive from home. My aunt and uncle had been providing regular cultural enrichment since my first holiday with them at the age of seven. In Adelaide, they took me to the art gallery, museum, zoo, botanic gardens, port, airport and Barossa Valley wine-growing region. When I arrived home, Dad had a surprise waiting in the paddock—a chocolate-coloured horse, 13 hands high. This new equine friend replaced my white Shetland pony, Tommy, who I'd been riding since the age of nine. The newcomer quickly earned the name of Nipper because he nipped my backside whenever he got the chance. I rode Nipper to fetch our cows for milking and to collect our mail from the cream-can letterbox around the corner.

Completing a great holiday, Corinella, who ran the children's page in *The Sun* newspaper, invited me to her annual party. Invitations were issued to children who won the most points in drawing and writing competitions throughout the year. The party included a ticket to a pantomime in Melbourne, and this was a big cultural treat for a bumpkin like me. I travelled on the train and my Great Aunt Della, who lived in the suburb of Elsternwick, looked after me.

Life appeared wonderful, and I strove to ignore niggling thoughts that something was wrong. In the past 12 months I had not menstruated and during the summer holidays had gradually—so that nobody noticed—dropped 7kg in weight.

In February I began the new school year, in Year Eight, a much happier, more outgoing child than a year before when I was withdrawn and frightened to speak. Classmates elected my friend Helen, who lived in Bairnsdale, as class captain and myself as vice-captain. Weekends were spent swimming, horse riding and helping on the farm.

Joy turned 16 in March and enrolled at a hairdressing academy in Melbourne. She had wanted to be a hairdresser since she was three. She often practised on me and one day had fed Tommy the Shetland a cup of sugar from the pantry while giving his beautiful long mane a crew-cut.

With Joy leaving home to board with our Aunt Marion and Uncle Alf for the next 16 months, I had our bedroom to myself.

The age of 14 was a period of stability, when I suppressed the nagging feelings and was pretty much free to be me. Home life seemed less stressful and I was happy—developing friendships, doing well at school, and helping my parents on the farm.

My weight stabilised between 46kg and 47kg; I won a Junior State Government Scholarship, was dux of Year Nine at school, was in the school hockey team and won a school cross-country race. One day my mother was called to the post office to collect a telegram from Sydney. It announced I had won a bicycle for having the most articles published during the previous six months in *The Australian Children's Newspaper*. I was chuffed with the award but, as my old bike was more suited to our gravelled and corrugated roads, Dad and I decided to sell my prize to a bicycle shop. I received $27, enough to pay for a 10-day trip with the Young Australia League (YAL) to Sydney and the Blue Mountains, more than 700km from home, during the next summer holidays. I was excited by the chance to travel and make new friends. Writing was starting to provide opportunities outside the valley but the farm was my major source of inspiration and contentment.

During this time I was conscious of my food intake, but managed to control it. If I wanted a chocolate bar, I would walk for an hour so that I could eat the chocolate as a reward. Anorexic thoughts remained, but I thought I was in control, turning to them as needed to supress anxiety.

Thanks to my father, I was even starting to think life had possibilities despite my gender. He never said: 'You can't do that because you are a girl.' His usual advice was: 'You won't know unless you try.' My love of, and affinity with, the land and the bush evolved from him.

Apart from hunting, which I learned from Dad, I loved to wander alone in the bush through the sweet-scented tea tree scrub, clambering over moss-covered rocks and across ferny gullies. I was not lonely. Kookaburras laughed overhead from branches in the big, shady gumtrees. Salamanders scarpered across rocks and fat goannas raced surprisingly fast to scale the nearest tree trunk or slip into the water. A platypus family lived in one section of the river. They playfully splashed and somersaulted near the bank while mid-stream, a pair of black swans glided by. The river and the bush, forever my friends, connected me with my soul and gave me strength to suppress my anxiety and food thoughts.

Almost.

4. SWEET SIXTEEN

At 15 years of age, I didn't look thin. I mean, I didn't look like I had a food or weight problem. I played tennis and hockey, enjoyed cross-country running, went to dances and worked on the farm; I ate most of the meals Mum dished up and, when visiting the homes of friends, I ate the meals there, too. This avoided many embarrassing moments, but I began to feel uneasy because I wasn't developing like other girls.

The breasts that had distressed me when I was 11 had disappeared and my chest was flat. Mum, concerned that I'd not had a period for almost three years, took me to a doctor in Bairnsdale. He wrote a prescription for tablets and said to take them for three months.

My girlfriends did not know about my secret. Totally outgoing, they were starting to socialise with boys and encouraged me to keep up with them. Several were joining the Glenaladale Young Farmers' Club and persuaded me to go along too. With 62 members, this was the largest and fastest-growing Young Farmers' club in East Gippsland, and one of the most active in the Victorian Young Farmers (VYF) organisation. Aged between 14 and 25, the members met at 8pm on alternate Thursdays, in the Glenaladale Hall. The club calendar was full of cultural, agricultural and social events—including dances, rabbit hunts, progressive dinners and debating competitions—which attracted young men and women from miles around. Some, like me, were still at school, but most were working—usually the young men were on farms and the girls, while living on farms, had secretarial, teaching or nursing jobs in town.

Within three weeks of taking the tablets prescribed by the doctor, my periods returned. I was relieved and so was Mum. Now that I was growing up she didn't call me Tim or Toby, and she encouraged my budding femininity by meeting me after school one day to shop for some teenage clothes: a pink jacket, a dark green tartan winter shift, a light blue pair of jeans, a pair of dark blue sneakers and pink lipstick.

To top it off, Mum bought fish and chips for me to eat on the way home. I was looking forward to finishing those tablets because although they had fixed me up and my breasts were filling out, they had made me gain weight. In 14 weeks I had gained about 7kg, making me 55kg. I was unhappy about this and tried to suppress growing unrest by helping on the farm and keeping fit. Sometimes on weekends, I milked the cows to give Dad a break, and I did more jobs on the tractor now that I had learnt how to change the gears. Running helped me feel stronger and happier and, being a member of the school hockey team, I regularly ran up the river and back for practice. All was going well but, after finishing the tablets, I missed another three periods. Mum took me back to the doctor and the news wasn't good: 'Becoming normal will take time, but don't worry. Take these tablets for another six months,' he said. 'I hope I won't get fat,' I said. Within a month my periods resumed and I felt relieved, having feared they might not come again.

The medication was stirring my hormones and desire for independence. My parents would not allow me to go on a date until I was 16 but a friend, Rodney, wanted to escort me to a Young Farmers' meeting. The VYF organisation was often referred to as a marriage bureau but I didn't think the regular Thursday-night meetings should count as a 'date'. However, Mum was adamant. 'No,' she said. She kept me on tenterhooks for several days before delivering this blunt judgement. My anxiety compounded to the point where I exploded, 'Why not?'

'Things happen,' Mum said, 'and I'll tell your father if you keep on about it.'

My courage failing, I blurted, 'Why haven't you told me about the facts of life? Why haven't you explained how babies are made?' During lunchtime at school my girlfriends had whispered about 'intercourse', and laughed when I asked what the word meant. They explained and, feeling repulsed and horrified, I took their suggestion and borrowed a book on procreation from the school library.

Despite growing up on a farm, where I saw bulls mount and enter cows that were on heat, and nine months later watched the same cows giving birth, I remained ignorant and naïve about this wondrous act.

Feeling increasingly stressed, I began to wonder what those tablets were doing to my hormones. For the first time in three-and-a-half years I began to count calories, allowing myself no more than 1500 calories a day, to give myself a sense of control and security.

I am on a diet! I want to lose 3kg.

I was progressively eating less and exercising more but Mum occasionally had some pull, usually when she made chocolate crackles. The sight of those rice bubble crunchies made me forget my diet. Momentarily. Eating sugary food was pleasant but guilt quickly kicked in and I would have to go for a long run to regain my sense of control. Being outdoors and being physically active helped me feel good within myself.

At home we were becoming more modern, the latest update being hot water from a tap. A Lindenow tradesman installed a hot water service and a new slow-combustion stove that, besides being used for cooking and baking, heated the water. Hot- and cold-water taps were fitted in the bathroom and our big cast-iron bath with claw feet was boxed in. I was pleased, as our bath had looked horribly old-fashioned with its feet on show. The copper and our big firewood box were taken out of the washhouse, making room for a shower to be installed.

Dad had the first bath using the hot water system. Until now water for our bath had come from kettles carried from the kitchen stove, or buckets carried from the washhouse copper or the briquette heater at the cow-yard. I had the first shower; I'd envied friends who had a shower in their homes. Until now I had used a dipper to wash my hair, bending over in the bathtub. Now, I stood as a continuous spray of warm water washed the suds from my hair and down my body. This was bliss. I hoped the household improvements would help me feel more like my friends. Something was preventing me from connecting with them—I was on the periphery, rather than within, their friendship circle.

Academically I continued to achieve and in October *The Examiner* newspaper in Tasmania sent a letter announcing I was the Victorian female winner of a 1500-word essay competition on the 'Apple Isle'. Dad was in the dairy when I told him and he left the cows alone for a moment to give me a big kiss. The prize for the boy and girl winner from each State was a week-long tour of Tasmania. This was exciting but, feeling anxious, I climbed high into the branches of the loquat tree outside our back door and ate bunches of the small yellow fruits, dropping their shiny round brown seeds on the ground below, until I felt bloated and sick.

At the end of the school year, just prior to Christmas, I joined other mainland essay winners and flew, on what was my first flight, from Melbourne to Launceston. From there we travelled with a chaperone in a bus around the island. We explored the former penal settlement at Port Arthur and, having recently read *For the Term of his Natural Life* by Marcus Clarke, I felt for the convicts at this isolated outpost, far from loved ones in England. We ate sample chocolates from the Cadbury's factory at Claremont, and went to the drive-in theatre, our bus parked sideways so we could see out the windows. By now I had a crush on Philip, the Victorian boy essay winner, from Portland. We sat together and Philip introduced me to French kissing; I remember nothing about the movie.

The next day we donned hardhats to learn about lead, zinc and copper mining in the towns of Zeehan, Queenstown and Rosebery. In Launceston we visited the huge Paton and Baldwin's spinning mill, which used power from Tasmania's hydro-electric scheme.

For me, the best was left until last, with a tour of the *The Examiner* newspaper press and printing rooms in Launceston. For the first time I began to think of journalism as a career, and boarded the plane for home feeling more sure about my life goals.

Philip and I planned to meet again over the coming summer holidays but, within a few weeks of returning home to celebrate my 16th birthday, between Christmas and New Year, another boy won my heart.

The first Saturday in January 1967 began like any other. After reading a book until 2.30am I had to get up at 6am to help in the dairy and, although I pleaded tiredness, Mum and Dad were adamant that I accompany them to the dance that night at the Glenaladale Hall.

Supporting the local community by attending dances was important to my parents. Adults who didn't dance played a card game, euchre, on trestle tables in the hall's meeting room; at midnight, the dancing and card-playing ceased and the trestle tables were carried into the main hall where everyone gathered for a sumptuous homemade supper.

As soon as I entered the hall that night I was glad my parents had insisted I go along. The three-member 'old-time band', comprising pianist, saxophonist and drummer, had never sounded so good. This was because George Coster, a member of our Young Farmers' Club, asked me for every dance. George, who lived on a dairy farm at Sarsfield, 40km away, not only danced with me but also sat with me. His twinkling brown eyes, framed by long curling eyelashes, brown wavy hair and sideburns, acted like a spell. My heart began to hop, skip and jump. George was 18, softly spoken and easy to talk to. Slightly taller than me, he was of strong and stocky build with biceps as big and hard as huge potatoes. We danced as one, as though we had been dancing forever, and had eyes only for each other. Mum and Dad had to remind me it was time to go home, and George walked me to their car.

This was the first time I had been escorted out of the hall by a boy. My parents had a strict rule that I wasn't to leave the hall during the evening, except to go to the toilet. About a cricket-pitch length from the Glen hall's back door, the women's toilet was cocooned in a rickety weatherboard structure that doubled as a home for spiders. There was no light and my girlfriends and I yelled if we touched a cobweb, and raced back inside. My mother regularly warned me not to leave the hall for any other reason because 'things do happen'. She would not elaborate but I guessed she meant that nine months later a baby might appear, and lives might be ruined. This train of events had happened to some of my girlfriends, who were sent away until their babies were born and adopted out. Falling pregnant when single meant shame for the girl and her family. Somehow the same stigma did not apply to the father of the child, who was free to get on with his life. George walking me to the car was okay, because my parents were walking with us. No time for even a quick kiss!

Now that I was 16, however, I was at the magical age at which I could start dating. Reminding my parents of this took courage. They probably did not dream that I would meet a boy within two weeks of my 16th birthday. Already I could hardly wait until the next Thursday night when I would see George at Young Farmers.

Tactfully, I asked Mum, and then Dad, if George could take me to the local dances and Young Farmers, and succeeded in getting 'yes' as an answer. I rang George and we talked for a whole hour. Mum was about to knock my block off but honestly George didn't stop talking. He was delighted with my negotiating success and said he'd pick me up at 8.45pm the following Saturday to go dancing.

A month later I spent Saturday morning picking a bucket each of beans and tomatoes down the paddock for Mum. I helped in the house too, trying to get her in a good mood to ask if I could go with George to see the movie *Dr Zhivago* at the Moondale drive-in theatre in Lucknow, near Bairnsdale but she said: 'No. You are not to go to the drive-in until you are 17.' I thought two rejections in a row would be too much so, while milking the cows that night, I asked if I could go to Warragul with George in April to the Young Farmers' State Achievement Day, and Dad said 'Yes'! Warragul was a three-hour drive from home and the Young Farmers were booking rooms in a motel to stay overnight. I gave Dad a big hug.

My heart sang as I returned to school in February to start Year 11—happy because of George and because I had finished those pills that made my periods come back—this time successfully. The prefects for the new school year were announced in our school general assembly. Seventeen were from Year 11 and three were chosen by popular student vote from Year 10. Out of more than 100 students, I was one. *'I must be normal,'* I thought, thankfully.

The school year had hardly started when I read a circular on the student notice board about an American Field Service Scholarship Scheme, offering a chance to attend school and live in the United States for a year. My imagination worked overtime. A fan of author Zane Grey, I saw myself as a cowgirl on a Texas ranch—riding a horse, cracking a whip and lassoing runaway calves. Dad liked that image too and said to me encouragingly, 'You won't know unless you have a go.'

The thought of pursuing a big goal like this helped to subdue my growing obsession with food. My days were increasingly defined by good days, as in being-in-control-of-food days, and bad days, when I ate until my mind was numb and my stomach about to burst. Farm work, and running along the river to Lambert's Flat, helped to ease my anxiety.

Trying to maintain a sense of control by counting calories was a constant challenge: one day I ate 10 apples. Clearly that was a bad day, because the apples were just the start. George said I was 'nice and cuddly'. This meant I was round and fat and I hoped I wasn't that bad. Another day, Mum had school canteen duty and brought home some leftover salad rolls; I restricted my school lunch to raw fruit or vegetables and had been in control all day, counting every single calorie, but in a weak moment I grabbed two of those delicious rolls and gobbled them down in two minutes flat. That's how long it took to break my false sense of security. Guilt was immediate and so was my punishment—I ran up the rocky river track and back twice, a total of 6km, in the dark.

One morning I arrived at school to discover my period had come early. I felt sick in the stomach but no wonder, because the night before I'd eaten a tray full of rich White Christmas slice and a large bag of grapes— *after* the evening meal.

Bulimia nervosa, the cycle of bingeing followed—in my case—by compensatory behaviours of exercising and fasting, was settling in. I did not know I had an illness. I thought I was weak for not coping. I wanted to be carefree like my friends but did not know how.

Amazingly, George seemed oblivious to my struggle. Going home after our latest date, a dance, he whispered in my ear as we cuddled in his car: 'I love you, and I mean it.' Not knowing what to say, I said nothing. I felt overwhelmed. This was the first time anyone had said to me: 'I love you'. Although I didn't feel worthy of his love, with George I could push my tormenting thoughts aside for a while and be myself; he became the centre of my world. He represented a rock-solid anchor that I could hang on to, against the pull of my eating disorder.

But I felt a growing urge to escape my nagging void within. I could not settle. Six months after George and I began dating, I mailed my application form for the American scholarship. Dad sent his confidential report too. I hoped that was not the last I'd hear of the scholarship because my eating problem was seriously sapping my ability to cope with the pressure of schoolwork, especially the twice-yearly examinations. While studying I either starved or gorged myself with food, food and more food. One evening I ate an entire 500g packet of sultanas after tea!

Sometimes I studied for seven hours and ate for seven hours. Then I would switch to stringently counting calories, thinking: *'If I control what I eat, everything else will be manageable'*. I felt happy, momentarily. I wished I had more time to help Mum and Dad with farm work and to ride Nipper. I also wanted to know if I should consider careers other than journalism.

Surely nobody could be as muddled, jumbled and undecided as me. I feel split between two worlds: I could leave school at the end of Year 11, live at home on the farm and work in Bairnsdale, or do Matriculation in Year 12 and go to Melbourne to university and get a really good job like teaching. The latter option is scary—I would surely get stressed out with study because I would feel I had to learn everything. I hope to win a scholarship to the United States to defer worrying for a while.

Controlling food intake was easier when the exams were over and I could catch up on some social life. George and I continued to go dancing every weekend and on our way home parked in the scrub off the Princes Highway, or up a seldom-used bush track, in his two-tone blue Holden. We had our favourite parking spots. Mum would have been impressed if she knew the effort I exerted to convince George we must not 'go all the way' because 'things do happen'.

But she seemed to resent my freedom and happiness. One Sunday morning, after I had three consecutive nights of coming home after midnight, she opened my bedroom door at 7.30am to remind me the cows were being milked and Dad needed help. She didn't care if I'd been out all night, saying, 'Get up and help your father, you know how tired he is.' Farm work was never-ending. There was no point saying, 'But I'm tired,' because her retort was swift: 'Your father NEVER complains.'

The following Sunday morning, I went to bed at 2.20am, and again Mum opened my bedroom door at 7.30am, calling 'Get out of bed. You know your father needs help in the dairy. You are either out with George or studying, you don't help on the farm any more, and you know how tired Dad is.'

This time my temper flew as I headed to the dairy: I slammed the back door, didn't say good-bye and left the front gate open, not caring if the chooks came in to the house yard and scratched for worms in the flower beds. However, Mum and I were back on good terms by nightfall. I felt guilty for not filling the role of a son, and guilty for being happy with the life I was starting to create with George.

I lived for the Saturday-night dances. My troubles were swept aside when George took me to the Sale Memorial Hall, where there was a large, polished floor and a band providing both old-time and rock 'n' roll music.

We hardly missed a dance and looked forward to our cuddle on the way home. These were the days before seatbelts were mandatory in cars, and George drove with his arm around me until pulling off the highway into our haven in the tea-tree scrub, and switching off the headlights. It was here one night that I eventually said: 'I love you'. Once the words were out, I repeated them. George had already told me about 10 times, and now that I'd told him we both felt very happy. I told him things I had wanted to tell him for ages, including about my struggle with food, and while George may not have understood, he was comforting.

We were devoted to one another. Then, a letter came. There it was, leaning against the vase of flowers in the centre of our kitchen table when I arrived home from school. Mum had placed it there for me to open. Nervously slitting the envelope, I gently pulled out the sheet of paper and began reading from the bottom up. The American Australian Association was inviting me to attend an interview for an American Field Service scholarship!

Mum and Dad shared my excitement. The AFS had started an international student exchange in 1946 to promote cross-cultural understanding. Since then, thousands of students had been exchanged and now I had a chance of being an exchangee too.

I told George but made light of it—if I gained selection, which was surely doubtful, many months would pass before my departure.

Dad drove me to Melbourne for the interview. I wore a new bright red wool dress with a belt and polo-necked collar trimmed in white. There were seven girls in my group and we were all nervous. We were asked to discuss two topics among ourselves. Then we were called individually to face a panel of six interviewers; two were ex-AFSers. I was asked many questions: about why I wanted to go to the USA, about Australian and American politics, Vietnam, home and social life. I wished I could speak more clearly but was heartened by the panel's interest in my essay-writing success and parting words, 'Expect a letter within two weeks'.

The letter came. I slowly opened it and then, as my eyes raced over the contents, yelled, 'I am being considered for a scholarship.' Mum and Dad were pleased. My Texan-ranch visions were becoming more real. There would be a home interview and later a group interview. The following day, a Health Certificate form arrived from the American Australian

Association. Its many questions included one about nervous breakdowns and psychiatrists. 'You have seen a psychiatrist,' Mum said, 'but we will ignore that question.'

My family preferred to think I was fine and I tried to appear fine because I didn't want people thinking I was strange or weak, but waves of torment were building within. One evening, nine months after George and I had started dating, I felt like howling when we had our first misunderstanding. I was at fault. He came for tea, and I was ready in my red dress to go dancing at Sale, when he said he had to visit some extended family locally instead. I didn't mind, but all we did was sit and listen and talk. Mum and Dad had gone out that night too and we were home before them: at about 11.30pm. I wasn't in a kissing mood and all sorts of things—the sudden change in plans for the evening, uncertainty about my scholarship application, essay deadlines, and the thought of no entertainment for the next two weeks while my exams were on—added up to make me very quiet and not altogether pleasant. Mum and Dad arrived home and George departed without kissing me goodnight. This was the first time he'd done that.

I could think of only one way to calm my anxiety.

After my parents went to bed I crept to the kitchen, opened the fridge door and ate an entire plateful of buttered drop-scones that Mum had brought home from her evening out. By now the time was 1.50am and, wide-awake, I read some magazines and listened to the wireless to calm myself. Next morning I didn't eat breakfast and with each new hour of not eating, began to feel happier. I didn't know what Mum thought about all her drop-scones disappearing. Wisely, she didn't ask. My spirits lifted further when George visited in the afternoon and I apologised for my rudeness. I loved him yet acted as though I felt the opposite. I didn't know what was wrong with me.

Another invitation arrived from the American Australian Association to a meeting in Melbourne, this time to meet other scholarship applicants still in the race. Seventy-five per cent of us would be placed with suitable families but final confirmation would not take place for another four months.

Uncertainty began to feed my waves of depression and I was grateful to my sunny-natured girlfriend Helen Edwards, who lived on a sheep grazing property at Fernbank, near Glenaladale, for keeping my spirits up. I called her 'Helen Eddy' to differentiate from my other best friend, Helen McLeod, who lived in Bairnsdale. I'd been friends with each since starting high school. Helen Eddy and I travelled on the same bus to school. Her strengths were the sciences, whereas mine was humanities. We were always concerned about our weight and joked about our diets, and how much we had eaten the night before. Helen Eddy was outgoing and more than anyone else encouraged me to join the Young Farmers' organisation. Boys and schoolwork were our main topics of conversation. Helen was of Swiss heritage and had long and glossy straight black hair, high rosy cheekbones and sparkling Sophia Loren eyes. She was beautiful, in both nature and looks. She was highly sought-after by boys and, at 15, had dated George before dropping him for one of my cousins. I had thought George was handsome and encouraged Helen not to drop him. Now, however, I was glad she ignored my suggestion, because six months later he had started dating me. At times Helen and I laughed so much on our way to and from school—sharing descriptions of our romantic parking adventures—that our bus driver threatened to put us off. We studied hard and our giggling fits left us weak and let the tension out.

However, my anxiety was increasing and I'd been feeling black for two days when Mum collected me after school one day to go shopping.

My depressed mood grew today and reached its climax when Mum picked me up from school at 2pm and went down the street. I ate some raisins (how fattening!) and bought an ice-cream—ugh! And on the way home I started to cry and I don't know why ... Mum doesn't either, I'm sure. I told her I was sick of rushing everywhere. Anyway, I gorged myself on apples and oranges when we arrived home and Mum made me eat all my tea and I also drank a litre of lovely pineapple drink that I bought. I'm out of my mood now and I am NOT going to gorge myself again, no matter how depressed I get.

A letter the following week confirmed my name had been sent to New York for an AFS scholarship, and only one step remained—that of being matched with a suitable family. I told Mum and Dad that if I received a placement, I'd prefer to stay home and work locally when I returned, as

I wanted to get married at the age of 21. Mum said: 'It will be a wonder if you aren't married before then!' Mum and Dad liked George, and also his parents, Charlie and Marion. Already they visited each other, and community and farming were common bonds.

Knowing we might be separated for 12 months, George and I made the most of our time together. On Saturday afternoons we played tennis with the Young Farmers' Club and, after milking the cows and eating tea, we dressed up and went dancing, usually at Sale. I wore a dress, stockings and squat heels, and George a shirt and tie, maroon sports jacket and dark sports trousers. We loved rock 'n' roll and old-time dance music equally and were on the floor from 9pm until the band stopped at midnight. We twisted, rocked and swayed with hit songs by Johnny O'Keefe, Col Joye, Normie Rowe, Elvis Presley, the Bee Gees and Buddy Holly. We sneaked a kiss and held each other tight in the slow Foxtrot, swung around in the Evening Three Step and looked forward to being in each other's arms on completing the circle in the graceful progressive Pride of Erin. I forgot my troubles while dancing; especially one night when in a romantic moment George whispered, 'I want you forever.'

I whispered back, 'You can have me.'

He said, 'I'll be waiting for you when you come back from America.'

This assurance was comforting but, a month before my end of Year 11 exams, dark moods swept in. I pitied everyone who came near me. The effort of trying to subdue my urge to eat so I could study was debilitating. Passing a subject was never enough—I had to do my very best and felt guilty if not constantly studying. Fearful of failure, I stopped playing tennis and curtailed seeing George. I memorised every page of class notes.

Stupid schoolwork; I am absolutely sure these will be my last exams, even though the Year 12 co-coordinator is insisting I go to university and do an arts degree.

George had left school at 16 to work on his father's dairy farm. He played tennis in summer, football in winter and participated in the Young Farmers' Club, and I wanted to be settled and content like him.

He influenced my decision making, because he was saying, 'We are going to be together for always.' George was already like a rock in my life. He was as steady and sensible as I was vulnerable and naïve. When he said we would be together always, I believed him, but still I was not happy with my body size. I'd lost 3kg in a month and he said: 'I like you as you are and don't want you to get an ounce heavier or lighter.' But I wanted to get thinner yet.

On weekends, in warm weather, I took my books down to the river's edge and sat on the rocks with my toes in a rock pool, soaking up the sun's warmth on my back, and feeling pacified in the peaceful setting. Such peace was short-lived. One day the sun got too hot and, returning to the house:

I ate and ate—and am not eating excessively again! I ate so much my stomach was turning somersaults: with peanuts, Twisties, ice cream, oranges, apples and dry biscuits. What a mixture! I thought I would have a feast seeing as the scales registered only 52kg when I weighed myself yesterday, but I can't say I was eating because I was hungry—must be tension.

Next morning on the school bus, I confessed my loss of food control to Helen. She had eaten a lot too, but surely nowhere near as much as me. We spent nearly all day laughing at anything, but mainly at the size of our stomachs. We'd eaten so much they looked as if we were having babies, and that wasn't exaggerating. Again, we couldn't stop ourselves laughing. Tears streamed down our faces; it was one way of letting the tension out, I supposed. Nerves, that's what it was.

I'm going on a diet starting tomorrow. I feel that sick from eating. Ugh!

With three weeks until my first Year 11 exam, determined to gain control, I adopted a strict routine, eating raw carrots and limes for my school lunch—the lime tree in what we called the 'old orchard' on the farm was loaded with fruit, and Dad grew the carrots, so there was plenty of both. Neither could be eaten quickly—the limes were sour and the carrots hard—so sucking on the lime and chomping on the carrots filled my lunch hour, if not my stomach. And the calories were easy to count.

Aerial picture of the family farm, Weeroona, at Iguana Creek. The windmill is in the bottom right corner by the Mitchell River.

Our farmhouse and the veranda I slept on in summertime during my childhood.

Age six, starting school, 1957.

With my big sister Joy.

The farmhouse and valley, 1950s. Notice the smoke coming from the kitchen chimney. The tank supplied the house with river water via the windmill. The dairy is down the hill on the right.

Me, age 13, feeding the calves—I loved helping my father with jobs on the farm.

Age 14, in Bairnsdale High School winter uniform.

Age 10, ready for the annual school sports day.

The outhouse: leave the door open while on the throne for a glorious view across the hills.

Age 13, on Nipper.

At Lakes Entrance, age 19, 1970.

Age 20, stuck in a cervical collar after driving under a loaded log truck.

Age 17, 1968: Sir Irving Benson presents me with a $50 award for winning a state essay competition on marriage. The money paid for my first manual typewriter.

Age 20. By now, my eating disorder had tormented me for almost a decade.

I looked at my friends happily eating salad rolls, meat pies and pasties, cream buns, vanilla slices and Paddle Pop ice-creams—all available at the school canteen, and marvelled at them eating such calorie-loaded food without being overwhelmed with guilt.

A few days before the exams began, Mum and Dad saw my principal, Mr Dyson, about my study options for the following year. Mr Dyson said I could start my Matriculation in February and, if I went to the USA in July, finish it when I returned home 12 months later. I didn't agree—I knew I'd be a nervous wreck.

Studying for the Year 11 exams was hard enough. One night my control broke. I tried to silence my anxiety, devouring a 300g packet of peanuts in less than an hour.

That was just the start. I ate enough to fill the world's largest elephant.

Amazingly, when the exams were over I weighed only 54kg in my school uniform. My relief was supreme and I looked forward to my 17th birthday. George and I celebrated this by doing the 'in' thing and going to the Moondale Drive-in to see a movie—well, part of a movie because we were distracted much of the time—snuggled up with cushions and rug in the comfort and privacy of his two-tone blue Holden.

We went to Lakes Entrance, a 45-minute drive from the farm, on New Year's Eve. In East Gippsland, this coastal town was the place to be on the eve of January 1, with two dances and a carnival in full swing on the Esplanade. As the night wore on, the crowd became merrier, yelling ''Appy New Year', to anybody or nobody, and motorists hooted and tooted.

At midnight George and I sat on the edge of the sea wall, the lights and the roar of the carnival behind us, and watched colourful fireworks shoot above the sand dunes on the far side of the channel. Afterwards we met up with Joy and her boyfriend Ray and squeezed around a table in a small, crowded café for a milkshake and hamburger with the lot—I figured I had danced enough to earn this treat. I was enjoying my hamburger until I went 'crunch' and realised the chef had served the eggshell too! George and I departed Lakes Entrance at 2.30am, stopping to cuddle for an hour in the scrub, and we crawled into our separate beds in adjacent rooms at his parents' house at 4.35am.

Sometimes I almost felt normal.

The year 1968 began with Joy and Ray announcing their engagement. I'd expected this for a long while and was delighted for them. Ray, a carpenter with a Bairnsdale builder, asked Dad's for consent down at the dairy after an evening of milking, and was so nervous he lit his cigarette at the wrong end.

In February I began my 'Matric' Year 12, studying English Expression, English Literature, French, Australian History and Biology. There had been no news about my American trip and I tried not to care. Just as I was going up the pole waiting, and Mum was about to topple off, the letter arrived. Encouraged by its big size, I tore it open to find a letter of congratulations on being selected as an exchange student. Almost a year had passed since starting the application process and I'd been afraid to think about going in case I wasn't selected. Now I could allow myself to feel excited. I ran to the dairy and tell Dad; he gave me two big kisses. Mum seemed to have mixed feelings. Joy was happy. I rang George at 8pm. He answered the telephone and as soon as I said 'Hello' he knew the letter had come. 'It has come, hasn't it?' he asked. 'I can tell by the sound of your voice that you are going to the USA.' He made me tell him that I'd won a scholarship and then he fell quiet.

I would miss George but my dream was coming true. Well, almost. My host family did not live on a Texas ranch. They lived on a Hampshire hog farm in Missouri.

5. ON EXCHANGE IN MISSOURI

I was set to depart for the USA in July 1968. For the next five months school continued as normal and I entered a national essay competition. My knowledge on the topic 'Looking Towards Marriage', was decidedly minimal but I developed some thoughts during a Year 12 religious instruction class. The Church of England minister lectured on SEX, which held everyone's interest and strengthened my resolve not to engage in a pre-marital relationship. The minister said: 'Girls give sex to gain love and boys give love to gain sex.' I didn't know about the first part but thought the latter was true. George was very passionate at times. I loved him but would not give in to my emotions. On our very next date I told him all that the minister said.

We had a deep and meaningful talk and shared our feelings for each other. George said: 'I'll have something to 'give' you in four or five years' time,' which I took as meaning he would work hard to provide us with a home. He also said that he would never get me 'into trouble' and asked if I still felt worried. Emboldened by his sincerity, I shared my secret about seeing a psychiatrist, in 1963. George was the first person I had told and his caring response increased our intimacy. If not talking about getting married we talked about my approaching departure. I wondered if we really would marry and what we'd be doing in five years' time.

My thoughts continued to go this way and that as I ran along the river track to Lambert's Flat and back for hockey practice, startling rabbits and dodging kangaroos on the way. I had told George that besides getting fit for hockey I wanted to lose weight. Not for the first time he said he liked me as I was; I reminded him that he'd said exactly that when I was 2.5kg lighter the previous year, and he said: 'But you're still developing.'

My life planning took an exciting turn one day at school when Mr

Dyson, called me to his office. The *Bairnsdale Advertiser* newspaper would offer a journalism cadetship in 1969 and, due to my essay success, Mr Dyson had put my name forward as a candidate. This news made my mind race and my heart leap with joy. If offered the cadetship, and if the job could hold until after my USA trip, I wouldn't have to leave my home district and, more importantly, George to study in Melbourne.

With my 'Marriage' essay in the mail to the judges in Melbourne, I wanted to learn more about the journalism cadetship. Mum picked me after school and we went to the newspaper office in Service Street, Bairnsdale, to meet the manager, Mr Don Yeates. A distinguished-looking, bespectacled man verging on middle age, with smooth light-olive skin, silver-grey hair sleekly combed back, came to the counter and invited me into his small office. He slid into his chair behind his paper-laden desk and I sat on a chair opposite, surrounded by piles of out-of-date newspapers. Mr Yeates said, 'A journalism cadetship on a country newspaper will provide you with a great grounding in skills that will be snapped up by larger newspapers. This is because on a country newspaper you learn how to do everything.' I liked that idea and began to feel more at ease. More so when Mr Yeates, who chatted with Mr Dyson at the weekly Rotary Club meetings, said he would leave the cadetship vacancy open until I returned from the US. Nothing was confirmed but I felt hopeful of getting the position. Mum and Dad approved of the job opportunity now, which was a relief.

My chances were boosted when a 50-word telegram from the National Marriage Family Week Council announced I'd won the Victorian section in the 'Looking Towards Marriage' essay competition. The awards were presented in Melbourne. I caught the Gippslander train from Lindenow South to stay with Great Aunt Della, who accompanied me to the prize-giving ceremony. Wearing a new light grey woollen winter coat and green beret, I shook hands with the award presenter, Sir Irving Benson, and nervously shared my views on marriage under the blaze of TV cameras. Aunty Della, standing regally close by, was enjoying the moment like a duchess on a royal outing. That evening, her chest puffed out a little more when a journalist and photographer knocked on her Californian bungalow door, and she was more excited than me when my photo and story appeared in *The Sun News* pictorial the next morning.

Hopeful that my essay win would further impress Mr Yeates of my writing ability, I spent my $50 prize on a manual typewriter. Uncle Alf took me shopping in the city to select this amazing little machine before catching the train home. Mum and Dad looked on with interest as I unzipped the smart black case and placed the typewriter on the farmhouse kitchen table. *Now I want to learn to how to touch type!*

Technological communications were slowly changing our world. Prior to my departure for the United States, an automatic telephone line was connected to our farmhouse and we no longer had to turn a small handle to raise the local exchange to make a call. Instead of 'Iguana Creek 3' and our timber phone box fixed on the wall, we now had a six-digit number and a black phone with a white dial face and handpiece on a black cord. The new phone sat on a small stand in our passageway. I felt excited dialling George's number direct for the first time—it seemed so modern! The communication update meant my Aunty Glad, who ran the Iguana Creek Post Office and Telephone Exchange around the corner, was out of a job. For years she had run the mail service and telephone exchange from a small weatherboard outbuilding beside her farmhouse front door. Shortly after the exchange closed, so did the post office.

Suddenly it was the week prior to my departure for the USA, and the Iguana Creek and Glenaladale community organised a dance as a send-off in the Glenaladale Hall. I felt like an adventurer departing on a great expedition, my sadness at leaving my home district countered by mounting anticipation of the unknown ahead. With my bags packed, I had one more important mission.

On the eve of my departure, with sandwiches and drink in a bag slung over my shoulder, I set off on a 12km trek from the farmhouse, along the river track, up over the blue hills towards the Den of Nargun, across to Friday Creek Road, which bisected my father's recently purchased several hundred acres of top country grazing property, known as Broadacres, and down the hill back to the house. As I walked I soaked up the sights, smells, sounds and feel of the land I loved. The eucalypt-covered hills, the green-skirted willow trees bordering the Mitchell River; the clear, mirror-like water, reflecting the ruddy cliffs above; the gullies' moss-covered rocks, tea-tree scrub and ferns; the log cabin on Lambert's Flat; kangaroos, wallabies and emus; fluffy yellow blossoms of wattle trees, the sweet scent of the pittosporum; the rumbling of the rapids, the call of the lyrebird, the warble of the magpie. I stored all these smells and images in my bank of sensory treasures to draw on when lonely or homesick during my year out of the valley.

The next day I was on my way to the USA with about 140 other American Field Service exchange students who had come from all corners of Australia.

Mum and Dad, Joy, Ray and George travelled to Essendon Airport to see me off on the first leg of the long flight. When we arrived at the airport, everyone but Mum stepped out of the car. I found her sitting in the back of Ray's two-tone green FJ Holden; she was crying. For the first time in my life I thought: *'Mum cares about me!'* Ray, who had been called up for National Service and was based at Puckapunyal for training, had come to the airport in his army uniform. Clutching a fat toy koala and wearing my grey coat, I stood proudly beside him for a photograph. The plane was nearby on the tarmac.

Dad gave me a big hug. George, his eyes filling with tears, gave me a kiss to last a year. The hugs and kiss said it all.

Now I was on the plane with other girls and boys and my adventure began. We had orientation sessions in Sydney and again at Stanford University in California. I learnt I was not to ask for a rubber in class, and if I became pregnant, I would be sent home. At Stanford it was summer vacation and we occupied a student dormitory. Being on American soil heralded a reality check—we would be 16,000 kilometres from home for 12 months. Suddenly this seemed an ocean of time as well as distance. A few students became hysterical at the thought, and were sent home. I had a more immediate concern—the bathroom. It was communal, with eight showerheads but no curtains. Most girls were from the city, many from boarding schools, and thought nothing of communal nakedness, but I was shy and self-conscious. My solution was to arise before dawn and have a quick shower before the others got up.

A week after leaving home, on August 3, I was settling in with the Edwards family on their Hampshire hog farm, northwest of St Louis, Missouri. I would write five letters weekly—three to George, and two to my parents—for the next 50 weeks. I did not know of any other Australians in Missouri and would not see any fellow Aussie exchange students for the entire year. Most of my host family was at the airport at St Louis to greet me. We had exchanged photographs and I quickly recognised my 'mom', Irene, with Pat, 16, Linda, 11, nine-year-old Terry and little Jimmy, aged four. The three girls were blond and blue-eyed, so my looks fitted in well. Livewire Jimmy had deep brown eyes and his big brother Johnny, 14, had dark hair and blue eyes. Right now, Irene explained, Johnny was at home with my host dad, Ruben, working on the farm.

The Mid-West's extreme humidity had almost zapped me when I stepped off the plane, and Irene and Pat insisted on carrying my luggage and loading it into the back of their big ranch wagon. Then we all piled in for the 120km ride to their farm, called Hamp-An Farms. The car had air-conditioning—a new and welcome experience for me.

Irene drove along Highway 70 partway to Kansas City, and took a right turn onto a series of smaller 'black-top' roads. For the final few kilometres she drove along a narrow dirt lane, bordered with low-lying trees and fenceless fields extending forever, before turning into an oak tree shaded driveway identified with a black-and-white 'Hamp-An' welcome sign.

We pulled up outside the red cedar ranch-style home and Pat, who was fast becoming not only my sister but also a lifelong friend, showed me to the room I would share with her.

Then it was time for the midday meal and there were more introductions as the men came in from the fields to eat and drink gallons of iced tea. I had not tasted iced tea before but Ruben assured me it was the best drink on a hot day. I'm sure it was thirst quenching but as it contained sugar, I pretended I didn't like it and stuck with 'hot tea'. Iced tea aside, new experiences abounded.

Ruben and I took a little while to understand each other. He had a deep, booming voice and his Southern drawl was strong. I quickly learnt he was the head of the family. He was a loving husband and father but his own children as well as the farm workers addressed him as 'Yes, Sir!' when he issued an order. The workers highly respected my 'mom' too, calling her 'Miss Irene'. She was always busy preparing meals for up to 14, at times dropping everything to drive as far as St Louis to run farm errands, such as collecting a machinery part, for Ruben.

Everywhere, the pace was faster than in Australia and everything from tractors to cars and combines seemed bigger, yet the Edwards family and my family shared similar values and work ethics. In Missouri, life revolved around family, farm work and the community, especially through the Southern Baptist Church at the nearby small town of Olney. The church was filled each Sunday. Like my parents, the Edwards lived about 32km from their nearest big town called Bowling Green. Bowling Green, like Bairnsdale, had a population of about 8000 people.

Land in Missouri was flat instead of hilly, and the Mississippi River, flowing southward just 50 kilometres from the Edwards' farm, was an ocean compared to the Mitchell River, but the warmth and friendliness of country people was the same. I was made to feel very welcome at both church and school. School was an adventure from the moment I boarded the yellow bus for my first day in the senior class at Wellsville High. There was no school uniform and, unlike at home, where we rode our bikes to the nearest main road, here the driver skillfully and determinedly steered down the narrowest of lanes—which were snow-covered in winter—to collect children at their farm gate or door. The school provided hot meals served by cheery cooks in its own cafeteria. I slowly developed a taste for baked beans with pork and sauerkraut, although usually I ate nothing because the calories were too difficult to gauge. The senior year subject range was extensive, allowing me to select both journalism and typing in my timetable.

The school year started in September and in some ways, while clothing was conservative, attitudes appeared more liberal. One girl in my Wellsville class was married; her husband was serving in Vietnam and, at 18, she had a baby to care for. At Bairnsdale, any pregnant girl had to leave school immediately, but here girls were encouraged to continue their studies. Some Missouri boys thought of me, a blond girl from Australia, as a challenge, like 'How far can we get with her?' I dated a few boys, but they were all disappointed. My feelings and thoughts were for one boy only, and he was back home.

Letters took a week to reach their destination, so when I asked George a question, I had to wait two weeks for his answer. I sat his portrait photo beside my bed, and looked longingly at his big brown eyes every morning and night. He visited my parents regularly and, in November, wrote with excitement that Mum had visited the newspaper editor, Mr Yeates, and was told that I had the cadet job FOR SURE!

This was wonderful news, but it seemed a long way off. When feeling homesick and lovesick for George, I ate and ate. Like my own mum, Irene was a great cook and prepared three hot meals a day. She creamed her own peas, lima beans and corn, and her homegrown ham and bacon were the best I had tasted. Crisply fried bacon and wholesome farm eggs were served on a big platter for breakfast every day but Sunday, when piles of pancakes, fresh out of the skillet and ready to be doused with maple syrup, were passed around our large oval table. Prior to each meal, including breakfast, everyone at the table held hands while grace was said. Even little Jimmy in his high chair took his turn. We went to church twice on Sunday and sometimes on Wednesday. Irene played the piano and sang. She was devoted to caring for her family and contributing to her community. Any spare moments were spent happily tending her flower and vegetable gardens.

I celebrated my 18th birthday with a pyjama party hosted by female classmates in a friend's house covered with snow. Their hospitality and acceptance inspired me to lighten up and make the most of my remaining seven months in Missouri. For starters, I determinedly stayed awake the entire night with my new friends. I returned to my host home about 2pm the next day and fell into a deep sleep on top of my bed. That was the moment George chose to ring and wish me 'Happy Birthday'. Irene shook me awake to take the call and George was not impressed with my sleepy response. Then several planes flew over his house and our phone connection was lost. Due to the high cost of the calls, we would not speak again until reunited in August. I went back to bed and sobbed. My parents had made their one call for the year two days earlier, at Christmas.

When I was lonely, Pat cheered me up. We talked late into the night; our beds were on castors, and we had fun rolling them around on the polished wood floors. Beside each bed was a desk and I sat here to do my homework and letter-writing. Often when I was writing to George, Pat was downstairs with her boyfriend, Lonnie, who was almost part of the family and like an older brother to me.

Thinking of George, I began 1969 determined to lose weight and lost 5kg in three weeks. But then I celebrated by gorging and felt angry at myself. I tried to eat normally but no more than two days passed before a gnawing emptiness overwhelmed me and I returned to continual binge-eating and drastic dieting. I envied my host family brothers and sisters, and my school friends, who ate normally. Even though we served ourselves from bowls passed around from the centre of the table, every meal was an anxious time for me. Irene's home cooking was delicious and calorie-counting was a never-ending challenge.

My silent food battle sapped my energy but with only 25 weeks remaining in the USA, I strove to live in the moment.

School was fun and my journalism and typing studies would be useful in my newspaper career. In the evenings, Irene accompanied me to address community organisations about life in Australia; sometimes I spoke several times a week—to church groups, 4-H clubs, farming organisations and schools. Gradually gaining confidence, I illustrated my talk with colour slides of my family, our farm and district. On weekends or afterschool I sometimes helped Pat feed and water the hogs. She drove a tractor just like I did back home. I missed the Australian cricket and football seasons, but made up for this by cheering at basketball and baseball games with my Wellsville school friends. The fervour with which my friends sang *The Star Spangled Banner* before each match stirred my emotions more deeply than a lifetime of singing *God Save the Queen*. The weeks began to fly by.

Sometimes, though, my efforts to manage everyday life by counting calories landed me in the pits. At Easter I sank in a quagmire of self-loathing. The school's big dance, the Prom, was only a few weeks away and I wanted to weigh 54kg. But instead of eating salads and vegetables, I was feasting on Easter eggs, marshmallows and peanut-chocolate clusters. I couldn't understand why I ate when I wasn't hungry and binged when I wanted to be slim.

I tried to focus on life 'out there' instead of being absorbed within myself. My school announced its Honour Graduates for 1969 and I was one of the chosen 12. My teachers persuaded me to sit for the entrance exam to University of Missouri-Columbia, which had a highly regarded school of journalism. I passed the exam and was offered a place. This was tempting, but AFS rules would require me to return to Australia for two years before taking up my place. Also, nothing could compete with my desire to return home to a life with George.

In April, the 'Senior Bus Trip' to Washington DC was a special time with my classmates, knowing I might not see them again after my return to Australia. When I returned home to my host family however, Irene called me aside for a quiet chat. Someone had reported seeing me walking and holding hands with a classmate, Marcus, in Washington. That was all we were was doing, walking and holding hands, but Marcus was black and the conservative Mid-West culture did not approve of a white girl holding hands with a black boy.

Irene called on my loyalty to George: 'What will he think?' As I was doing nothing wrong, I didn't think he would mind, but I deeply respected my host family and did not hold hands with Marcus again. Another classmate, Harrel, took me to baseball games in St Louis, and we became close friends. This was acceptable: he was white.

Keeping busy, attending Year Book meetings and social events, helped take my mind off matters not under my control. Right now I was in the school gymnasium with hundreds of teenagers and parents at our school's Queen of the Prom dance. The school band was playing and the Master of Ceremonies had announced the coronation ceremony was about to begin. I was wearing a full-length, fitted, sleeveless pale blue gown, with white lace on the bodice—borrowed from Pat. I was also wearing a pretty corsage, presented by my Prom partner on arriving at the farm to collect me in his pickup truck. We'd whirled on to the polished floor as soon as the band struck up, but we lacked rhythm and my thoughts were of George, dancing close to him in the Sale Memorial Hall far away. Suddenly I was nudged—the MC was calling my name, and everyone was cheering and clapping. I was the Prom Queen! Led to the dais, I sat like a startled rabbit on a wicker throne under an arch decorated with colourful paper maché flowers. Smiling radiantly, the previous year's Queen, who had returned from college for the event, crowned me with a silver tiara. '*I don't deserve this,*' I thought, but here was more applause, and I danced the rest of the night as in a dream. There were beautiful and popular girls in my Senior Class who were slim and didn't go home and binge after eating a big slice of pepperoni pizza, and I was sure they were far more worthy of wearing the glittering crown.

As departure from my host family drew near, I numbed rampaging emotions by gorging on peanut butter and jelly sandwiches, chocolate, icecream and chocolate chip cookies until 3pm, or 4pm, or 10pm—however long it took to grab hold of myself. Sometimes it was a few seconds to midnight when I managed to stop and write in my diary, 'A new start tomorrow'. Thoughts of leaving my friends and my host family, the upcoming end-of-year AFS bus trip, the plane ride home, meeting Mum, Dad, Joy, George and Ray, and my friends back home all swung back and forth like a pendulum in my mind. In control, out of control; that was me.

The sadness of farewelling the Edwards was eased with assurances of 'I'll be back' and 'Remember you have promised to visit'. My relationship with this loving family would last our respective lifetimes. They stood by the road and waved as I began the first leg of my homeward journey on a two-tiered Greyhound bus bound for Washington DC. I was the only Aussie among about 40 AFS students from 27 countries. For the next 21 days, every hour became packed with memories to cherish. One day I sat with a Turkish friend, the next day a Filipino, Polish, Vietnamese, French, Nicaraguan, Chilean, German, Brazilian, Japanese or Scot. We were like a little United Nations, sharing thoughts and feelings on everything from boy-girl relationships to hopes for the future. Chaperoned on our 2000km journey by three young-at-heart Americans, we were billeted with families along the way. We expressed our appreciation at each stopover with a concert rehearsed during our long hours on the bus. Our concerts took place in community parks, and families came with a picnic basket to share afterwards. Like junior ambassadors for world peace, we linked arms as we sang and entertained through music and song, our many cultures rolled into one.

But part of me was holding back. Weighing 53kg, I was 3kg off my latest goal weight. While my friends sang, acted and played the guitar with carefree exuberance, I mimed along, convinced my voice sounded like a frog with a sore throat, and calculated if I had done enough walking that day to allow myself a leg of fried chicken or spoonful of macaroni cheese with my usual lettuce leaves and carrot sticks. I fought to maintain control so I could enjoy the moment. The more we travelled, the higher our tempo became and the more our bus exterior became decorated with happy banners promoting international goodwill.

All went well until July 11. That morning we left Montpelier, Vermont, at 10.30am and stopped at a shady park for our usual picnic lunch. Then we departed for Cape Cod, through Boston. I was sitting with new friends Liza, from the Philippines, and Cristina, from Brazil; we joked and laughed together. But that afternoon our bus driver, a recent immigrant to the USA, lost his way in Boston and drove under a 3m-clearance railway overpass. He forgot the height was insufficient to accommodate the two-level Greyhound bus and without warning the entire upper level was battered in on top of us. Bang, bang, bang!

I was on the upper level, sitting next to the window with Cris. The roof and luggage racks above our heads caved in and were pushed back, the windows fell out, and we were trapped. Police, ambulance and fire brigade arrived within minutes, sirens going everywhere, and we were all safely rescued. I fell out of the window headfirst into the arms of a helpful fireman; this wasn't very ladylike, but being in shock I didn't care. Most of us were uninjured but eight were taken to hospital. The rest of us stayed at a hostel at the Massachusetts Institute of Technology for four hours until another bus and driver were organised to take us on to Cape Cod, two hours away. We were tired and distressed, and worried about our injured friends. On a brighter note, we received mail, and my 11 letters included three from George who was counting the days until I arrived home. Crawling into bed at 1.30am, I hugged his hand-written aerogrammes filled with loving scrawl. I was billeted with a strange family who lived in a huge 17-roomed, two-storey house with cats that peed in my shower. The stench permeated my bedroom and I yearned for George and home.

The next day, reports of our bus accident appeared on the TV and radio news and made front-page headlines in Boston's main newspaper. Of the 75 buses travelling across the USA with AFS students, I was on Bus 34, the only one that crashed.

With our year coming to a close, we pushed on and five days later were bound for New York City. We arrived at the United Nations Building on Manhattan Island at about 9.30am and from there were free to explore. Salva, from Argentina, and I paired up and, except for the heat, the smog and the dirt, we had a memorable and exciting time. Firstly we went to the AFS office and I met some Aussies for the first time in a year. They laughed at my Southern accent. Salva and I went to Macy's, a large store, to Chinatown and Greenwich Village and boarded a ferry to Ellis Island to see the towering Statue of Liberty. We rode a subway train, clinging to each other as it raced and lurched through tunnels with carriage doors wide open, and took a bus or two. New York was huge and I marvelled at the thought that two-thirds of Australia's population of 12 million could fit into this one city. When I looked up, between the tall skyscrapers, the sun shone like a Chinese lantern masked by a haze. Beside me in the streets, fire hydrants were turned on, delighting barefoot children from the high-rise flats who ran and splashed in the cool water as it gushed along the pavement and down the gutters.

The children were confined, yet making the most of where they lived, and I envied their seeming liberty. I was captive to something within that had me gorging on macaroni and cheese and angel food cake one day, and starving myself on cans of Diet Coke and one pear the next. Apart from the cat-in-the-shower house, all my billets had been with caring families and the mothers asked: 'Are you feeling unwell?' when I refused their beautiful home-cooked meals; I hated myself for appearing rude. I wished I could be normal. If only I didn't binge, I wouldn't need to starve.

By July 20, I was in Reston, West Virginia, where we AFSers staged our talent show for the final time. Then we were invited to different homes to watch television because Neil Armstrong was about to leave Apollo 11 and take the first step of Man on the Moon. I tried to imagine the men way up there and wondered if moon travel would be common one day.

That night was one to remember forever. Ten of us, each from a different country, sat cross-legged on a lounge room floor, watching the screen, cheering as Armstrong left his spaceship to walk on the moon. Every now and then we scooped our hands into a large, white plastic container of melting vanilla ice cream sitting on the floor between us. We had no spoons, so we licked our sticky fingers and hugged and cheered as man stepped beyond our world.

The following day we went to Georgetown University in Washington for our big AFS Mid-Way Convention and reunion. Our bus became one of 75 converging on the huge parking lot, and we stepped into a swell of more than 3000 students walking around, seeking a familiar face. National flags waved like beacons, leading the way to our countries. I embraced my Australian friends. We laughed at our accents and at the differences a year had made—several girls laughingly admitting they had gained 15kg. I was amazed that they didn't care. Although weighing 3kg less than when I arrived, I felt fat and wanted to lose more.

On our next day out in Washington the 3000 AFSers sat on the White House Lawns, clapping loudly when President Richard Nixon appeared on a balcony, waved and addressed us.

My food obsession accompanied me everywhere, even on this memorable day when I saw the President of the United States. As I packed my case that night, I wished I could be like my carefree and confident friends. We had been out having fun until after midnight for 10 consecutive nights. When with friends, I scarcely ate but when alone, I binged.

On July 23, we hugged and said sad farewells. I had been reunited with my Australian friends but already was missing everyone on Bus 34. I coped by eating one egg, one apple and half a pear for the day and dreamed of travelling the world to see my friends again. For now though, I was heading back to Australia—and to George.

He was alone at Essendon Airport to greet me on August 4. Family groups were waving balloons and banners, greeting other students, but George was my sole welcoming party. He was all I wanted. We had been counting down the days to this moment for so long that in my excitement, I lost my voice. His Australian drawl hurt my ears for a 'toime' but he looked the same, his warm kisses were the same and in a short 'time' he sounded the same, too.

The drive to my family's farm took about four hours and my voice gradually returned. We stopped at a roadside café for lunch and I insulted a waitress by asking for a cup of 'hot' tea. 'Our tea is always hot,' she said. She didn't know I was fresh from the land where iced tea was served as a matter of course.

I fell silent as we turned the home corner and drove up Findlay-Alexander Road, past the Morrison, Hammond and Morton farms, to the farmhouse at the head of the valley. I had travelled far and seen much but everything in the valley looked the same as when I departed 12 months before. Time seemed to have stood still.

After greeting my parents and sister at the front gate, I raced up the garden path, through the back door and into every room. Somehow there was comfort in seeing everything in the same place. In the kitchen fireplace, slow burning logs glowed a warm welcome. Yes, it was good to be home. But I was not alone. Niggling thoughts were urging me to eat today and diet tomorrow. So I made a thorough pig of myself. A thick crust piled with butter and Vegemite was followed by a crumpet with honey and butter, cake and biscuits; everything that I hadn't tasted for a year; pumpkin and curry too.

Everyone seemed pleased to have me home and this was where I wanted to be. My challenge would be to settle into local rural life, which appeared quiet and slow after living in Missouri, and to manage my growing inner chaos.

6. ENGAGED AT 19, MARRIED AT 20

Three days later, Mum and I drove to Bairnsdale in our faithful FJ Holden, which seemed small after the Edwards' ranch wagon. We went to the newspaper office and, after welcoming me back, Mr Yeates asked me to start work on the first day of September. This meant I had three weeks in which to learn to drive, so I'd be busy. I also needed to learn shorthand. At least I could touch type. I felt I had hit the ground running.

That night, George took me to the Young Farmers' District Council annual meeting at Bruthen, about 20km up the Alpine Highway from Bairnsdale. On learning I was becoming a cub reporter, the members voted me as public relations officer. Talk about getting back into things! I was glad though, and felt great reconnecting with my friends, who milled around and laughed as they listened to my Mid-Western speech. While I was in the USA, George had turned 21 and had been elected president of the Glenaladale Young Farmers' Club. This meant a busy social life, attending Young Farmers' activities three or four nights a week around the East Gippsland region.

My friends did not know of my secret battle. The morning after the meeting at Bruthen, I ate a pile of crusts and crumpets dripping with butter for breakfast—and hated myself for the rest of the day.

I tried to ignore the nagging emptiness by unpacking my suitcase and boxes. There were gifts for my family, clothes to sort and keepsakes to store. Every keepsake had a memory attached. Out came Percy, a bright pink and green toy turtle, an 18th birthday present from my Missouri girlfriends; a bracelet from Marcus; my 'Class of '69' gold ring and *Chanticleer* school year book that I'd helped create; a black baseball cap emblazoned with the Edwards' 'Hamp-An' farm logo; an Indian arrow head, found in the woods and given to me by a Missourian deer hunter; an intricately carved, hand-made leather wallet bearing my name, a gift from my host family; several charm bracelets from classmates; and a 'quarter' coin flattened by the funeral train carrying the body of former USA President Dwight D. Eisenhower. When the train trundled through Missouri on its journey from Washington, D.C. to Abilene, Kansas, my friends and I placed coins on the track and stood back to watch in respect as many carriages passed by, then stepped up to gather our mementoes. I also had hundreds of photographs and colour slides to sort and, among my clothes, favourite mini skirts and figure-hugging, skinny-rib tops.

After the midday meal I walked along the river to the log cabin, thrilled to see salamanders, their tails in the air, running across the track for a dip in the water. I took deep breaths and soaked up the smells and sounds of river and bush, reconnecting with the place I loved. Later, I gave my parents a break and milked most of the cows, and washed the yards down. After a year on the hog farm, I hadn't forgotten how to milk cows. I was trying to adjust to my new situation but food thoughts hampered my efforts.

Within two weeks of returning home:

I am feeling sick, mad at everything and everybody, including myself, because I regularly eat non-stop and then starve myself for the next 24 hours while trying to catch hold. I look forward to starting work, hoping to establish a fresh discipline and routine.

A few things, I was discovering, had changed while I was away. One was fashion. Even my conservative mother laughed at my 'mini' skirts. Hems had gone up and up but not in Missouri. I put on each dress and skirt and stood on a chair while my cousin Denise pinned them: at least 8cm shorter on each, and 12cm on some. I hoped Mum or Denise would stitch the hems, as my attempts failed—either the stitches showed on the front side, or the hemline ran up and down like a yoyo. I chopped a kilogram of raisins to help Mum prepare Joy's wedding cake mixture and fed hay to the cows for Dad, these jobs being more to my liking.

Preparing to take my driver's licence test also gave me something to focus on, but the big day, a Friday, didn't start well. Mum woke me at

6.30am to go to the dairy and milk almost all the cows. That job took two hours. I then reversed the FJ Holden out of the car shed and drove down the paddock for a final practice, driving around the hay bales and reversing between wooden boxes. I managed to do all this without grating the gears. At 10am I drove, with Dad beside me, to the Lindenow police station. The lone policeman was a big, jovial man. I hoped he'd remain jovial. I had an eye test, an oral test and then a driving test, a rather wonky one. I scraped the entire right side of Dad's shiny, immaculate car on the big, round wooden gatepost as I followed the policeman's instructions and drove around the grounds of Lindenow Football Club. Dad, sitting in the back seat, said nothing and the policeman, sitting beside me, calmly continued issuing instructions. I managed to return us to the police station without hitting anything else, feeling sure I had blown my chances. However, despite my brush with the post, the policeman announced: 'You've passed.' Fearing he would change his mind, I gave him a big smile and quickly paid the $8 licence fee. I bought the mandatory pair of 12-month, red-on-white 'P' probationary plates, and Dad bravely let me drive us home.

Now I was ready to start work the following Monday. Work could not come too soon. The damage to my parents' car increased my desire to achieve financial independence as soon as possible. That night, however, George swept my anxiety aside, taking me on a 75-minute drive up the winding Alpine Highway to a Young Farmers' Ball at the small town of Swift's Creek. We danced as one, our rhythm unbroken by our year apart. The judges in the Princess of the Ball contest were impressed, awarding me with a blue sash, inscribed with gold lettering. After the presentation, George and I took to the floor again. It was then that I noticed, as we whirled around the hall, that several other young men were catching my eye.

Suddenly I wished I could date each of them. I wanted to be sure about George. After all, I was only 18 and each of the boys was from a respected farming family. However, the next day when I shared my thoughts with Mum, she said: 'How can you possibly think in such a way? George has waited a whole year for you to come home. Take a good look at yourself. You can't possibly hurt George's feelings now by going out with others. I'll talk to your father about this and I know he will be very disappointed.'

Guilt and uncertainty swept in and, unsure how I should think or feel, I binged until my mind was numb.

On Monday, September 1, I got up at 7am, ate two boiled eggs for breakfast, reversed Joy's blue and white Vauxhall out of the stable and drove her and myself the 32 kilometres to work. Joy worked in a hair salon in Dahlsen's Arcade in Nicholson Street, around the corner from the *Advertiser* office. She had suggested that I buy her car. She would not need it after her marriage to Ray in a few more weeks, as they would live in the town and share his car. She had the Vauxhall valued at $650, and offered it to me for $600. I had accepted, thinking this was a good deal and would start payments with my first wage.

I walked into the newspaper office carrying a small cane basket in one hand and typewriter case in the other. A desk had been cleared for me outside the office of the editor, Mr Ted Forwood. He introduced me to the small team of journalists. Several were members of the Yeates family and they were multi-skilled, doing everything from writing cricket results to taking pictures at balls, working on the linotype machines and delivering the newspapers to newsagents in outlying towns. Mr Forwood and I were the only two full-time journalists who were not family members. The family members did whatever had to be done to get the newspaper out on time. Mr Forwood showed me how to use the telephone and handed me a list of calls to make. I did simple jobs at first, like checking a lawn bowls result, confirming the spelling of a name in a caption, calling for fishing reports, and seeking school council news and the outcomes of monthly branch meetings of the Country Women's Association. I met office and printing staff during morning and afternoon tea breaks and began to make friends. Payday was every Friday and after a probationary period my work hours were generally 9am to noon, lunch for an hour, then 1pm to 6pm.

Mr Forwood had come to Australia from England and I liked him immediately. He took me under his wing and promptly set about shaping and honing my journalistic skills. The *Addy*, as it was called, was published Mondays and Thursdays and *The East Gippsland News* was published on Fridays. I tapped out my stories, double-spaced, on small sheets called copy paper, and Mr Forwood corrected them while I stood beside him and watched. The stories were set in lead by the linotype operators and placed into galleys in preparation for publication. A favourite place was the darkroom where strips of negatives hung about and black-and-white prints were pulled from troughs filled with smelly chemicals and pegged to a line to dry.

The newspaper employed a cadet photographer, Robert, and we often went on jobs together—I got the story while Robert took the pictures. We enjoyed getting out of the office and returning with news for the next edition.

I quickly grew to know and love the sounds and smells of the newspaper office and print room: the clickety-clack of the office typewriters, the louder clunks of the linotype operators setting the metal type, the smell of printer's ink, the molten lead and the huge rolls of newsprint.

My favourite sound was that of the presses starting up to print the latest newspaper edition. Grabbing a new edition as it rolled hot off the presses always gave me a little adrenalin rush.

George and I were together on weekends and during the week when we could manage it. Whenever returning home from a date or Young Farmers' event we pulled off into the scrub in George's Falcon 500 ute —which he had bought new before I went to Missouri—for an hour. One night he had difficulty returning to the road, spun the wheels and suddenly took off backwards, reversing into a stump. Thump. Getting out with his torch to inspect the damage, George was not pleased. A dent near the tow bar made that night's cuddle expensive, but we knew better than to park outside my parents' front gate. If we sat in the car for more than a minute when George pulled up at the gate, my mother got out of bed and called through the window, 'June, is that you? Is that you, June? Get inside ... Now!' So we parked in the scrub, just like we had before I went away. George had noticed other boys looking at me, and one night while we were parked, he said: 'I am afraid I'll lose you.'

'You don't need to worry,' I said, thinking of my parents' insistence not to date anyone but him—to do so would indicate for sure that my AFS year had been a waste of money and morals. But George wanted more reassurance. 'I want to become engaged on your 19th birthday,' he said. Despite this pressure, I didn't feel ready to be engaged, and distracted George with a kiss. He wasn't giving up. He said: 'Your birthday at the latest.' That night, after George dropped me at home, I went inside and ate until I felt like bursting.

At least I enjoyed my first week at work, and felt journalism was the right choice of career. My first pay packet was a sure sign I was on my way to independence. Aside from car payments to my sister, early purchases included a pair of bathroom scales. Mum and I stepped on — she weighed 54kg and I weighed 55kg.

Joy, meanwhile, had a severe case of pre-wedding nerves. She worried so much she cried and got sick. She wouldn't explain what she was worrying about but I was glad she had waited for me to come home so I could be a bridesmaid. Ray had completed his two-year army training and resumed employment in the Bairnsdale building trade.

George continued to hint that he wanted to become engaged, but I wanted time to work out who I was and where I was going with my life. I didn't know if I was doing what I wanted or what others wanted me to do. I ate either too much or too little and lacked confidence in making decisions.

Less than a month after starting work I wanted to disappear down a rabbit burrow forever. There were several reasons, the major one being that, when backing out of the Nicholson Street angle parking after work, I scraped the car belonging to David Yeates, the chairman of the board of directors at the *Advertiser* office. My car was unscathed but I'd damaged his. Two men, both strangers, helped me straighten my car and reverse out of the fix. I thanked them and, too embarrassed to look them in the eye, walked back to the office with leaden feet to confess to David. He responded calmly and kindly, saying: 'Don't worry, insurance will take care of the damage.' David immediately became my friend forever, but I felt awful and shook all the way home.

Secondly, I was being called 'Tubby' at work by one of the typesetters: what next? I didn't know. And thirdly, George had come into town for lunch hour and bought me a huge pineapple milkshake. Of course, I had drunk it all. On arriving home I ate six of Mum's freshly baked Anzac biscuits that were as big and flat as saucers.

I was sure 'weakness' must have been flashing like a neon sign across my forehead. I felt unworthy of myself, and more so of George. At 8pm I tried to regain control, writing: *'I'll stay on an 800 calorie-a-day diet for three weeks. Do or die.'* For my night was not over: George was calling in

30 minutes to take me to Young Farmers and our activity was a rabbit hunt. All I wanted to do was go and park somewhere in the scrub with George. Oh, to disintegrate!

A few days later my food battle resurfaced when, arriving home from work, I fainted. I must have hit my head a beauty as it still ached. Mum was worried and accompanied me to see a doctor. He concluded I was okay, which was a relief, but the cause remained a puzzle. I knew that eating three balanced meals a day would help a lot but while this sounded easy, I found it impossible to do.

Joy and Ray married in St Andrew's Presbyterian Church in Bairnsdale—she looked beautiful, like a porcelain doll, and Ray looked spunky with his slick, rock 'n' roll hairdo. Afterwards about 130 guests attended a reception at The New Norfolk, a popular pub and reception venue in the tiny railroad town of Lindenow South. Besides being a bridesmaid in pink, and supporting my sister, the wedding gave me an opportunity to catch up with relatives I had not seen since departing for the USA.

Everyone knew George had waited a year for me, and was asking: 'So when are you two getting engaged?' I stayed at George's place that night and got to bed at 3.30am. We could park outside his parents' back door as they didn't come out and yell at us to get inside.

I was happy with George and at work but feelings of emptiness persisted. Bingeing stopped me from thinking but made me feel worse. Since arriving home two months earlier, I'd gained 2kg and felt ashamed when George held me.

Sometimes I wanted to cry. Mum constantly grumbled, and when she said that she and Dad had to repay my Commonwealth Scholarship money because I didn't complete Year 12 in Australia, I wished I hadn't gone to the USA. I would have paid the money if I could. I resolved to focus on controlling what I could in my life, by staying on a three-meals-a-day balanced diet, squeezing no pimples, recording my expenditures and caring for myself.

That resolution did not last 24 hours. Next time I saw George I was wearing a new white blouse and blue slacks and he said: 'You look beautiful.' He often told me this but I didn't believe him. I loathed myself. Some nights I awoke sweating in bed and was starting to think this was due to my stupid eating habits.

My relationship with Mum hampered my efforts to take a hold. Dad was blockheaded at times and she unloaded her worries and blues on me. When I came home from work and said, 'Hi Mum, I'm going to stay at George's house this weekend,' she would respond with a list of jobs: 'You should be helping your father. You know it hasn't rained and there's irrigating to do. The bougainvilleas need trimming and the chook house needs cleaning out.'

George lived 40km away so we saw each other more if I stayed at his farm. He milked his father's cows twice a day, seven days a week —weekends were no different to any other day. With my newspaper work, plus wanting to be with George, I hadn't time to work as much on my parents' farm and felt I was letting them down. Part of me wanted to be what my mother wanted—'Tim' the farmer, helping Dad, but then I wouldn't be me—June the journalist and girlfriend of George.

By November I'd reduced my weight to 54kg and was starting to feel I was over the settling-in disturbance. During one sunny lunchbreak I sat with other workers on the lawns in Bairnsdale's beautiful Main Street gardens and ate a salad roll—an amazing achievement. Usually I ate nothing. Right then, a Young Farmer friend, Neil, walked by and stopped to chat. He had grown up on a dairy farm in my home district and was working in town as an apprentice motor mechanic. Another lunchtime, after going to the grocery store to buy canary seed (I had 16 birds in a large aviary on the verandah at home), Neil drove by and suggested we eat lunch in the shade by the riverbank on the edge of town. So I hopped in and impressively ate another salad roll, and Neil dropped me off at the newspaper office on his way back to work.

Halfway home that night I remembered I had left the canary seed on the floor of Neil's car. I hoped he would not see it.

But I had hardly parked my car when Neil pulled up beside our farmhouse front gate and walked up the garden path with a big smile, holding the birdseed and saying: 'Hey, guess what you forgot?' I thanked him profusely and almost shooed him away. Mum was helping Dad finish off at the dairy and I hoped she would not see Neil, but no such luck.

'What was Neil doing here? So why were you in his car? Who do you think you are, behaving like this?' On and on she ranted.

Mum accused me of things relating to my love life; things I realised with growing anger she could know about only from my diary and letters. Neil and I had exchanged letters while I was in the USA, as we liked each other—to what extent we would never know as circumstances limited us to friendship. Mum revealed she had found an old letter from Neil in my coat pocket, read it and destroyed it. I was incensed.

My mind askew, I accepted that my parents knew best, but the canary seed experience fuelled my desire to put some distance between us. Planning a wedding with George grew increasingly attractive.

On the evening of November 29 George drove to the farm, went to the dairy, and asked Dad for my hand in marriage. I was 18. Of course Dad said 'Yes'. Both families were delighted. Our next step would be to choose a ring. George's Mum referred us to a family friend who was a jeweller, as we had no idea what to look for.

I remained dubious about becoming engaged so young, but there was no backing out. The formal engagement announcement appeared in the *Addy*, in January 1970, shortly after my 19th birthday. 'You're a baby, too young to be engaged,' my editor, Mr Forwood, said reprovingly. 'I love George,' I assured Mr Forwood and, being happy for us, he published a picture of us celebrating with our families in a Bairnsdale restaurant. Our wedding date was set for April 10 1971, and I began counting the weeks.

I remained opposed to sex before marriage, but some friends and colleagues had more liberal views. While driving to Omeo with Bill, a photographer, to cover the town and district's annual agricultural show for the newspaper, our conversation turned to sex and marriage. Bill, in his 40s and happily married, was amazed to learn I'd be a virgin on my wedding night. 'But how will you know you are sexually compatible if you don't try it beforehand?' Bill said. 'I just know,' I said, faithfully believing that great sex would flow naturally from true love. Luckily, George was patient. He was waiting more than four years to go to bed with me.

Privately I yearned to be as disciplined with food as I was with sex but I was hopeless. I felt angry and disappointed for being weak. I wanted to set myself free from food torment before I married George.

My weight was 55kg and I wanted to be 50kg. Months were slipping by and I was as fat as ever. In July, a cow trod on my foot in the dairy and I cried, not because it hurt badly, but because I felt unsettled and didn't understand why. Perhaps I'd suggest to George that we postpone our wedding for a year. I loved farming and journalism but they didn't seem to mix. I wanted time to learn shorthand, and to study for my Year 12 English.

However, the urge for something definite like a marriage date to focus on, to repel my invisible tormentor, increased my resolve to wed on April 10. I loved George and I'd live for him. Blow my career. If I couldn't cope with the pressures of working in the newspaper, I'd stay at home and work with him on his parent's farm.

Two days after my 20th birthday, I became an aunty when Timothy was born to Joy and Ray. I was pleased, rather chuffed really, to think my nephew had my childhood name. I had been Tim the girl and now Timothy would be Tim the boy. While I was glad for my sister, babies were not on my agenda and three months before my wedding day, I mustered the courage to see a gynaecologist about birth control. The doctor, understanding and matter-of-fact, issued a month's sample supply of Nordiol-28, which he said was called 'the Pill', and a six-month prescription. He suggested I start the pills on the first day of my next period, so I would be 'settled in' by my wedding day.

Sometimes, my silent food fight manifested outwardly.

Gee—I never know what the next day will bring—I washed my hair in the bath tonight, and as I was getting out, I started to get dizzy and my heart went bang, bang. I got out and opened the door, sat on the chair and then I blacked out and I don't remember what happened next. Must have fallen on the floor with a bang, 'cos Mum came running. Must have given her a bad fright. She ran up the passage and shouted for Dad, and then I came round. I lay on my bed and oh, I now have a very empty tummy. Mum wants me to go to the Doctor, but I feel okay now, and Dad says that's the main thing. Don't think I'll ever wash my hair in the bath again ... Mum says I need rest and food (?!). I told her I won't be late to bed.

I was eating enough food, but was stuffing myself one day and starving myself the next. I tried, but could not eat three meals a day like 'normal' people.

With only a few weeks until my wedding, I strove to care for myself. I'd found a bridal gown I loved at the rapidly expanding Chadstone Shopping

Centre in Melbourne. My bust size impressed the woman in the bridal shop, and she asked: 'Where did you get your nice full breasts?' I hinted that farm work and plenty of fresh cows' milk in my childhood was the secret, but thought the likely reason was the hormone pills taken as a teenager to restart my periods. I loved my gown the moment I tried it on— it fitted my slim waist and ample bust perfectly; it had a high neck, long see-through sleeves and a train. To top it off, I would wear a short veil.

The gown was carefully wrapped in layers of soft white tissue paper and placed in a large, rectangular, flat, white box for the journey home to the farm. Mum liked my gown too and suggested we place the box on the double bed in the top room of our house.

The next day I was at work when Mum rang to say, 'Something terrible has happened.' She was sobbing and I braced myself for something really terrible. Mum rarely called and rarely sobbed. Cuddles, a longhaired white kitten given as an engagement gift, had entered the spare bedroom while Mum was feeding the chooks. Leaping on the bed, Cuddles discovered the big box, which had its flaps open, and jumped in. His claws sank into the tissue paper, which made a delightful rustling sound. Thinking this was a game, an excited Cuddles burrowed deep. Returning to the house, my mother heard the rustling and ripping sounds as she entered the back door. Running up the passage, she entered the bedroom to find Cuddles happily ensconced in shredded tissue paper. Unfortunately the paper was not the only casualty—my gown was torn as well.

The gown would not be perfect for my walk down the aisle, but I didn't feel perfect either. A Bairnsdale seamstress, who had made pale blue gowns with short puffed sleeves for Joy as matron-of-honour and cousin Denise as bridesmaid, mended my gown beautifully. Nobody would notice it wasn't perfect. But the incident seemed ominous. I constantly felt that 'something is not right' but 'if I weigh 50kg everything will be right'. I didn't know such thoughts were not normal or that my incessant battle to ease anxiety by counting calories was a sign of illness. Food consumed most of my thinking time. As for the gown, Mum was more upset than me.

I didn't feel worthy of a perfect gown.

Easter Saturday, April 10, dawned a beautiful sunny day. I was due to walk down the aisle of St Andrew's Presbyterian Church, Bairnsdale, at 4pm. Joy was expecting me in the hair salon at 11am to style my hair, and I would stay in town, dressing in my bridal gown at her home, a short drive from the church. My day didn't begin as planned.

April 10, 11.15am, Hairdressers: ... I was up soon after 7am. I had a bath and washed my hair and then I had a blackout. I have a big headache from when I hit the floor. I lay on Mum's bed until I recovered —my stomach lost its contents! I weigh just 8.4 stone (53kg)! I had trouble remembering what day it was. Had two mugs of soup for breaky—not eating anything more until the reception. I'm going to eat each of the four courses!

The reception, like that for my sister's wedding, would be held at The New Norfolk. Dad walked me down the aisle at 4pm on the dot; I didn't want to keep George waiting one moment. He had waited long enough! I felt wonderful standing beside him at the front of the church, saying our vows. He didn't know about my blackout that morning, as, according to custom, we'd not spoken since the day before.

About 130 guests sat down to a four-course meal at our reception and I ate everything on my plate. I sipped a little champagne but preferred the punch. I'd not wanted alcohol at my wedding but Dad insisted and, as he was paying for the reception, jugs of beer appeared on the tables. Speeches were made, telegrams were read, including one from the Edwards family in Missouri, and George and I cut our two-tiered wedding cake, a fruitcake baked by Mum and decorated with white almond icing. A band struck a note and George whisked me onto the small dance floor for the Bridal Waltz. He held me close and everyone clapped. We could have danced all night, but this was our special night—tonight we wouldn't be parking in the scrub!

The time came to change into my 'going-away' outfit—a mini-skirted brown and pink floral suit. The figure-hugging jacket had short puffed sleeves, a Chinese collar and covered buttons. I loved it. But where would I dress? George was heading into the only available changing room. I turned to my sister for help and she laughed and said: 'You're married now, silly. You can go in the same room as George!' Amazing, I thought, how a marriage ceremony could make what one moment was wrong behaviour, suddenly right!

We returned to the dance floor to much applause. Our families and friends linked hands and sang *'Auld Lang Syne'* as George went one way around the circle and I went the other, everyone wishing us well and giving us big hugs and kisses. Then we dashed for the door to escape in our getaway car. George thought he had organised this well, with his four brothers, but our Young Farmer friends, who had hosted a kitchen tea in the Glenaladale Hall for us a few weeks earlier, outsmarted him. They grabbed George, held him upside down and poured confetti down his trouser legs. Tin cans and toilet rolls had been tied to our car's rear bumper bar, and 'Just Married' was scrawled in lipstick across the rear window. Managing to get in and close the doors, we headed off, amid much cheering, rattling, tooting and hooting, on our honeymoon.

Our first night was at the Nowa Nowa Motel, about an hour's drive away, between Bairnsdale and Lakes Entrance. Being Easter, and now past midnight, George gave me a 200g chocolate rabbit. I ate it immediately. *'Eat today and diet tomorrow'*, I thought, sitting in bed in my sexy lace nightie. Whether that was before or after we made love for the first time, I don't remember.

Next morning we headed further north, stopping for a few days in Sydney and then on to Queensland's Gold Coast. Two weeks later we returned to George's home district of Sarsfield to set up home in an old rented farmhouse beside the Nicholson River. We had three new items to start our marriage: a red lounge suite, a double-base bed and a twin-tub washing machine. The remainder of our furniture was second-hand. The main thing, we agreed, was that we had our own nest now.

From the start, George and I helped each other. This was different from our parents, where the man did not help in the house—that was a woman's job. I'd milked hundreds of cows and driven tractors, but had not used a washing machine. George helped me work out the instructions before leaving to work on the farm for the day. We lived across the paddock from his parents' dairy farm, 40km from my parents' farm and 12km from Bairnsdale. With George back at work on the farm, I returned to the newspaper office, where everyone congratulated me on becoming Mrs June Coster.

In May the speedometer on my blue and white Vauxhall passed

the 74,000km mark and, with winter settling in, I took the car to the mechanic's shop to have two tyres recapped. They were to have a short life.

The morning of Friday, June 18, started badly. George and I slept in until 6.45am, and arose to find our hot and cold water taps frozen. Most annoying! George went to milk the cows and all I could do before leaving for work was vacuum the floors and make the bed. While doing so I ate 10 fruit scones to quell my nagging emptiness. I had been married for two months and already my happiness was being sabotaged.

Driving to work along the Omeo Highway with my mind sluggish and my stomach stuffed with scones, I was driving up a long slope known as the Sandhill when I pulled out to overtake a loaded cattle truck on its way to market day in Bairnsdale. The truck seemed to blow brown exhaust smoke across my windscreen and, unable to see, I started to return to the left side of the road, in case there was oncoming traffic. At the same time, I reached for the wiper switch on the left of my steering wheel to improve vision, but before I could, I was knocked unconscious. Then I felt like Alice in Wonderland, being drawn up out of a deep, dark burrow. I slowly opened and raised my eyes and began taking in my surroundings. Blood was trickling down the breast of my pale grey woollen coat, the dashboard was covered in shattered glass, and I was slumped on the passenger side of the front seat.

This was like a bad dream, but as my eyes gained focus, reality dawned: I'd run into the back of a big log truck, now stopped in front of my car. There were three huge brown logs on it. I was sandwiched between the cattle truck, which had stopped behind me, and the log truck.

7. LOG TRUCK ACCIDENT

The truck drivers assured me that help was coming. A local vet, Mr Green, on his way to service a call on a nearby dairy farm, had stopped at the accident scene. He put a green tarpaulin—normally used to keep cows warm—around me and called the police and ambulance on his radio before driving on down the road to tell George, who was doing the morning milking. The ambulance arrived and the officers asked, 'Do you feel any pain?' I said: 'My neck.'

As the officers carefully lifted me out of my car, I observed that it had no roof. No windows, either. By now the police had arrived and were admiring the fact that I was alive. My mother was selling cakes on a church stall in Bairnsdale's colourful Main Street gardens when the ambulance raced by with me inside, lights flashing, and siren blaring. 'Some poor soul,' she said to a friend.

My face and knees were dripping blood as I was unloaded from the ambulance and wheeled into the emergency room at Bairnsdale Hospital.

George arrived, relieved to see I looked in better shape than my car that he had passed on his way to the hospital. Nine stitches were required on the outside of my left leg and facial cuts were cleaned up. The major problem was my neck. X-rays revealed a spinal fracture. My head was placed in a neck clasp and sandbags were provided for pillows.

The police ran checks on the cattle truck, and found nothing amiss. They were so impressed with my survival they placed a photo of my car in their station window. A compulsory seatbelt-wearing law was about to be enacted in Victoria and a policeman said: 'If you had been restrained by a belt, the big log that went through the windscreen over your steering wheel might have decapitated you.' Privately, I believed my scone binge may have clouded my driving judgment, but dared not mention it. People would think I was silly. The facts were I hadn't seen the log truck and had been transported 'to the other side' where peace reigned, and drawn back again. Everyone agreed I was lucky to be alive.

Within 12 days I was home, but my body was in shock. My skin became uncomfortably puffy with a fluid build up and I lost 3.5kg in one night when my kidneys suddenly started to work. I had awful dreams, often screaming in terror. *George must feel like throwing me away.* Determinedly, I slowly resumed living. Knitting a jumper for George was good therapy for me while he was busy milking the cows and, to start regaining confidence, I drove his utility around the paddocks while he fed hay to the cattle.

George was worried about me, though, and Mum insisted on accompanying me to the clinic. The doctor decided my nerves weren't right, but he didn't know this was due to my long-time torment as well as the log truck. He prescribed tablets to keep me calm, and tablets to help me sleep. The doctor also prescribed a laxative to get my insides working. Thinking a little retail therapy might provide some cheer, Mum and I shopped for a midi-dress. A new style, opposite to the mini, the midi's hemline went almost to the ankles. There were some pretty outfits, but I realised my first shopping priority must be a car.

GP Motors in Bairnsdale had a suitable vehicle, a second-hand, two-door Torana SL, white with pale blue interior. I paid for it with my savings of $500, plus a $500 loan from George's Mum, and $450 that Dad could claim in insurance from the Vauxhall. Dad added $105 to the insurance money. I planned to repay my loan by Christmas. The Vauxhall, which I'd finished paying for only weeks before wrecking it, was worth $30—the value, the wreckers said, of the battery and spare tyre.

More X-rays revealed my neck had not mended. Instead it was worse. My doctor phoned a Melbourne orthopaedic surgeon, Mr Kevin King, and arranged an appointment for the following week. My doctor thought it urgent, that I'd need the bone taken out, and I'd need to travel the 273km to Melbourne in an ambulance.

Lying on my back for four hours each way in the ambulance was uncomfortable, and I was crestfallen in Mr King's consulting room at the top end of Collins Street when he said: 'You need to wear your brace for another six to 12 weeks.' No mention of an operation. He said: 'You are very lucky, as the injury has missed the most important part of your spine by 1.5mm.' Mr King was surprised I'd 'come out of it all with so much neck'. I returned to work in late July, driving my Torana, but my freedom was curtailed when my local doctor found out and said: 'No more driving until the brace is off your neck'.

'Why do I have to wear the brace, when the bone won't mend?' I asked.

The doctor illustrated with X-rays that the brace was necessary due to squashed and bruised discs in front of my neck, and because the bone segment had yet to reattach itself to my spine.

My pre-existing anxieties and spinal injuries together gave my marriage a rough start. George for evermore would say: 'You were never the same after your accident.' However, we were getting into a fresh rhythm of shared domesticity. I did the grocery shopping and cooking and, on Saturday mornings, while I washed and baked, he vacuumed the floors and cleaned the bath and basin. But my moods changed more often than the weather.

One Saturday George's mother invited us to lunch with family visiting from interstate. We gathered on the Coster homestead's front lawn, in the sun, against a backdrop of shady camellia and peppercorn trees. A red-and-white gingham cloth spread over a trestle table, set up on the verandah, was barely visible beneath platters of ham, chicken, creamy potato and Waldorf salads and buttered bread rolls. I rapidly calculated I could eat several lettuce leaves, two tomato slices and half a boiled egg. I was struggling for control and strict calorie counting was vital to avert anxiety. Everybody was piling food on their plates and I marvelled at how they could eat and not think twice about it. The aunts and uncles were kind, but in asking about my accident, they said, 'You are looking well.' I had binged the previous night and their comments confirmed I was fat.

I began withdrawing from conversation to deal with my thoughts within. Pavlova, pineapple cheesecake and trifle—each piled lavishly with freshly whipped cream—were served for dessert. Everyone was eating at least one serve. George's Mum loved preparing and eating rich food. Her desserts were delicious and the guilt of declining to eat any added to my self-loathing. I felt increasingly suffocated, trapped. *'I do not belong.*

I do not want to be here,' my mind was screaming. '*I need to escape.*' I whispered to George: 'I want to go home. Now.' I felt removed from, and uncomfortable with, the warmth and love around me. Things came to a head when George reluctantly left the family gathering to return me to our house. He yelled and I howled. 'You could have waited until we'd had a chance to have a chat with our visitors,' George said. 'They will think you are rude and self-centred.'

'I can't help it,' I shouted, hating myself, and bursting into tears.

George disappeared back to his family. I collected some wood for our open fire and cut some kindling, took our washing off the line, did the ironing and put our clothes away. Doing something physical helped my anxiety to subside and I had regained a sense of calm by the time George returned home to change into his dairy clothes. I helped him do the milking, and we put one of three lots of hay out for the cows for the following morning. We decided to have a date that night, in bed. We'd try to ignore my neck brace and the bone that that clicked so loudly George could hear it.

Fifty days had passed since my neck was placed in a brace, and there were 35 more to go. Certainly I hoped it was no more. A neck brace wasn't the sexiest thing in bed.

More X-rays at the end of August revealed the bone hadn't moved and the three discs had not returned to their normal size and never would. My local doctor reported the discs needed time to harden before worrying about the bone, which was stuck between two vertebrae. After seeing the doctor, I completed my newspaper workday and waited for my ride home to help George milk the cows. It was 7pm when we went inside to fix some tea. I cried when we got to bed, tired with all the work, my eating hassles and the worry of my neck.

We had barely fallen asleep when we were woken by the sound of rocks and stones hitting and rolling down our iron roof. So soon after my accident, the banging terrified me. Before George had a chance to get up, people were lifting the sash of our bedroom window and climbing through it. Naked except for my collar, I screamed and hugged the sheets. George managed to pull on a pair of pants before a light went on.

Our intruders were members of our Young Farmers' Club, who had come to 'tin kettle' and treat us to a 'newlyweds' house-warming'. By the time they left, we were exhausted. Our new bed had been tipped upside down and the mattress was marked with muddy boot prints; we had sugar in our salt container and salt in our flour. We had onions in our oven and oatmeal stomped into our carpet. We'd been to several 'tin kettles' ourselves and they had been pleasant social events. However, in recent years, some outsiders had begun to go feral with their antics. We didn't know the young people who'd caused our property damage, and didn't go to Young Farmers much after that. I had great difficulty socialising and, like other couples, we had our careers and family life to think about. The great rural organisation's heyday was almost over.

My newspaper hours were irregular. Sometimes I'd be rostered to report on a night meeting, anywhere from Lindenow to Lakes Entrance, and George drove the car for me. Arriving home from a night meeting could be scary. Our rented house was infested with rats, which entered the kitchen at night and scuttled across the floor. One almost tripped me up, when I switched on a light to make a hot cup of Milo. I was having nightmares and the house was giving me the creeps. We decided a caravan would be more cosy and economical, and found a second-hand one in Bairnsdale. It was 8.2m long with two rooms—a blue-carpeted bedroom and a kitchen-living area. There was a sink, fridge, gas hot plates and oven, cupboards, two stools and divan.

George's mum loaned us the money, which we would repay within a year. We gave a month's notice on our rental accommodation and George towed the van home with his ute. He positioned it at the rear of his parents' house, which meant we'd be handier to the dairy. George and his dad erected a roof over the van to provide shade and shelter and I set about creating a flowerbed beside our door.

By October I had been wearing my neck brace for four months and I'd another appointment with Mr King. This time he decided to wait another six months, saying my headaches and backaches were not serious enough to warrant the risk of surgery. At least I could take the brace off. 'You will have to put up with the clicking and grinding,' Mr King said.

I had to tolerate my neck, but George had to tolerate me. We had little time for leisure; about the only time we were together was either milking cows or in bed. We agreed that when our van was set up, probably in January, we'd have a weekend 'escape'. This would be our first break since our honeymoon eight months before. George, meanwhile, was planning a surprise. In November I came home from work to find a chocolate-coloured pony waiting in the cow yard! I called him Jason. Almost three years old, he was not tall, but a good height for me. George paid $260 for him, which was a lot of money, and I said Jason would be the equivalent of both party and present from George, for my 21st birthday the following month. Jason was so well trained I could duck between his back legs. I rode him to fetch the cows for milking before going to work at the newspaper office and felt free, cantering over the paddocks in the morning breeze.

Unfortunately I did not feel as free in the caravan, metres from George's parents' back door. I hardly saw George alone; he didn't get in from the dairy until 7.30pm, and in the mornings returned from the dairy as I was leaving for work. Other family members were often around and, while they were cheerful and did not pry, I felt stifled. I couldn't go out our caravan door without having to smile and greet someone. I was constantly fighting an urge to isolate myself from social situations and began to feel jealous of time George spent inside his parents' house, talking to them, instead of being in our van with me. The stable qualities of his loving and caring family clashed with my insecurities. Something would have to be done, or our marriage would get near to failing.

Living in the van, though, was convenient for George and he did his best to make it comfortable. He poured a concrete floor outside our van's front door, extended the shed roof, erected fibro cement sheeting walls and created a bathroom with a shower heated by a small gas-fired hot water system. I enjoyed making our van more home-like and baked a fruitcake for Christmas in the small van oven. My little cottage garden was blooming with zinnias, cosmos and portulacas.

In January 1972, we had our longed-for weekend away, staying at a motel in St Kilda, an inner-city seaside suburb of Melbourne. For two days we became childhood sweethearts, George and June, again. We went shopping, saw the stage show *Charlie Girl* and an Australia versus Rest of the World cricket match at the MCG. We returned home with intimacy renewed, but my internal struggle remained. Within a week I was bingeing, angry at my lack of willpower, and tearful. We'd been married almost a year; sometimes George said he couldn't understand me, and I began to suspect that something stronger than me was affecting our marriage.

'Let's have another weekend away,' George suggested. 'That will give us something to look forward to.' But finding someone to milk the cows for a night or two was difficult. I began a diet of 1200 calories daily, believing life would be manageable if I controlled my weight. Although I had failed countless times before, I had to have faith that this time I would succeed.

I have started my DIET! Yes, I am most determined that this time I am going to reach 50kg. I have changed the calorie allowance to 1200 average per day as I think I need that much when milking the cows of a morning. I weigh 63kg—13kg to lose, and I will lose it all at least by our first wedding anniversary on April 10! That is my aim: if I reach it by then or before then, I treat myself to a new outfit—no new clothes before then!

But several days later:

I was in the doldrums last night and have vowed I'm never going to be in such a depressed-at-myself state again. I was so angry at my lack of willpower I cried—yes, I ate too much! But today I am back on my diet, starting at 62kg, and am determinedly adhering to it until I reach 52kg! From now on I am keeping to a stringent set of rules on eating so that I don't ever get so upset again.

Bulimic thoughts were intruding increasingly on my daily life, but suddenly I had something else to think about. On the evening of March 22, I dreamed I gave birth to a baby boy! I rarely remembered my dreams, but this one was as bright as day. Now I wondered, *'Will my dream come true?'* I hoped so!

In February my doctor had said, 'Now that you have been on the Pill for 12 months, I want you to stop taking it for one month to check that everything is working well.' George was to take precautions for that time. That was a laugh. I went to the chemist to buy a packet of condoms because George was too embarrassed to do so.

The night after my dream, George and I made love in our van. The packet sat unopened on George's bedside table. Our lovemaking intensifying, I reminded him of the condoms. He paused to pick up the packet, tried to open it, gave up and tossed it on the floor. 'I might get pregnant,' I whispered. 'I'll be happy if you do,' he said. I guessed I would be, too. The next morning my abdomen had a dull ache.

We had wanted to have our family while young, though I wanted to complete my Year 12 English studies and my cadetship first. A week went by and it seemed I would need to do some rethinking. I was not imagining the ache in my stomach and there was no sign of my period. Within six weeks my pregnancy was confirmed and the due date was set at December 14. With luck I would at least be able to sit for my English exam before giving birth.

Being pregnant gave me fresh impetus to be at peace within myself. After a few false starts, I began trying to control my bingeing by focusing on the next doctor's visit and the term of my pregnancy.

I was depressed all morning, and got just so sick of myself I have made a big resolution which I am determined, utterly determined, to carry out to the full. As from 8pm tonight I am going on a diet—600 calories average daily until I weigh 57kg, and then 1200 calories average daily until I weigh 54kg. I'm aiming at weighing 55kg by the time I go to see Dr on May 26.

I recognise my mood changes:

I am as changeable as the wind! Now on the last diet I am ever going on! Basically, 3 meals a day, and NOTHING to eat between them except fresh fruit or health bars, an ice-cream on Sundays! So tired of upsetting myself—never again!

By the time baby arrived, I was determined to have silenced the thoughts that made me unsociable and restless. For four months, I showed no weight gain and was pleased. Baby was growing bigger and I was becoming slimmer.

In September, Mr Yeates asked me to finish work at the newspaper office, saying: 'I don't want you giving birth on the office floor.' I had completed three of the four years of my cadetship, and wanted to work another two months. But Mr Yeates would not negotiate so, with no maternity leave entitlement, I worked on the farm while waiting for baby to come, enabling George to look for work elsewhere.

George, who had worked full-time on his parents' farm for seven years, was annoyed at his dad, who was in his 70s, for offering little incentive to stay on the property. He offered what he believed was a workable 'farm succession' arrangement but his father did not agree —and now George was talking of us leaving his family farm and share-farming elsewhere.

A short-term employment solution was found when he obtained work off the farm, on a new bridge being built over Ramrod Creek on the Omeo Highway, an hour's drive from home. Although a steady job would be best, every bit of extra work meant extra money. Drought had set in and job prospects were poor. We doubted we'd make any hay that year and finances would be grim in 1973. George enjoyed his bridge work, especially the pay packet, and I helped by milking the 70-cow herd night and morning. George's dad helped too. Several times a week I drove a ute-load of hay 12km out a bush track to feed cattle on George's 80ha bush block that we called 'Shady Glades'. For the past year, while I was working in the newspaper office, George and his father had been busy clearing land, and had sown some to pasture. It was a big step forward to have some cattle there, even though the pasture had dried off in the drought and hand feeding had become necessary in summer.

My English exam was over and baby was six days overdue when I was making one of those trips to the bush block. I enjoyed driving along the winding, dusty track, listening to the bellbirds and watching for kangaroos jumping in front of me. Today, though, a low back pain was a distraction, hinting labour was setting in. My pain increased but I resolved to tell no-one until George returned from his bridge work. I threw the heavy oaten hay bales to the cattle, drove back to the farm and, with George's dad, had completed the evening milking when George arrived about 6pm. As soon as I told him how I felt, he insisted I call the hospital right away and, after I'd had a quick bath, took me in for admission.

I was hungry but was given no time to eat my evening meal. After a long day's work on the farm, I was in the room, shaved and scared, lying on a high and hard, narrow bed, by 9pm. My gynaecologist's black gumboots stood ominously by the door. My night was lonely, filled with moans and groans. George stayed for a while but the nursing staff, concerned he would faint, sent him home.

Shane Lindsay arrived with the aid of instruments at 10.45am the next day, December 21, weighing 4.3kg. We took our 'big little treasure' home four days later, on Christmas Day. The nurses had not shown me how to bathe Shane or even change his nappy—after each feed he had been cocooned in a tightly-wrapped bunnyrug and whisked back to the nursery—but I was happy to be going home. I weighed 55kg and was determined not to let my weight bother me again. George had cleaned our van all spick and span but while collecting us a reddish-brown dust, fanned by a hot north wind sweeping over our neighbour's freshly ploughed paddock, flew in the open windows, settling over all the van's contents. Not to worry, we had our little bundle of joy.

We placed Shane in his dark blue bassinet on the divan in the kitchen part of our van. The first nappy change was a challenge. George and I carefully undid the safety pins, unwrapped the wet flannelette nappy and folded the fresh one to look the same.

With five feeds, nappy changes, washing, folding and ironing every day, Shane filled up my day. His birth was our 'bumper crop' in what was otherwise a serious drought year. No rain fell in December and I hoped 1973 would bring us plenty of it, plus money and a new home.

I am breastfeeding my three-week-old son but...

I'm being a naughty girl—eating all sorts of delicious things that I shouldn't be eating. I weighed a pleasing 53kg this morn and figured I'll go on my grapefruit diet as from tomorrow until I weigh my much-longed for 50kg. Then, I'll be very happy!

My eating patterns became more chaotic and my anxiety continued into 1973:

Gaw, I'm so confused and unhappy ... think I'm almost going around the bend.

By mid-January the bridge work had finished and George was disillusioned. He and his dad discussed a revised farm management plan and decided there was not enough productivity potential on the farm to sustain two families. It seemed Shane wouldn't be growing up at Sarsfield. We started to peruse advertisements, for station hands and share-farming, in Australia's largest circulating rural newspaper, *The Weekly Times*. George found a few possibilities but the jobs were too far from home.

Shane was a month old when we had to start buying grain feed for our dairy herd, and I wondered if I should return to work at the newspaper office to help meet the cost. Mum and Dad understood the dire situation and seemed to suggest I return to work in May. I phoned the newspaper office and with relief learnt I was likely to get my job back. I had worried it may have been given to someone else. If George also obtained a job off the farm we could stay in the district. This seemed our best plan.

Suddenly I was in a whirl. Mr Yeates phoned on January 23, asking me to return to work not in May, but on February 5, when Shane would be six weeks old. He wanted me to work three days a week for three weeks and then on February 26 resume full-time. He said if I didn't accept these conditions he would have to employ someone else. I hadn't wanted to work while Shane was a baby. I'd been hoping to breast-feed for six months but needed the job. I was in great pain, eliminating feeds and weaning Shane in two weeks so I could return to work. The two grandmothers were offering to share the care of Shane, but as they both lived miles out of town I'd be unable to race home to see him, or feed him, in the middle of the day.

Sitting on the laundry's concrete step at the back of my in-laws' farm house, I put my head between my knees and bawled. I loved my baby and felt a mother must need a heart of steel to return to work when her baby was six weeks old. My heart was soft. I coped by thinking I was returning to work so George and I could create a home for our baby and us.

If we both worked we could buy a house in Bairnsdale through a housing co-operative that offered loans at less than five per cent interest. George got another 10-week temporary job a on a bridge within an hour's drive of the farm so our prospects looked brighter, but he wanted to be a farmer, not a bridge builder.

At work, I became riddled with guilt for leaving my baby. I felt older women, particularly, were staring at me when on assignments, and imagined them saying to each other: '*What sort of a mother is she, leaving her baby and returning to work so early?'*

From 5.30am until 10pm I was on the go. It was good to be busy, but oh! George was of three minds: whether to move into town, stay on his parents' farm, or go to another farm. I said he must choose and Shane and I would support him. I wanted the three of us to be together.

We signed papers to buy a house in Bairnsdale but before we'd moved into it, and two months after I returned to work, George obtained a share-farming position on a dairy property. The position was at Stanhope in the Goulburn Valley region of central Victoria, a six-hour drive from Sarsfield. We were assured of $6500 a year, which was a good wage. I hoped we would like the farm and would stay there for at least five years.

The job required two milkers, and, as our start date approached, I wondered how I'd look after Shane and milk 140 cows twice a day.

8. BABIES

We were committed to the share-farming job and, by the start of May 1973, had sold our caravan, said farewell to Sarsfield and leased our house at Bairnsdale, and were settling into a fibro-cement share-farmer cottage a few miles from the small dairying town of Stanhope. As envisaged, my days became filled with milking cows, caring for Shane, housework and more cows. My only break was a short visit into town to collect mail, newspaper and groceries. We were milking 83 cows in a herringbone shed, but this would increase to 140 in spring.

Each day became the same as the one before and after it; milking cows was like that and, socially isolated, I felt trapped. I ate and ate and became FAT. I tried the grapefruit diet, low-carbohydrate diet and counting-calories diet. Each failed. Each time I binged and let myself down, depression took a greater hold, sabotaging my relationship with myself and with George. By mid-June I was thinking *'I'll go bonkers if we don't have some variety in our lives'*. Editing the Victorian Young Farmers' newspaper was my only creative outlet. By July I was feeling a little resentful at us moving to Stanhope, as George was already talking about returning to Gippsland. I'd given up breastfeeding Shane, then my job, to go to Stanhope and two months later we were talking of leaving. I was tired of being mixed up in both my inner and outer worlds.

On one matter I was not mixed up, however, and that was the effect of our situation on five-month-old Shane. One wintry night I rugged him up in his pusher and wheeled him through the mud to the dairy. He couldn't be with George and me in the cold and wet herringbone pit, where there was risk of flying hooves and cow muck landing on one's head, so I left him strapped in his pusher in the wash-up room. Shane could see us working but he howled loudly, his misery making us all unhappy. Being busy, I could not leave the pit to comfort him. About to wash the mud off a cow's teats, my frustration spilled over and I squirted the cold-water hose at George instead of the cow. Now the three of us were yelling. I wheeled Shane home. He didn't stop howling until he was on the lounge room floor in front of the oil heater without his nappy, playing with his toys; then he was content.

Shane was independent, strong and adventurous; when we tried to cuddle him we were likely to be socked in the face with a flying hand. But I knew our baby shouldn't be left alone. My mother had taken me to the dairy when I was a toddler, but she worked in a small conventional shed, which was more child-friendly and the pace of milking was slower. An early memory, when I was three or four, was of squatting by the copper fire, the precursor to the briquette heater, while my parents milked a few metres away. I would collect the white plastic caps off discarded penicillin tubes, that Dad used to treat milk fever, push them on a twig and poke them in the hot ashes to melt them and make interesting shapes. This kept me amused for hours. Sometimes I'd wander off and look for eggs in the nearby haystack, climbing up and down the bales. By the age of five I was starting to help in the dairy, shooing the cows in from the outer yard, and hosing the yards at the end of milking.

But times had changed. Herds had increased in size and dairies had expanded to achieve faster throughput. They were a dangerous place for crawling babies and toddlers. George and I had heard of toddlers losing fingers in the fast-moving pulley belt of the engine room or disappearing for a moment and drowning in a cow trough. Being hundreds of kilometres from family, not knowing anyone locally and with no access to a child-minding centre, keeping Shane in the house seemed our safest option.

Another evening I barricaded Shane, eight months' old by now, in our heated lounge room on a rug with his toys and television on for company while I was at the dairy. I returned two hours later to find a very happy little boy. He had been industrious, pulling the books out of the first three shelves of our book case and extracting my leafy pot plants from their containers, ripping the leaves apart, probably devouring a few, and playing in the dirt he had spread over the carpet.

A letter from George's mum revealed that his dad was planning to sell his cows. This meant the family farm at Sarsfield wouldn't be used for dairying again, not by us, anyway. George's dad maintained that if George wanted the property he'd have to pay five-sixths of the farm price to his five older siblings, and was resolute, despite some siblings saying this was too hard on George financially. His father's firm stance helped George accept that he had to seek fulfillment elsewhere.

But Stanhope was not the answer. A lecture from the farm owner on everything we were doing wrong provided fresh incentive to depart. I was expected to help in the dairy from start to finish—that was, until all the washing up and yards were done. But I already spent two hours a day milking in the dairy, and refused to leave Shane alone in the house for longer than that. George was told he wasn't doing enough work and shouldn't wear rubber gloves when milking because they 'lacked sensitivity'. I'd bought the gloves for George a few days earlier to protect his hands from the cow kicks and mud, which had caused sores. I thought the farm owner's attitude was harsh, and George was annoyed.

The next morning we were up at 5.05am. I fetched the cows in on my horse, Jason, who had travelled to Stanhope with us. At 7.15 I returned to the house and ran to Shane, who was yet again crying in his cot. I felt upset, seeing him like that.

The wettest winter in 50 years didn't help. The water table rose so high, the bowl of our septic tank toilet overflowed, and George had to fetch the tractor to pull the car out of a bog in the tin shed that served as our garage. The final straw came when I became pregnant and suffered a miscarriage at eight weeks.

We looked in *The Weekly Times* for another job, one requiring only one milker. I would be happier when pregnant again and when we were settled. We didn't have to wait long. In September George was accepted as a farmhand at Kilmany Park Farm Home for Boys, near Sale, in our home region of East Gippsland. Only one milker was required. 'The wage is not high, but we're going,' George said. His decision inspired me to stay on my latest diet. The move represented another chance to control my inner self.

Two days before we departed from Stanhope, another pregnancy was confirmed. This was the best news to come out of our five months at Stanhope. My goal for the next eight months would be to not exceed 60kg. My pregnancy would be a time for losing and controlling weight, not gaining it, in a bid to silence my taunting thoughts.

We moved to Kilmany Park, an institution run by the Presbyterian Church for young male wards of the State, in September. The boys lived with their carers in a mansion on a big farming property that had one of the first rotary dairies in Australia. The cows stepped on a slowly revolving platform and were milked by the time they completed a full circle and stepped off. The rotary design enabled many cows to be milked at one time and was a big advance from the conventional dairies George and I had grown up with and the herringbone, in which we'd worked at Stanhope. George was one of several farmhands operating the dairy, situated 500m down a dirt track from our living quarters—a three-bedroom brick home in beautiful rural surrounds. The house was the most modern we had lived in—it had new striped acrylic carpet in the lounge and bedrooms, and for the first time we had an inside toilet. The property was a 70-minute drive from my parents' farm, and 90 minutes from Sarsfield. I'd not need to get up at 4.30am anymore to fetch cows, and, more importantly, leave Shane alone. I enjoyed taking him for walks in the stroller around the bumpy farm tracks and down to the dairy to look through the fence at the cows being milked.

Now that I was pregnant, it was easier to control my weight:

I'm happy because I've started a diet published in a 'slimming' magazine and I am confident of and determined to staying/stay on it until I weigh 53kg. I'll ... begin summer on the right foot, keeping my weight down so that I'll weigh not more than 63kg when fully pregnant.

However, being a full-time mother was not enough to quell my tormenting thoughts.

Within two weeks of moving to Kilmany, restlessness drove me to the Commonwealth Employment Office, on the corner of the Princes Highway and Raymond Street in Sale, to seek part-time typing to do at home. However, the employment officer said: 'You can do more with your skills than stay-at-home typing,' and arranged for me to sit for a Public Service Department examination. This, he said, would qualify me for a clerical job in the public service and my name would be put forward when a local position became vacant. George, meanwhile, was disappointed with his new employment; he was low on the pecking order of the farmhand team and without a specific duty or responsibility. In April 1974, five months after starting work at Kilmany Park farm, he announced: 'I'm fed up.'

'Take your gripe up with the foreman rather than going off to me about it,' I said. I reminded him happily that we were about to start our fourth year of marriage and our second child was due in four weeks.

Because Shane had been a bit 'over-baked' when he was born, with dry skin peeling off his feet and hands, the gynaecologist at the Gippsland Base Hospital in Sale took no chances with my second child, inducing my labour on May 11. This labour was easier than my first, and in less than five hours, our second son, Rohan Charles, was born. At 3–4kg, Rohan was of average weight and in excellent health. Like George, he had a dimple in his chin. 'Amazing', I thought, and then realised George had been leading me on for years. He had told me that his dimple developed because he leant on his pencil point in primary school. And I'd believed him.

George and I had a pact whereby I would name our sons and he would name our daughters. I'd chosen 'Shane' because I liked the 1953 Western movie of the same name. The source of Rohan's name was more regal—he was named after our Victorian Governor of the day, Sir Rohan Delacombe. Sir Rohan retired after 11 years as Governor on May 24, shortly after Rohan's birth.

With two little boys to keep me occupied, everything was rosy in my world except for the sleepless nights, the problem of George being dissatisfied with his job, and my inner void. Within a few weeks of Rohan's birth, my bingeing caused upsets in my breast milk and consequently upsets in Rohan, who vomited three times in one night. This regular occurrence and Rohan's distress added to my self-loathing. I feared he wouldn't register a weight gain on his visits to the infant welfare centre, and that the health sister would label me an unfit mother.

Striving to eat only the right amounts of nutritional foods, I started a diet diary, telling myself that by stringently sticking to my rules, I would cope, but within two days another binge would occur. Somehow, Rohan gained a little weight each week but I was distraught, aware that my weakness was affecting not only me but, through my milk supply, my baby. Even while I held my baby in my arms, and Shane was not yet two, I began yearning for the contentment, and sense of control, that would come with another pregnancy.

If only George was happy in his job, but he was not. 'For many reasons, I believe we should stay at Kilmany,' I said. 'In three to four years you will be foreman, most likely, and have status and responsibility, plus we have a home and security.' A Toy Tots Childminding Centre had opened in Sale, so I could work too, knowing our children would be in good care.

Rohan was six weeks old when I had a severe binge. He vomited twice because I was upset, and that upset me further. The infant welfare nurse did not suspect a problem at his weigh-in, but I began to wean him to avoid the impact of further binges. They were difficult to avoid at the moment because George, intent on being his own boss, was looking for a dairy farm to buy. At first I felt depressed and ate myself numb; then crawled out of the blackness, determined to make the most of yet another change, another fresh start.

However, I was slipping and sliding into dark ravines. Each failure to feel settled caused my slips and slides to be steeper and more frequent than the one before. Rohan was three months' old when my craving for stability intensified the desire for a third baby. George agreed, and the hope of pregnancy gave me something to cling to.

I had more to hold onto in September, with the offer of full-time employment as a clerk in the Sale office of the Department of Social Security. I didn't know what a clerk did, but would soon find out, as I was to start work within a week. I phoned the childminding centre, arranged an inspection and enrolled the boys, now aged 21 months and four months. I would miss them, but work would help me feel I was sane.

Scanning the *Gippsland Times* newspaper property section, George found a listing for a 131-acre irrigation dairy farm at Airly, near Sale. 'It sounds a good buy. Let's have a look,' he said. The present owners had eight children under eight and were struggling financially; they wanted a quick sale so they could return to family in Melbourne. We bought the property, walk-in walk-out, in joint names, and received 80 cows, plus machinery, with the land. We would take possession prior to Christmas, and I would keep working to help pay the bills.

My third pregnancy was confirmed on Shane's second birthday, the news coming the same week we moved to our farm. Everything seemed to be happening at once, but moving into the former Soldier Settlement house with its white weatherboards, corrugated galvanised iron roof and three bedrooms kept our feet on the ground. Chooks had been roosting on the laundry troughs and the smell of their manure in the house had me holding my nose and running outside to gulp fresh air. The hot water was dirty, noisy rats were chewing in the thin walls at night and the rooms had been painted in gaudy colours. But this was our house and our farm, and we'd overcome these little problems.

We forgot our challenges for a few hours while we ate Christmas lunch with George's parents at Sarsfield, a 90-minute drive away, and returned home about 4pm to milk our cows. I walked into the kitchen to find a mouse running across the kitchen floor and dead blowflies everywhere. But by the following day, Boxing Day, the house was beginning to look like home, that was, apart from the many blowflies, which we would discourage by installing flywire on the windows, and the mice, which we would trap and bait—we'd killed a total of five that afternoon, hitting them on the head with the hearth brush.

I turned 24, and 1975 dawned with fresh optimism. All went well until a little drama unfolded while I was at work in late February. Mid-morning I felt my tummy had been wrenched. Thinking I'd stretched a muscle helping George to move an oak wardrobe from the house to the machinery shed the night before, I feared my doctor would criticise me for lifting something heavy and delayed seeking medical advice. I was feeling nauseated at lunchtime but ate a salad roll and drank 600ml of milk, thinking nourishment for my baby might help. At 2pm at work I had to lie down, and 45 minutes later a colleague and friend, Julie, offered to drive me to the medical clinic.

I sat on the wooden bench outside my gynaecologist's consulting room but he kept overlooking me and seeing other patients because I did not have a regular appointment. At one stage I rushed to a toilet down the corridor to be sick. As the minutes ticked by, I could hardly sit up. The clinic was closing at 5pm, and members of the clinic staff were going home, when a GP at the end of the corridor seemed to take pity and offered to see me. He found a sore spot on my right side near my hip. He checked my tongue and my rectum and took a urine sample. After quickly conferring with my doctor, he told me to go straight to the maternity ward of the hospital next door and book in.

My mind was foggy and I battled to explain that I was worried about nine-month-old Rohan. Shane was at my parents' farm for a holiday but Rohan was at the child-minding centre which, like the clinic, was about to close for the day. George was milking cows 8km away on the farm and our only car was where I'd parked it that morning—at the child-minding centre in town. The clinic staff assured me they would notify Toy Tots and arrange care of Rohan until George could collect him.

George eventually found me by phoning Toy Tots, wondering why Rohan and I had not arrived home, and called a taxi to take him to the hospital. I didn't know about this because my mind became increasingly groggy. On admission to the maternity ward I was placed on a gurney and a medical team converged, swiftly swapping my work clothes for white cotton cap, boots, jacket and pants. Someone penned crosses on my tummy and at 6.45pm I was wheeled to the operating theatre to have my appendix out. The emergency operation was a close call, more so because the surgeon needed to cut around my baby.

'If you had been one more month advanced in your pregnancy, I would have taken the baby out with your appendix,' my gynaecologist said. By the time George arrived, I was being wheeled to a ward to start recovery.

Within two weeks, I was back at work in the Department of Social Security, checking people's eligibility for the aged or disability pension. George, meanwhile, was working hard to improve our farm which had potential but, like our house, was run-down. New cattle troughs, fencing, laneways and pasture improvement were some of the jobs he tackled. He prepared soil and fences along our farm's perimeter in readiness to plant hundreds of native trees that we bought in 15cm tubes. We planted the trees together on weekends and looked forward to watching them grow to provide shade and shelter for our herd.

We spent $200 buying polythene piping to improve our water system and I was starting to conclude that money didn't go anywhere on farms. My mother had learnt this lesson long ago. As a child, when I asked for a new toy or a treat, she would respond, 'Money doesn't grow on trees'. She repeated this in response to another frequent request, 'Mum, I want a brother to play with.' I kept asking until I was 11 years old and, trying to be helpful, planted a sixpence in the garden at the back of our house, hoping it would grow and solve my mother's money problems so I could have my playmate. Unfortunately the sixpence didn't sprout roots and now I understood Mum's wisdom. To have money I'd have to earn it, and even then things might not go my way—my off-farm income, instead of providing funds for house renovations, was meeting our living costs. I hoped our hard work and farm improvements would pay off.

My pregnancy continued and, with the birthdate set for the first week in August, I began 12 weeks' paid maternity leave at the end of June. This was the first time maternity leave had been available to me and it helped greatly with our finances. Determined not to allow my thoughts to upset my breastfeeding with my third baby, I tried to establish a healthy eating pattern before the birth. I wanted to breastfeed for the first two months at least.

Benjamin George arrived in a natural birth on July 27, weighing 3.9kg. George, who had become accustomed to the birthing process, said, 'He's beautiful'. And he was; Benjamin had dark hair and already I could tell he'd have brown eyes: the Coster trademark. I chose 'Benjamin' because I liked Ben Hall, an Australian bushranger who lived from 1837 to 1865. A television series about Ben Hall, who became an outlaw after a few misunderstandings, was screening at the time son Ben was born.

With a wonderful husband and three beautiful sons I had every reason to be happy but felt depressed. Within a month, I resumed stuffing and starving myself. My breasts were overflowing with milk one day and drying up the next. Somehow Ben coped admirably, and at night often slept 12 hours straight.

Oh I am a silly billy. I ate like a horse all yesterday arvo till I felt quite sick. Now I am overflowing with milk! I only had a cup of tea for breakfast and I'm feeling better already. I'm going to go on the low carbohydrate diet—got to do something.

I've started a health book and will buy a new set of bathroom scales this week—my present set have never been quite the same since Shane put them in the bathwater.

Ben was a month old when Rohan was admitted to hospital with gastroenteritis. We took two-year-old Shane for a visit but, unknown to us, Rohan had been placed in isolation. Only the parents were allowed admission. Shane couldn't understand why he was unable to see his brother. He had been a good little boy and yet felt he was being punished. When we returned to the farm, he expressed his displeasure by disappearing from the house, finding George's hammer and smashing the tailights of our new tandem trailer. George was annoyed. Shane was a very lively and we couldn't guess what he would do next. One day, George was having a cuppa inside before the afternoon milking, and heard the tractor start. He raced outside, jumped a barbed-wire fence and reached the tractor before Shane took off.

Shane was equally creative in the house. My white wedding shoes that I continued to wear for best befell the same fate as my bathroom scales: 'Look, ships in the bath, Mummy,' a gleeful Shane said.

Some mornings, while the three boys were asleep, I walked 100 metres to the dairy to help George clean the machines and yards after milking. I would return home shortly afterwards to find Shane had opened his bedroom window and tossed all his bedding outside—along with sheets and blankets from Rohan's cot. Fourteen-month-old Rohan would be standing half-frozen in his cotton bunny outfit on the bare mattress, shaking and rattling the sides of his cot for attention.

Shane was always one step ahead in deciding his next adventure. If Rohan didn't come when we called, we knew where to look—in Peta Rabbit's coop, on our front lawn. Rohan, a snowy-haired, self-contented little boy, didn't mind Shane shutting him in the coop after letting Peta out for a play. Both boys looked on bemused as George and I crawled through the undergrowth of our cypress hedge, calling sweet things to Peta in the hope of recapturing her. Luckily we always did, and she lived for eight years.

The children were a divergence from my eating disorder, but my depression was worsening:

I'm starting to wean Ben today or tomorrow—I've started my diet and I am really determined to stay on it as I want to weigh 50kg; more than any other thing I can think of, that is what I want for my own self. And I am going to make it this time—don't know how long it will take but it will at least be before I turn 25.

But two days later:

I've had so many false starts it isn't funny any more.

Ben was two months old when I began weaning him and became clucky again. I reasoned that I'd like one more child and then, instead of taking the Pill, I'd have my fallopian tubes tied. Having a goal helped me push my tormenting thoughts aside.

By now we'd been on our farm for almost 12 months, and making sufficient income was a struggle. The UK had joined the European Economic Community in 1973–74, and shut the door on its imports of Australian dairy products. Many small family farms, like those of our parents as well as our own, were no longer viable for dairying. My father, who had helped us out with some cows when our herd was found to have bovine tuberculosis, was switching to vegetable growing and raising beef cattle, while George's parents were retiring, selling most of their property, and moving into Bairnsdale. George was not dedicated to farming any more—he couldn't see the point in continuing to struggle—and told my dad we were tidying our farm to put it on the market. Dad was in favour of this; he was as fed up as us of the soaring costs and depleting farm incomes. We figured we'd need a month to complete the fences, plant the trees, finish the track and paint the house.

I agonised over whether we were making the right decision, but George was definite and said, 'If we get a buyer, we'll sell.' We did get a buyer, miraculously making a small profit, and paid cash for a four-bedroom brick veneer house in Sale. Sale's economy was booming and the township was expanding due to development by Esso and BHP of gas and oil reserves off the Gippsland coast. Settlement day for our house was set at January 21, 1976.

The year on our farm had been hectic, and we felt older and wiser. In the first week of January, George obtained a job at the Murray Goulburn Milk Factory in Maffra, 15km from our farm. We still had cows to milk morning and night, and I helped as much as I could with three little boys to look after. I wheeled the three of them, crowded into one pusher, down the gravelled laneway that ran through the centre of our property, to fetch the cows for the afternoon milking. Sometimes, with the summer sun beating down as we followed the cows home in the dust, I put the boys in a cow trough to cool off. They laughed and splashed, and I wished I could get in, too.

A few weeks later we moved into town. We hadn't lived in a town before, with neighbours next door. I was not impressed when the little ginger-haired boy from across the road visited with his daddy's golf club one day, and belted the heads off my large bed of colourful poppies. Not even Shane had thought of doing that.

Our main bedroom had an en suite bathroom and our family room had a beautiful parquetry floor—great for dancing, if we had the time. We'd hardly unpacked our boxes, however, before my restlessness resumed. It would not let me be! Work seemed my only answer. George's factory wage gave us enough to live on and in my heart I wanted to be with my boys, but my head wanted to escape my tormentor. I thought I'd regret working through the boys' infant years, but my depression was affecting us all. At the end of February I returned to work in the Social Security Department, with the boys being looked after by a Jane, a capable young woman, in our home.

George was trying to persuade me that we had enough children; being the youngest of six, he was adamant he wanted no more. My head agreed with him, even if my heart didn't, as two or three children was being widely accepted as the limit if the world was not to explode with people. When we first married we said two was enough. Then, because we didn't have a daughter we said we'd have one more, and that would be our limit and our luxury, so perhaps we should have stuck with that thought. But we hadn't accounted for the views of three-year-old Shane. The very next day I came home from work to learn that Shane had announced out of the blue to our babysitter Jane that he was getting a baby sister for his next birthday. George heard him tell her. When I arrived home an hour later, Jane said: 'Shane, tell your mum what you want for your birthday.' With a grin, he said: 'A baby sister.' We decided to try and grant Shane his wish.

Within six weeks, I was pregnant. But my body was tired. There were signs a miscarriage may occur and one evening, after work, blood loss led to a hospital admission. I prayed and asked God over and over to save this baby. In return I promised to take better care of my baby and me. Earlier that evening I had stuffed myself with food, including a huge feed of wild duck, which my brother-in-law Ray had shot, and my mother had baked.

Next morning my doctor confirmed my baby was intact and allowed me home, providing I rested in bed for several days. He said my problem was due to some placenta coming away. I was to take two iron tablets a day.

Ben turned one at the end of July and now our sons were one, two and three. I affectionately called them Huey, Dewey and Louie, after Scrooge McDuck's nephews in Disney's *DuckTales* series. All we wanted was a Daisy to complete our little team. But this pregnancy remained a struggle. Depression flowed from guilt after each bingeing bout. I tried a high-protein diet as set out in a slimming magazine. Desperate to achieve my goal of 50kg after giving birth, I tried any diet that offered some sense of control. Success was vital—this was my last chance.

However, a routine doctor's visit in October landed me back in hospital. I had been losing water and my doctor said my membranes had ruptured. I went home after a few days of rest but had to take it easy. The good news was that I didn't need to work any more before Bubsie's arrival and so could relax with the boys in front of our first colour television set, which we'd bought to watch the Montreal Olympic Games in July. The TV was a great entertainer for the boys. In the mornings they watched *Play School* and *Sesame Street* while I washed breakfast dishes and hung washing on the line. I tried to tell myself to relax and enjoy my boys: all I had to do was stay well and lose weight. But by November, my gynaecologist was worried about Bubsie's size and by the small amount of fluid around him or her. He admitted me to hospital again, this time for a week. My body continued to lack iron, among other things, and injections were ordered. The doctor was not worried about the baby being small, but about it starving, and ordered 24-hour urine tests to check the food intake. He didn't know about my years of roller coaster eating patterns or dark moods.

Four weeks prior to my due date, my gynaecologist said, 'What a scungy kid you've got in there.' He was the same doctor who'd left me waiting when I had appendicitis. His words stung, but I had to remain his patient because he was the only local doctor who performed the tubal ligation operation.

Bubsie was almost due when George came home with cheerful news from his employer. He had been working in the milk factory as a cleaner since we left the farm, and had been promoted to the position of operator in the carton milk section. This meant more shift work, but the shifts were generally eight hours only and the pay rate was higher.

A few days later, on December 22 at 12.17am, 17 minutes after Shane's fourth birthday, George and I became parents of a daughter. The labour ward staff were as excited as us, and celebrated with a glass of champagne. Amanda Anne weighed 3.2kg at birth. Shane had his birthday present and his sister certainly wasn't scungy; she was beautiful.

George, from a family of five boys and one girl, was especially happy to have a daughter and chose her name, 'Amanda', after Mandy Rice-Davies, a British socialite invovled in a Parliamentary scandal known as the Profumo affair in 1963. Now our family was complete but the torment in my soul remained.

On Christmas Day I was feeling a little down because my breasts were engorged and painful, and because of the upcoming tubal ligation operation. Through tears, I growled at George and said: 'I've done my bit for our family. You should have a vasectomy; it is simpler procedure than mine.' However, he wouldn't budge. 'I'm a coward,' he said. I agreed. He left me no option but to have the operation, as we could not afford more children.

A tubal ligation would also prevent my use of pregnancy as a lever to fight my thoughts, and this worried me. My gynaecologist said: 'I would prefer you to be 30 before operating, but because you have four children I'll do it now.' He preferred to wait eight weeks after the birth, to allow my uterus to contract, but if I went home without the operation, I knew my thoughts would rage and I would want a fifth baby. Rather than tell the doctor this, I said I'd have difficulty organising childcare to return to the hospital in eight weeks: I wanted the operation now. It was scheduled six days after Amanda's birth, the day after my 26th birthday.

On the eve of my operation I received a phone call from Shane, who was staying with my parents. He said: 'Happy birthday, Mummy,' and after a small chat he asked: 'And how is Amanda?' I felt deeply touched and longed for the six of us to be at home together.

The next day I awoke from the anaesthetic, telling myself 'I'm a free woman'. No more pregnancies for me. Not the brightest or best feeling right then, but at least my tubes were tied. Amanda and I went home three days later, on New Year's Eve. She'd already had an effect on her father. Our neighbour invited him to drink a beer, 'to wet the baby's head', and George did so. At the age of 28, this was his first glass of beer. Amanda was our pot of gold at the end of a beautiful rainbow. Like our sons, she was priceless.

So ended the childbearing phase of my life.

9. RETURN TO THE LINDENOW VALLEY

Four children under the age of five kept George and me busy, even with Council Home Help coming for several weeks after my operation. But being busy did not stop my niggling thoughts, and within weeks of Amanda's birth I began thinking about returning to work. The problem was to find someone capable of minding four children, the eldest of whom was yet to start preschool. With a gorgeous baby girl to love and hug, I felt silly to be talking about returning to work.

Emotionally my heart struggled bigtime, but mentally, I did not have a choice. My mood swings were such that George and Joy together convinced me to return to work. The break from home would be good for the children and me and, although half my wage would go on childcare, every dollar was useful. Unemployment in Australia was 12 per cent, the highest since World War Two.

I arranged to return to work at the start of April, giving myself time to wean Amanda and start a new diet in a bid to be free of depression, grumpiness and unhappiness. My many failed attempts to appease the tormentor in my mind were reducing my self-belief to rubble. I couldn't have any more babies, and dieting was not the answer. I had to clutch at something to raise myself out of the darkness that had deepened through 15 years of dieting, each failure increasing my frustration and depression. Work was reassuring because, when I completed tasks and did a good job, I felt a little 'normal'. A mother and daughter, Hazel and Janet, came to our home each day to care for our children, and everyone was happy except me, mainly. I supposed this was because I was mixed up. Always driven to have a goal, this time I aimed to control my eating so I could leave work as the new me when George found a secure job.

He wanted to return to farming and within a month accepted a job requiring an experienced man for milking, with regular days off, on a farm at Neerim South, 20 minutes north of Warragul, in West Gippsland. This was two hours west from where we currently lived.

The thought of another house move dismantled my latest nutritional rules in a flash. A binge later, I wrote another plan, outlining a fresh strategy to weigh 52kg—believing this would bring me peace. I ignored the fact that on the rare occasions I had attained my weight goal, contentment was fleeting. I could not satiate my gnawing emptiness, and yet trying to control myself through food was the only way I knew to repel the blackness. At most, I gained momentary relief, before slipping back into the emotional quagmire.

Maybe the answer would be to stay home and face my fears. I'd find out at Neerim South. This would be the first time I had not worked since we married, although I supposed that with four children, I would have enough to do. Shane had started preschool in February and already had been suspended once for knocking everything over in the dolls' corner.

George had told my mother about our latest plans, and she had not contacted me since. Therefore I was thinking the worst—she didn't approve. I wanted to call her but feared she would upset me. I cried at night, thinking Mum disliked me—probably because I wasn't a boy —because she rarely praised or showed an interest in anything I did. George's parents, despite being 20 years older than my parents, were less judgmental and more understanding, and therefore more approachable.

I regretfully handed in my resignation, giving a month's notice, to the Department of Social Security. The job was secure and well paid, despite its lack of excitement, but George said resigning was the right decision.

We were moving to Neerim South in four weeks and I'd not packed a thing. The packing and the shifting, and leaving our comfortable home, deterred me most. Moving to a small, old farmhouse a few miles out of Neerim South was not what I wanted. George became irate if I said anything but I doubted that milking someone else's cows, 200 of them, twice a day at Neerim South would be the answer for him. Maybe, however, the cause of my constant uncertainty was within me, and had nothing to do with George. I did not know what to think any more.

We arrived at Neerim South just prior to spring. Faded paint on the weatherboards made our 'new' home look shabby, but inside we found it clean and comfortable. The house, with a rusting corrugated iron roof, was about 100 years old. It nestled near some big cypress trees and old shedding on the side of a steep hill, about 3km out of town and 2km from the main homestead and dairy. The children immediately relished the freedom of living in the country again.

George was busy with work and I became involved at the local pre-school, which Shane attended four days a week and Rohan three days a week. We were welcomed into the local congregation of the Uniting Church in Australia, and I developed a friendship with another young mother, who also had young children, on an adjacent farm. But my dark thoughts raged against these efforts to develop a sense of belonging in the community. Within two months I feared I was losing my mind.

I am having great trouble adjusting from being pregnant, having babies and working, to this plateau of seemingly nothing.

I could not accept the nothing. I was fighting it, and looking for something but didn't know what. It wasn't morning coffee parties, one of which Rohan, Ben Amanda and I had attended the day before. Such events were enjoyable but not substantial. I needed to do some study, or get a part-time job reporting, or take up something new like dressmaking, all out of the question due to the geography of where I was living. I loved my children and enjoyed looking after them, but something was missing. A hole within could not be filled. My great fits of depression were no good for George, the children or me.

I compiled a list—the latest of thousands—and vowed to check my progress daily:

1. *I'll not be happy inside until I weigh 50kg. I'll eat nothing today and thereafter 1000 max. calories a day until I do so. Today, only tea, coffee, lo-cal lemonade.*
2. *Today I'll go into town and look for a suitable knitting pattern to knit up wool I have. This will keep my fingers busy.*

3. *I will look forward to the day when we are again in a house of our own.*

   Food has made me a moody person since I was 11 years old—15 years. I must come to grips with the situation.

Within 48 hours I'd tear this list apart, having let myself down with a fresh binge. Depending on the seriousness of the binge, days would pass before I found the strength to push the darkness away, rise up and start again. November arrived and I remained in the doldrums. Silly, I thought, when I had a supportive husband and four lovely children. I wondered if the reason was because so much had happened, every year for 10 years, and now, nothing. I needed something to interest me besides the children and George.

Going on the Israeli Army Diet to gain momentary relief seemed to be my only option.

George came home with bright news: he'd have two days off at Christmas, which meant we could make the two-and-a-half hour trip to my parents' farm and visit our families. I wrote to Mum, pleased to have an event to look forward to.

On December 8, her letter of reply sent me on a downward spiral. She stated plainly that there would be no room for us at the family farm at Iguana Creek that Christmas because my city cousins would be staying there. She suggested she could house one of us, Joy could accommodate three, and George's mum possibly two. But we didn't want to be split up. George's mum would have others staying with her, and Joy had enough with her own family without us. The bottom line was that my cousins, who could easily afford to stay elsewhere, were my parents' priority.

Mum suggested we make a daytrip the weekend before Christmas but George said firmly: 'No, we will celebrate our Christmas at Neerim South.' My depression hit a new low. I had always felt Mum and Dad didn't like me but had no idea why. 'The less we see of them the better,' George said, 'because they upset you.'

On December 15, I summoned courage to phone my mother. She always had a list of things gone wrong and this time her lead story concerned the pet house cow. 'Ginger has died, struck down by milk fever,' Mum said. 'Your father is very upset.' Dad had milked Ginger by hand since he went out of dairying. Then she asked, 'Are you visiting at the weekend?'

'No', I said. She started to carry on, reminding me that they had enough worries without me behaving like this. She called for Dad, and I lost courage and put the receiver down. Dad phoned a few minutes later to put me in my place, but although tearful I managed to say, 'My cousins are adults now and could find alternative accommodation at Christmas. Why do they come before me? I love you but feel second rate, as though I am not liked.' We finished civilly but I was confused. Maybe I was imagining the rejection, but Mum had been upsetting me for years and perhaps I had to explode, sometime.

On Shane's fifth birthday, December 21, I remained depressed. I cared for my children but, driven by incessant inner unrest, I wanted one more shift, one more new start, to a home of our own. George was reluctant because for once he was feeling settled—he liked his farm job. 'We need to get out and socialise, and spend a little time together without the children,' he said. 'Let's make an effort to settle at Neerim South.' We maintained church attendance and, with Shane at kindergarten, I was meeting new families and the community was friendly.

Shane began school at Neerim South Primary in February 1978 and Rohan and Ben were attending four- and three-year-old pre-school respectively, so our little family was growing up.

In March, Mum and Dad turned me away again. I wrote to say we could stay with them at Easter—but Mum replied there would be no room, because friends and relatives from Melbourne would be visiting. I felt unwanted. 'We will stay at Neerim South at Easter, as we did for Christmas,' George said. I didn't mind relatives and friends having priority when I was young, but I did now that I had my own family.

My parents' latest rejection knocked my sense of self 'for six', and three months slipped by before I grabbed hold and pulled some of myself together. George tried to cheer me, assuring me that we would purchase a property locally within the next few months.

I've taken a hold on myself—have stopped falling into pieces and have started to pull myself together. George still doesn't know for sure where we'll live, but he does assure me we'll be out of this house and into one of our own no later than August 12.

We watched a movie 'Hawaii' on tele last night and it went for 3 hours, till 11.30pm, and after we came to bed I broke down and had a long sob—the culmination of many feelings—my longing to be free from the effects of anorexia nervosa and bulimia, my longing to be in our own house and settled, my longing for more company. Well, now that George has assured me of a date I will show myself that I can be a new person. No later than August 12 I will weigh 49kg to 50kg and I'll never again weigh more than 50kg. I'll be free of the illness that has plagued me for 16 years. Commencing today.

No matter how hard I tried, I kept slipping. I looked for something else to grab a foothold. We started looking for a house to buy.:

We're shifting into our own brick veneer house here at Neerim South by the end of July! We will be settled! It's a wonderful relief! Now I know our date, I will lose my weight.

With my childhood home out of bounds at the most meaningful times of the year, George understood my need for us to live in a home of our own.

Our children helped me to live in the moment, although at times I worried for their safety. Shane and Rohan enjoyed exploring the old sheds near our house. One day they found an axe and decided to be helpful by chopping some wood. I was busy in the house with Ben and Amanda when Rohan came in the back door leading Shane, who had blood dripping from his blond hair, over his face and down his clothes. Our robust little boy was decidedly pale and shaky. Pushing aside flashbacks of my bus and log truck accidents, I struggled to stay calm. Running to fetch a fresh towel, I wrapped it around Shane's head like a turban, and sat him on a kitchen chair. Too scared to inspect his wound, I gave him a glass of lemonade and a biscuit and we sat and waited for George to come home at lunchtime. Carefully we unwrapped the turban and found the cut was only several centimetres long, on the crown of his head. Shane had reversed the axe and hit himself on the upswing when it slipped. I did what my mother had done with me when I became caught in rusty barbed wire as a young child, and bathed Shane carefully in warm water, adding a good dash of Dettol antiseptic. Being resourceful and resilient was part of my heritage. My parents had taught me that physical challenges were acceptable as part of life's struggle—Shane was soon running around again—but mental problems were a weakness to be ignored.

For many reasons, I would be glad to leave the house that had been our home for almost a year. One wintry night I sat in the small, heated lounge with the four freshly bathed children, watching television while waiting for George to come in from the evening milking. I had a routine and it worked well. I placed the children in the bath together, and took them out one at a time to dry and dress in their pyjamas. The last one out had the biggest play in the water. As each child was dressed, I sat them on the sofa and gave them their dinner. Usually they were ready for bed by the time George came in from milking the cows. This particular night, something dashed out from behind the heater in the old chimney at the end of the room. A bat! It flew from wall to wall, darting here, swooping there, its wings spread wide. Amanda was sitting on my lap and I tried to protect her head. The boys, especially our nature-lover Rohan, watched the zooming bat with interest until it left as silently as it had come.

At four, Rohan was observant and perceptive. One day, he set off to collect the eggs from our small family of chooks that lived in an old wire-netting pen downhill from the house. He returned, calling: 'Mummy, Mummy, look what I've found.' I ran to the back door and stopped. He was happily swinging a dead rat by its tail. It had drowned in the chooks' water bucket. I could do without rats.

But even Rohan's tolerance of wildlife was sorely tested one night when he awoke, yelling. George and I rushed in to find bees in his bed. Already he had been stung five times. One finger was so swollen the fingernail looked ready to pop off. Bees had built a hive within the house walls and were oozing out of keyholes and wherever they could find a crack. They had homed in on Rohan and left the rest of us alone. The property owner quickly arranged for an apiarist to take the bees to a new home but I remained on edge and, when a house across the road came on the market, George agreed we could buy it. We moved in within 30 days; this would be my best new start of all time.

Living in our own home increased our sense of belonging in the Neerim South community but now I wondered if the key to quelling my persistent restlessness was not here but in my childhood district of the Lindenow Valley. Perhaps I needed to return there to discover the reason for my inner turbulence.

Fearing another rejection at the forthcoming Christmas, I wrote to my parents, sharing my thoughts and hoping they would reciprocate. It would help us in our long-term planning to know if Dad wanted George to work on his farm eventually or not. George and I thought not, but we'd settle at Neerim South more easily if we knew for sure. Knowing my parents' plans for their farm would free me to make my own life plans. Perhaps this was the root of my torment. I'd probably get 'blasted' for daring to broach the farm's future, but I loved the property; hopefully we would learn where we stood and be free to move on. We'd return to the Bairnsdale district if Dad wanted us to carry on the family farm because, apart from George and our children, I wanted to honour my heritage. If Joy were to have the farm, George and I would concentrate on settling at Neerim South. 'Better to know than to wonder,' we thought.

My parents responded with a letter containing unexpected news. Part of the Lindenow Valley's fertile river flat country, belonging to the highly respected Rathjen family, was on the market. Situated between my parents' farm and the primary school at Woodglen, the land would be auctioned in two lots at St Andrew's Hall, Bairnsdale, in four weeks, on September 18. 'Perhaps you are interested?' my mother wrote. George and I thought the larger of the two blocks, which had the better house, would suit us at the right price—if we knew we could one day work my parents' property and our property together. I explained this in a phone call to Mum and she said she'd talk to Dad and phone back. We'd soon know if we were wanted at Iguana Creek. If we were to buy 'Rathjens' we'd need to sell our house at Sale and the one we had just bought at Neerim South, in a hurry.

Mum phoned back. As for running the two properties together one day, she said, 'Dad says he thinks things will work out the way you want'. That was the extent of his assurance, and we decided to run with it. We would bid for the Rathjens' home block of 94 acres and four-bedroom house. Because we needed time to gather our funds, Dad said he'd help us make the 10 per cent deposit, which could be as high as $10,000 if it went for $100,000. We hoped it would be less, but we'd go that high.

On September 18, less than three months after purchasing the house at Neerim South, George and I sealed our future to a certain extent. The auction was nerve-wracking. The large hall was filled with farming families talking heartily to each other until the auctioneer rang his bell, read his preamble and began calling for bids. Our hearts thumped as George raised his hand and placed our first bid. The larger lot was auctioned first and, at $1250 an acre, went too high for us. However, we bought the smaller lot, of 78 acres. We paid $1100 an acre, $86,976 total, which was more than we planned but an extra bid made all the difference. My father encouraged us, whispering: 'Offer what it is worth to you.' We were farmers again! We would grow vegetables and raise beef cattle.

We were 'going home':

Oh boy it will be good to be back at home. No more depressing moods for me—I know what I'm doing, where my future lies now, and from today on forever, I am a new person.

I have decided this muddled year will give me at least one achievement. I weigh 56kg and will weigh 49kg–50kg by the end of the year. I'll start my new life at Woodglen as a new person, rid forever of the nasty effects of anorexia nervosa which have plagued me since I was 11 years old. I'll be a new me!

No more depressing moods for me now I knew where my future would be! Now, it wouldn't matter if my parents had no room for us to stay because we would be living close by. Perhaps I had to go back to Iguana Creek and Woodglen to free myself of problems that had plagued me since I was in Grade Six.

George and I returned to Neerim South to give notice, attend to the sale of our properties and pack our belongings, for the second time that year. Our Woodglen home would be a small, rundown fibro-cement cottage— the sole residence on our land. Our big debt was set to get bigger because we would build a new house. Thinking of this challenge spurred me to stay on a diet for 30 days' straight, breaking all records. If I adhered to my diet I was sure that every challenge, no matter how difficult, would be achievable.

The cottage was falling apart but we would make do in its four small rooms while organising for a kit house to be built over and around us. Already I was thinking we would live much of our own lives at Woodglen. I wanted to talk about the past to make sense of my present, but Mum always said, 'That happened a long time ago, we don't talk about that.' I wished she understood that answers were essential to clean and heal my emotional wounds, real or imagined.

The good news was that I had stayed on my diet and weighed 52kg when we moved house at the end of December. This wasn't quite my goal of 50kg but was the least I had weighed since my wedding day, almost eight years before. My challenge was to maintain this control. On our first morning at Woodglen I looked at the pile of packed cardboard boxes and didn't know where to start. There was a mess inside and outside our cottage, which had been vacant for months. Instead of lawn there was tall, yellowing grass, and I warned the children to look out for snakes. Eventually I began to clean and unpack in the kitchen. This didn't take long as there were few cupboards. We erected temporary drapes of eiderdowns and blankets over windows in the bedrooms, nailing them to the rotting window frames, and pretended to the children that we were camping.

As for our paddocks, we couldn't see them because they were full of thistles and blackberries. George drove his tractor into the paddock next to our cottage and I could see only the funnel moving like a periscope above the fluffy purple thistle tops.

We had some idea of the physical challenges facing us in developing our land and building a house. But the biggest challenge of all was lurking in my mind.

10. LOSING MY SENSE OF SELF

The New Year began with me 'having it out' with Mum. Living 'just around the corner' was not helping our relationship. For several days she had been niggling me, warning if I returned to work at the *Advertiser* office she would not look after my children. My job was to work on the farm. I decided we were highly incompatible; she didn't listen and passed judgment before words were out of my mouth.

I know I am wallowing in self-pity and I hate being this way—for my own sanity and good I know I need at least a part-time job working in Bairnsdale. I can't do the garden (no garden, and no point trying to make one while the house is being built) or anything else round this little humpy. My depression has led me to 'gorging' myself this past week—understandable too, but today I must start lifting myself out of the doldrums.

Wanting to please my mother, I pushed aside my desire to return to the newspaper office. Determinedly, I showed I remained 'Tim' at heart by becoming a picker in my parents' vegetable paddocks. This work involved bending over long rows of vines which lay on the ground, picking bucketful after bucketful of prickly little green gherkins for $6 an hour. The gherkins went from the bucket into hessian bags, which were tipped into wooden pallets at the old dairy—now a cool room for the vegetables. From there the gherkins were trucked to Lindenow to be graded for the Melbourne markets. After a few days, my back ceased to ache. The work was therapeutic in a way: I liked feeling physically fit and strong, and in the paddock I was unable to binge. My hands, squelching in puddles of sweat in cotton gloves within pink plastic gloves, were busy and my mind was free to roam. Gherkins loved hot weather. In the heat, the yellow flowers turned into market-sized gherkins, about 10cm long, overnight. Miss one, and it swelled into a largely worthless cucumber. As I picked the gherkins I wondered whose plate they might land on, and whether they would be eaten with crackers and cheese, or in a big brand hamburger. I thought of what I would do with my day's earnings too. An hour's picking, I calculated, would earn enough to buy a leg of lamb to roast for our dinner, and four hours' work would buy a light fitting for one of the children's bedrooms.

George was working full time at a local quarry to build up funds to get our farm going. My thoughts turned back to the newspaper office. My hourly earning capacity there was twice that of vegetable picking. I liked paddock work, chatting to fellow pickers who came from all walks of life and, despite the flies and heat, being outdoors. But I loved writing; words remained a best friend and I felt comfortable with them. My parents didn't understand. They believed I wanted to work in the newspaper office because, 'You think you are too good and above others to work in the paddock.' Dad was so angry, he spat in disgust. I wanted to resume my journalism career but this did not fit my parents' image of what they wanted me to be. I'd done little newspaper reporting for six years, and if I didn't return to it now, my chances of a job would diminish.

Feeling guilty at disappointing my parents, I binged to numb my anxiety. I despised myself for wallowing in self-pity, but to build self-worth knew I needed a job in the newspaper office. After several weeks of paddock work, my mind was made up. I'd inquire about a job and if I got one, then I'd worry about finding a babysitter. Deciding my way ahead was one step; finding the courage to act on it was another.

My home situation spurred me on: I couldn't do the garden or anything else around our fibro-cement shack while our new house was being built. Parts of the old house and parts of the new lay about around the house yard and we had to be careful where we stepped. The mess made my mind increasingly volatile and one morning, halfway through January, one of my swinging moods caught George on the hop in our tiny kitchen. We had received word that our house would cost $10,000 more than anticipated. My brain went into overdrive, calculating the number of vegetable-picking hours required to pay for it. The prospect reduced me to tears and I said, 'I wish I could work at the *Advertiser*.' In frustration, George, who was about to leave for the quarry, smashed his drink container of orange cordial, which I'd fixed for his lunch, with his fist. Cordial flew everywhere, over table chairs and floor, creating a sticky mess. I bought that container for him when we were on our farm at Airly. George walked out and I had to wash the floors by hand; I'd only washed them the day before, with a rag and water as someone had broken my mop. The cordial flew over a letter to my cousin Leila that I'd just finished writing at the kitchen table—so I would need to rewrite that, too.

After the flying cordial episode I worked in the paddocks for four hours, picking cucumbers and zucchinis this time. Shane helped; at six, he was already a great little worker. The work was better than nothing, but my mind was rampaging. A few days later I gathered my last little piece of courage and phoned my former boss, Mr Yeates, at the *Advertiser* office. He wasn't available so I had to re-use my little piece of courage to ring again later—this time I connected straight away. Unprepared words tumbled out. They must have worked, as Mr Yeates invited me to call in the next day to discuss a position.

I could start part-time work the following week, and a full-time position was promised when another journalist moved on. This was great news. It was short notice, but I accepted the offer. George would be home with the children for the first day. He and I were friends again—inevitable of course, because we loved each other so much. We'd faced many pressures since arriving at Woodglen; the amount of work to be done, and the amount of money to be found, was at times overwhelming.

Thankfully, by now Mum was happy about me working in town and offered to mind the children whenever she could, so this made me happy, too. Rohan and Shane were excited about starting classes at my old school, Woodglen Primary, a kilometre from our farm; Ben would attend preschool at Lindenow and Amanda would be at home for another year.

My days became a mix of taxiing children, working in the newspaper office, picking vegetables and housework. Working six-and-a-half hours a day in the paddock and three-and-a-half at the office left little time for the children. We were cramped in our four small rooms, with the framework of our new house taking shape around us. Early one morning I awoke at the crack of dawn feeling someone was being amorous, and it wasn't George: a cow had put her head through the open window behind my bed and was licking me with her raspy tongue! The children thought our open house was wonderful.

Gradually I worked more in the newspaper office and less in the paddock. Besides his quarry work, George was busy in the evenings and on weekends, slashing and clearing our paddocks of blackberries and thistles, and helping our brother-in-law Ray who was building our house. We were both busy working and didn't notice immediately that three-year-old Ben was becoming a bundle of bones, was hallucinating and seemed to have a high temperature. Two days later, during my lunchbreak, I took him to the doctor and described his vomiting, lack of appetite, fever, drowsiness and lethargy. The doctor decided Ben should see a paediatric neurologist in Melbourne. He said there might be 'something going on' in Ben's head; hopefully nothing serious, but until we knew we would worry.

George's mum took Ben home after we'd been to the doctor. He cried, as he wanted to 'go home with Mummy', but as the men had the roof off our cottage that day and I was working, it was best for him to go with his Grandma Coster to Sarsfield. She would love him and look after him, I was sure, but my heart went out to my little boy.

We saw the neurologist in March, and tests confirmed Ben was suffering migraine attacks. There was no history of migraines on either side of our family, and we hadn't known they could affect someone so young. Ben would be on medication until he was nine years old.

On a free day from the office I drove around to my parents' farm to pick gherkins, but instead received a lecture from Mum. 'You are a disappointment and a worry,' she said. She compared me with local farmers' wives and I didn't rate well. They were happy with their lot; they were content to stay at home and didn't want to chase a career in the town. Leaving the gherkins on their vines, I went home, ate all day and became terribly grumpy.

Maybe the strain of trying to be mother, vegetable picker, journalist and wife in the mess of a half-built house is getting to me,' I thought.

Beyond all that hid my tormentor, my negative voice, gnawing in my soul. No matter how busy I tried to be, it would not let up. I could not escape it. The possibility that I was sick, instead of weak, did not occur.

I was being gnawed at, within and without. The rat-infested old part of our humpy-house turned my stomach. Discovery the previous night: rats were munching apples out of a box in our bedroom – the only place where there was a spot to store them. Discovery that very morning: rats had chewed into my muesli, in the one and only kitchen cupboard that had a door that actually shut. As I wrote at the kitchen table, a rat scuttled across the ceiling above my head, and there were great gaps in the ceiling for easy access to the floor. I wished the renovations were finished. This place was a muck hole.

Unable to control the rats, I focused on my eating:

Began a new lease of life today and shall put yesterday's woes behind me. I am today starting a strict eating program—3 meals a day and only fresh fruit or vegies in between, or milk/health drinks. Sugared drinks in rare moderation—and with that under control, I'm confident all else will be controllable and I will be a much more relaxed and capable person (journalist/mother/farmer/and sometimes wife).

Six months after arriving at Woodglen, our new home was taking shape and we had almost completely vacated our old house. Rohan, Shane and Amanda were sleeping in the new lounge room until their bedrooms were finished, and Ben was sleeping where our backdoor would go for a little longer.

George and I were in our new bedroom and we were using our new kitchen. Unfortunately, the rats were using it, too. One night George was late home from work and I was cooking spaghetti for tea. I switched on the ceiling fan above the stove while the pasta was cooking and there was no whirring sound. I looked up and saw something white and furry. The fat belly of a rat was stuck in the fan. I called the four children and we stood, spellbound, watching the now squealing rat. If the fan cover fell under the rat's weight, we would have extra meat in our pot of bubbling spaghetti. Thankfully, the rat scampered out of the way. On digesting our latest rat tale over dinner, George put bait in the ceiling of the new part of our house; trouble was, the ceiling opened into the old end of the house and the rat procession was endless.

We continued to provide open house to district rodents throughout winter. One morning a dying rat was writhing under our kitchen table. Luckily George was up first. He finished it off outside and threw it as far as he could into the paddock. I wished I could dispose of my eating problems as easily. My attempt to eat three 'normal' meals a day had failed many times over. Each failure concluded with me making a P-I-G of myself. The pressure was great and I struggled to gain a balanced perspective. I couldn't be happy with the world until happy within myself. Calorie counting seemed the only the answer to achieving peace; it never lasted long, but perhaps this was because I was weak.

I added to my woes at work, reporting an important Bairnsdale Town Council resolution completely in reverse and, to compound the error, it was the lead story on the front page. I concluded that my mind was overloaded. I felt sorry for my children, as I seemed inadequate not only at the newspaper, but in motherhood as well.

As predicted, despite living closer, I saw little of Mum and Joy, who were in constant touch with each other. Joy called in to see me for a few minutes one afternoon on her way home from a visit. I felt on the outer, thinking '*I might as well live 200km away instead of just a couple*'. Joy was expecting her fourth baby in September—she would have a girl and then, like me, would have three sons and a daughter in the same order.

George and I were not getting along well. We needed to go out and have some fun. But, for a while at least, work was necessary to pay for our house, the new irrigation system, shedding and fencing. Many marriages were breaking up, but I didn't want ours to end. George was my best friend, my only ever lover, my rock. He had a quick temper, took a long time to forget a grudge and was rather serious, but he was my Number One.

I felt dreadful that he and the children suffered while I tried to deal with my inner torment. Food was the only way I knew of coping and controlling my reactions to adversities. When tired, I binged, and lost confidence and the ability to cope with my busy schedule.

George came home from the quarry at lunch time one day to find me a miserable heap of woe, hunched over my typewriter at the kitchen table. Shortly I would depart for the newspaper office to work a 2pm to 10pm shift. The children would be asleep when I arrived home. George comforted me and I felt better. I had growled at the children that morning and felt bad about that. They were laughing, banging their wooden building blocks, but the repetitious sound echoed loudly in my head. When I growled, the children stuck together like glue. George was doing his best to help. I surely could not manage without his support and love.

I was working in the office 40 hours a week by September and hoped my extra income would enable George to stop work at the quarry, as he was not happy there. If one of us needed to work off the farm it was better to be me, as I earned more and generally enjoyed it.

Almost a year after moving to Woodglen, I unpacked our last box from Neerim South. Our house was complete and the children moved into their bedrooms. They deserved their bright new rooms after sleeping here, there and everywhere. Building our home while living in it with four children under seven had been hard slog, but was easy compared with the struggle raging within me. Building a house was finite; it had a start and a finish; my tormentor—a combination of eating disorder, depression and anxiety—was grey and black, an untouchable voracious mass in my mind:

I will get hold of myself one day. I hope I can do it without requiring special help. I figure it's probably me and my instability, insecurity, that's caused us to have so many shifts and probably my unhealthy, erratic, gluttonous diet that causes most of our arguments.

When I think of all the troubles in the world, mine are very small and I must overcome them before they destroy my life.

The pressure of working 18-hour days to make the farm viable weighed heavily. I didn't need a husband for financial security, but I did need my husband for love and friendship, and lately George had no energy to give me either. Days passed without him saying 'good morning', let alone kissing me.

Increasingly I feared I was going around the bend and thought I'd do our family and me a favour by seeing a psychologist. By evening most days my head felt as delicate as a thin eggshell. Without any buffer I screamed at the slightest provocation or noise. The sound of a child tapping a teaspoon on the table, while waiting for dinner to be served, resounded loudly in my brain and sent me running, holding my head, to the other end of the house. My tormentor thrived on such chaos. I called it a 'tormentor', because at times I felt I could almost put my hand into my head and pull this dark, horrible mass out. My monster was becoming almost real, almost tangible.

I began to think my instability and insecurity had caused our shifts and arguments, and my tormentor wanted to destroy my marriage and my life. An example was the children's Sunday School Anniversary. Normally on a Sunday morning I took the children to Sunday School at the Uniting Church in Lindenow. However, the final Sunday School session for the year was special, taking the form of an afternoon concert so families could attend. George and I had both worked hard that morning. I'd pushed our lawn mower over our dusty and rocky, acre-sized front yard that I was trying to turn into lawn and followed up by mowing the lawns at my parents' property. I also had sprinklers going on my fledgling flowerbeds.

George had been on the tractor, raking our ryegrass and inbetween preparing the ground for our next gherkin crop. He came home at 12.20, expecting lunch on the table, intending to gobble it down and do more raking before the concert at 2pm. Lunch was not ready, and I was worn out from almost four hours continuous mowing. I prepared his lunch quickly, and he threw it to the ceiling where it splattered and fell to the floor. George stormed out and returned at 1.45pm, to go with us to the concert. Unfortunately he said: 'I am going to the concert for the kids' sake, not because of you.' Tempers re-ignited. George stormed off again and the children and I went alone. The children were well behaved and pleased with their book prizes. When we returned home, I did housework before going to the newspaper office from 6pm to 10pm, typing and sub-editing the weekend sport results, the usual routine on a Sunday night.

Home by 11pm, I slept on the family room couch and found that it was comfortable. That was the first time I was too upset to sleep with George—I wanted him to apologise for his behaviour and he would not do so. The next day I forgave him anyway and bought him some much-needed new clothes during my lunch break. Thinking our arguments perhaps resulted from work pressure, I said we must pay someone to help in our house at least two days a week, to make life easier for us and our children.

The end of the 1970s was looming, and George and I reflected that we had achieved a lot in this decade. In the past year alone we had settled at Woodglen and built our house. We wanted to start 1980 with George at home on the farm fulltime but he returned to the quarry in mid-January, much to his disgust. We needed the quarry pay packet, at least until the farm started to generate income. This seemed a long way off when flooding rains fell throughout the night and day, drowning our contract green bean crop.

George was a picture of gloom and I was, too. The beans were to have been our major farm income for the year. I was in a mess trying to sort out my inner self, without farming's uncontrollable factors and George's unhappiness at the quarry. He was becoming depressed, coming home grumpy, saying degrading things about himself and his work. 'If you dislike your job so much, leave it and farm fulltime,' I said, not knowing if George and I, or only my own inner troubles, caused the tension between us:

I do not think I am going to succeed in my quest for 'normality' on my own.
I'm going to need some help. This afternoon, while out hoeing weeds in the gherkin patch, I decided I should/will go talk to a Dr, and seek his advice on whether my problems are just silly make-believe fantasies which can be brought under control by myself, by using some professional help to get myself under control. I feel I haven't been 'normal' since I was 11 years old, and worry I will spend the rest of my life riding waves of depression, at the expense of happiness to myself and our family. I've got to the stage where I don't know what the answer is, except I do know George and the children are important to me. Do I need a good long holiday with George, should we be working together, should I be working at all, should I be near my parents? I don't know. I do know I am mentally in a mess.

I didn't know any answers and feared that if I described my battle a doctor would declare, 'You are unfit to be a mother.'

This fear compelled me to try alone once more: if I could follow a healthy eating plan, surely my sanity would return.

Next day:

I will make it on my own, with encouragement and understanding from George. By following a healthy eating plan, I'm confident my sanity will return and my weight will drop.

As a diversion I booked at the hair salon for Joy to perm my fine, straight hair. I returned home to a mixed reaction from the children over my curls; at first they doubted I was really their mum, but were convinced when I began to growl. The pampering lift was momentary. The following Saturday I fell further into my deep, dark pit and feared afresh I was going crazy. Engulfed by blackness, I broke out in a hot sweat and began wailing while making lamingtons before lunch. My children were outside, but Shane came running. I raced to the bathroom and splashed cold, running water over my face to regain composure. I detested myself for losing control in front of my children.

Any affirmation that I had made the right decision in returning to the Lindenow Valley may have eased my anxiety right then. Instead, it intensified when I learnt that George and I were not invited to join other local young married couples at a dinner dance in town. I mentioned this to Mum after mowing her lawns yet again and she, who already knew, put the problem squarely at my feet and said: 'You should make an effort to visit the other 'girls'.'

'Well,' I said, 'and what do these girls do? They don't work a 40-hour office week like I do, or pick gherkins, or mow huge lawns. They have time to sit and chat and gossip over cups of tea while their children are at school.'

Mum had the final word: 'If you are so busy, stop work.'

I couldn't win. George and I needed my income to help develop our property, but mostly I worked to hold onto my sanity. I wasn't like 'the other girls'. My inner chaos encouraged social isolation. Obviously it was making me appear unfriendly to the outside world.

Because Mum refused to talk about my childhood, I knew she would scoff if I mentioned my fear of losing my mind.

I wanted to know why she had called me Tim, when I was good, and Toby, when I was not so good, when I was a little girl. Several years earlier, an older cousin had confided my birth was premature and difficult, resulting in my mother being unable to have more children. I asked Mum if this was true but she was furious I had been told and would not answer. I wondered if she resented me for spoiling her chance of having a son, or for being a daughter instead of a son.

Unable to get answers, I concluded I was a big disappointment—and was continuing to be one. My passion for writing was stronger than that for farming, and I didn't fit the all-important mould of a stay-at-home farmer's wife. To feel better, I counted my many blessings:

I know I have a lot to be grateful for: I have four lovely children, a good husband, we all have good health; and knowing that makes me just so mad I'm the way I am.

I really feel I've hit the bottom of the deepest pit and from now on, I will improve. Perhaps I am capable of helping myself. I really must have one more do-or-else-see-a-Dr try—starting tomorrow.

Two nights later I went completely 'crackers' and George broke down too. He felt powerless to help me. Afterwards we comforted each other and midnight passed before we collapsed into sleep. Next day I broke down again at lunchtime. I said to George, 'I've had ups and downs since I was 11 and I have always got up. But now I am having grave difficulty getting up, and this time I need to get up to stay.'

That night my tormentor took over my mind. I ran from the bedroom to the kitchen, pulled a knife from the drawer, began slashing my nightie and was threatening to slash my throat. I wanted to cut out this thing that would not leave me alone. George chased me, seized the knife, and quickly set about taking and hiding the other sharp knives in the kitchen; some of the children woke with our screaming and shouting, and peeped out their bedroom doors, only to run and hide under their bedcovers.

I'd hit rock bottom. I had to seek help. I wanted to see my children grow up. For their sake I wanted to recover. I had to get this monster out of my head. The next morning, I called the medical centre in Bairnsdale and asked to see a doctor urgently.

11. SEEKING HELP

I didn't know where to start sharing my problems of the past 18 years with the middle-aged male GP sitting opposite me, but he was patient. He didn't say I was silly and wasting his time; he listened. He was understanding and said I should have asked for help years ago. He explained how a brain worked, sending messages through the nervous system. He said my brain had a gap or deficiency, which affected large brain messages—to do with mood, memory, self-esteem and so on. Possibly, a lack of oxygen to my brain had occurred in the few hours before I was born, but he assured me, 'The type of person this happens to is usually excellent in every other respect.'

This was reassuring! He wrote a prescription for pills, called Tryptanol, to compensate for my deficiency, and said: 'You will be a new person.' He asked to see George, saying: 'He will have conditioned himself to bearing up with the way you are.' I was to return in a fortnight.

I'll do whatever the Dr says. To be carefree and fun loving will be truly wonderful.

My illness had a big head start, but my battle to beat it had stepped up a cog now that I had sought help. I had a restless first night, waking up off and on. Those tablets seemed to set something going in my head. I felt strange. The next afternoon I had one of my thumping 'car accident' headaches. Also, I had a dry mouth and throat as predicted by the doctor. I didn't know how long I would be on the pills, but could see that adjusting to a normal life would take a while. At least I had made a start, and was on my way to saying 'Goodbye' to those horrible depressions.

Two weeks later I saw the doctor again. I was sleeping easily but having many dreams and feeling nauseated. My doctor was pleased, saying this confirmed his diagnosis. 'You have a chemical deficiency in your brain,' he said.

The pills, the GP said, were making my body produce more of the substance required to overcome my chemical deficiency. 'Because you have suffered for many years you are a chronic case and will require the pills for six months or longer to return to normal,' he said. 'This happens only to the best people,' he added, smiling at me, and said to George, 'You must be a special man to have put up with living with a depressed person like June for this long. People as depressed as her are not easy to live with.' The doctor assured George: 'In another six months you will have your fun-loving June back'. Right now, while suffering side effects, I found the new me hard to imagine, but looked forward to it. The doctor said I might suffer side effects for some weeks and gave me a month off work.

The month went by but my recovery did not leave first base. The doctor changed my tablets, stating I was to take one of the original prescription and two of another, each day and return in a fortnight. He said to extend my leave to three months off work and not make any major decisions until I was 'right, which might be a long way off'.

Staying home was good in that I had more time with my children but not good in that I was less able to divert my tormentor. Five days after stopping work, I feared I was 'cracking up'; I was bingeing and, although living in my childhood district, felt isolated, like I didn't belong.

Completely out of control today, and I hope never again will I sink to such low ebb. When I get so low I would end it all if not for George and the children.

I have found I go to pieces when left alone. I eat, eat, eat and eat. It's a wonder I haven't burst. When I get like that I do wonder if it's pills I need, or psychiatric help, or both.

I need George more than ever, and don't like being without him, even for an hour, but of course he has to work.

Most of my emotional energy was absorbed in day-to-day inner struggles. I'd washed the floors one morning, and was almost finished when a kindly church member called in to ask after me. 'Okay,' I said. I didn't know how to start explaining to someone that I felt sick in my head. The weather was a safe subject.

My parents were unable to understand my need to seek help for my mind. They were more into 'just getting on with life' and letting bygones be bygones. Mum seemed to have a knack of enforcing the feeling that I was weak for not coping. 'I'm feeling tired,' I said one day, and she responded, 'Your father is the one who is tired, working long days on the farm, but he never complains.' She might as well have said, 'You have nothing to complain about and should be helping your father.' So I no longer shared that I felt tired.

Encouraged by our doctor, who said my illness had plagued me not 18 years but all my 29 years, George and I organised a two-week holiday as a diversion. We flew to Western Australia to visit my childhood Sunday School teachers, Mr and Mrs James Findlay, who with their three sons had departed the Lindenow Valley in the early 1960s. The family had developed farming country at Narrikup, near Albany, in the southwest corner of Australia. On their departure from Iguana Creek, Mr Findlay, who was born in 1900, and I became firm penfriends. More than 17 years later we continued to share a beautiful friendship, our 50-year age difference of no consequence. While I'd relate the birth of a child, he would describe his latest heart attack; I did not tell him about my fear of madness but my troubled mind must have been evident.

At 54kg, I was determined this holiday would mark the start to the new, carefree me. However, despite my medication, my mind remained in its old pattern when I returned home and my doctor decided a return to work might help. I was to stay on my pills and see him in three weeks. To alleviate pressure at home, we employed a family friend, Lorna, to mind our children three or four days a week. Lorna was like an angel. She looked after the children, had tea ready to cook when I arrived home and helped with the housework.

Back in the busy newspaper office and doubting the effectiveness of my medication after a restless night's sleep, I asked my pharmacist: 'What is Tryptanol supposed to do?' 'Calm one down and pep one up,' he said.

Well, they don't do that with me at all. I find it very hard to wake up of a morn ...

I don't think those pills are helping me any, nor of course is the mounting pile of bills. I don't feel like working; yet we need the money, and I'm not sure the best thing to do is stay home. In fact I'm not sure of anything. I don't know what role I should be playing—or what is best for me.

I still go crazy if there is any repetitive sound, and I almost feel I'm like I was before I first went to see the Dr.

My doctor encouraged me to keep working: 'Because,' he said, 'you're not a cat, you're a cougar, and your intelligent mind is too active to stay at home all day. Don't feel guilty about working and spend your free time at home with George and the children—forget that 'dirty pile of clothes in the corner' or whatever.' My doctor said to cease the medication but to remember his advice on taking time out. 'Moreover,' he said, 'George is not to consider himself a failure but a success.'

George began our second spring on the farm by giving notice at the quarry, to farm full-time. I earned enough for our family to live on, and George would meet the farm costs and payments. This was good news, but my black clouds were returning. Something, I was convinced, was stopping me from being 'normal'. George couldn't understand me and neither could I.

Depression lurked like a black octopus in my brain, its tendrils sabotaging my emotions. Again, I felt I could almost touch it; its presence was so real. I felt sure that if I could expose it to the light, it would die and I would be free. But I did not know how to achieve this.

I was going down, down, down. I feared returning to the doctor because, having sought help once and failed, I was worried he would say there was no cure. My 30th birthday was looming and George was tired of me moping about—he didn't seem a degree brighter either, but maybe I had made him that way.

I tried to grab hold:

Well I've actually spent a day as a normal person might: muesli for breakfast; salad lunch; orange, apple and 2 radishes for afternoon snack, roast dinner and ice-cream for dessert.

If I had faith in myself to continue along that line, it would be great, but

No, I believe I should go talk to the Dr once more and try and explain that all the problems re our farm of the past 12 months are only the 'icing on the cake' so to speak—the root of the problem lying way back when I was 11 years old. I don't think I've been a free person ever since that time. Food being my greatest bugbear of all.

I was tired of being 'obsessed', tired of my mind being knotted like a tangled ball of yarn, my nerves as brittle as burnt eggshell. I was trapped and ready to snap.

The doctor said he had prescribed pills, to see how things went, but 'Obviously, they have been treating only the effects of your problem, not the problem itself'. He referred me to a clinical psychologist at Hobson Park Hospital, a mental health institution, 100km away at Traralgon. The appointment was in four weeks.

Work at the *Advertiser* was a struggle but I persevered, hoping to feel differently after the psychologist had untangled my mind. Nothing I did had meaning and George said I was as cold as ice. I was too tense to make love, even to kiss. After going the wrong way for so long, I hoped I could be helped and we could make a new start and have a happy family life.

My inner battle left little energy for communicating in my outer world. Joy phoned and 'socked it to me', accusing me of being unthoughtful by not staying in touch. She began interrogating me as to why and I thought what the heck, and said: 'I'm seeing a psychologist next week.' Joy had the answer to my problem. 'It's simple,' she said. 'Pull up your socks and think about other people instead of yourself. You are going down the wrong road, putting your needs before others.' I am sure she meant well but her words amplified 1000 times in my mind and converted to the self-accusation that 'I am weak, weak, weak'. I felt speared by guilt. George said I should have clamped the phone down on my sister.

On the day of my appointment with the psychologist, I travelled to Traralgon alone, taking time off during a busy day in the newspaper office. The psychologist indicated I was a complex case but was keen to help unravel my muddled mind. His first step was to eliminate the chance that my sporadic eating was caused by 'functional hypoglycaemia'. He arranged for a glucose tolerance test at the East Gippsland Hospital, Bairnsdale. This would require a urine sample and, after consuming a glucose-rich drink, blood tests every hour for five hours. 'There is only a 50 per cent or less chance this is the cause of your woes,' the psychologist said, 'but I want to eliminate it before going into other things.' He intended to put me on high doses of vitamins after the tests.

The day after the tests was a Saturday, and I didn't think I could go much lower without leaving this world and entering the next. I didn't know what triggered my unhappiness. I supposed, as usual, a number of things. George had been slashing our crop of Brussels sprouts that morning, and had driven the tractor over an irrigation terminal, breaking it, and repairs would be expensive. Then he had brought a baby hare, which he had found in the paddock, home for the children; he put the hare in the rabbit hutch and within half an hour one of the boys took it out and lost it. This upset me more than the broken terminal. I was angry and upset at the boys, more so because they wouldn't say who did it.

George took the four children to the football while I stayed home to recover and do some jobs. I baked two batches of cornflake and yo-yo cookies, which George liked, and two teacakes. I mowed the front lawns and was ironing clothes when the family arrived home about 5.30pm. The children had enjoyed their day out and were full of chatter. I was a mess and full of tears; I'd eaten all day and had my period too.

On the following Monday, three days after my blood tests, I was told the results were abnormal, and I was to see the psychologist the next day, again at Traralgon. I felt a little ray of hope; maybe this time I was on the right track to the new me. Sometimes my head was so weary I thought no one could possibly fix it up.

The psychologist illustrated, on my blood test graph, how the sugar substance that I had swallowed had raced through my blood stream. 'Sugar gives you a 'high' and then leaves you feeling deflated and depressed, like air escaping from a balloon,' he said. My pancreas didn't seem to be working properly either, and he recommended a hypoglycaemia diet 'to see how you feel'. Although sceptical, I agreed to try it. The diet was high in protein, low in sugar, and I was to take three lots of vitamin pills at 10 times the normal dose. My psychologist said he would see me again in six weeks, at Bairnsdale.

I learnt more about hypoglycaemia in a book from the health food store next to the newspaper office. I read that it was the opposite of diabetes—

not enough sugar in my blood—and my blood test results indicated a severe case of the disease. Knowing there was a medical reason for my confused state gave me hope of becoming normal. I had to hang on to this hope.

I tried to believe the hypoglycaemia diet was helping but was fooling my psychologist and myself. I was trying to fix something within me and yet my reality was I had a job to do and four children and a husband to go home to each day. My confidence was zero. When reporting on local government council meetings at Bairnsdale, Bruthen and Omeo, I felt that the councillors looked at me strangely when, during morning and afternoon tea breaks, I asked for 'hot water please', rather than tea or coffee, which were banned on my diet. I wanted to hide rather than draw attention to myself.

Summer arrived and the heat affected me, especially returning home from the newspaper office in my un-air-conditioned car and with low tolerance levels. The result one evening was a big 'barny' with George, in front of our children. George had had a hot and bothered day too. I walked in and without thinking, said 'The house is a mess,' and wham! Sparks flew. At times like this being a working mother didn't seem worth the tension, the arguments, and the extra strain. But we were living on my wage.

A month after starting the hypoglycaemia diet:

Had a 'bad' day, by that I mean I yawned incessantly all day—the action alone wears me out—let alone the cause, whatever it may be. I got very little work accomplished because of my drowsy state. I am wondering if this diet and all these 12 tablets a day are doing me any good at all.

Rather than wait for my next appointment, I called my psychologist and was told to cut out the Pyridoxine tablets, and halve the Vitamin B tablets, leaving the ascorbic acid the same. A week later, I remained dopey, dull, unenergetic and prone to headaches. Suspecting thyroid trouble, the psychologist arranged more blood tests. These led to a diagnosis of migraine headaches, of which I was not convinced, and that there was nothing wrong with my thyroid, of which I was convinced.

By November, the psychologist assessed that I was no longer depressed, but confused. 'What makes you confused?' he asked. I didn't know. I wanted to be happy at home, looking after our family and writing, with George the leader in our family. I didn't like being the main breadwinner.

The psychologist suggested I stay on the diet for another month and, two weeks later, he met with George and me to resolve my confusion. 'Set aside 20 minutes each night to talk to each other about yourselves, and go out one night a week without your children,' the psychologist said. But we worked long days and our blues continued. Too tired to give each other sympathy or understanding, we saw each other only at mealtimes, with four lovely chatterboxes in between. Frustrated, I went off the hypoglycaemic diet, and tried to eat like a normal person. I failed of course, within two days, and returned to the diet, but it did not seem the answer. I remained restless for something—more like a craving—an insatiable craving to be relaxed, to take things easy, to read awhile, to have fun with George and the children.

First, however, I had to fill my void within, and I was going crazy trying to do so. George's mum, who kindly accompanied me on one of my trips to see the psychologist at Traralgon, visited the farm one Saturday afternoon soon after. She sat on the couch in the lounge while I darted about making a cuppa, folding the washing, doing the ironing and picking up after the children. She said, 'The trouble with you, June, is you don't know how to relax.'

George came in for an afternoon tea with his mum and said he missed me when I was at work and wanted me to stay home, but work was helping me stay sane.

By early 1981 I had been on the hypoglycaemia diet for six months. My psychologist said to remain on it and take the vitamin pills to reduce stress. Our child-minder, Lorna, was continuing to be a wonderful helper. With Ben joining Shane and Rohan at primary school, Lorna cared for four-year-old Amanda at least one day a week at our house and did a stack of housework. She also looked after the boys when they arrived home from school. The children loved her, and many fireworks were avoided between George and me by coming home to find the children happy, the floors clean, the washing folded and a meal ready to eat.

Having home help alleviated pressure, but I missed my children due to long work hours. A night meeting meant I was away from home from

8.30am until 11pm. Sometimes Amanda was asleep when I departed for work, and asleep when I returned home. I loved my 'Missy' or 'Apples', as I called her, and tried to explain that I worked to help pay our bills. Amanda seemed to understand and, knowing she would be at school next year, I decided to keep working. Amanda was happy—a little sunbeam. If she was not with Lorna at home, she was at preschool in the mornings, and with her Grandma Alexander in the afternoons, often attending Glenaladale branch meetings of the Country Women's Association, or the Lindenow Bowls Club, where my mother played lawn bowls. George also enjoyed looking after Amanda if he was not busy with tractor work.

One night, Amanda made me laugh. She said: 'I don't want you to go to work tomorrow.' I said: 'I'd better talk to Dad about stopping,' and she replied, 'Yes, tell Dad to stop paying bills.' I hadn't mentioned bills to her for days. She was a bright button, a deep-thinking one too. I liked to dream about staying home. As it was, the children made mistakes and called me 'Dad' and George 'Mum'.

I wished for time to do craftwork and play sport, to break up my set routine of work in the office and at home. But even if I had time, I would feel guilty using it in that way. Saturday was my 'free' day when I baked our week's supply of food. My only break was taking the children to Sunday School at Lindenow, where I enjoyed teaching a small class.

The hypoglycaemic diet wasn't helping and I was 6kg 'overweight'. Fed up, I sent a four-page letter to my psychologist and hoped he could find a solution. I hadn't been falling into the dark, deep pits of despair I'd experienced the previous year, but was heading that way. To be able to eat without food dominating my thoughts was all I wanted.

Mum telephoned to say Joy was having a difficult time with Ray, who had developed rheumatoid arthritis. I thought Ray might also be having a difficult period with Joy, and suggested my sister spent too much time at the family farm, but Mum did not agree. 'It's her home,' she said. I thought a wife's first duty was to her husband's home. Not that George and I were picture perfect. We continued to have colourful times. That morning, Ginger Cat jumped on the kitchen bench, looking for a drink. George swung him in the air by the tail. I was drinking a cup of warm water, and hurled the contents over George. At least he let the cat go. I was cross at him for being cruel and he was cross at me for being foolish.

Our children looked at us. The previous night I had smashed one of my vitamin jars so hard on the table the lid came off and white pills rolled all over the floor. Oh dear, oh dear. Time to slow down.

S-L-O-W D-O-W-N, June.

Another week-end coming to a close. What I miss most in my life right now is walking. Walking through the paddocks, through the bush, along the river bank. That is what I miss the most. And I feel I need. Starting next week I believe I shall re-organise my schedule so that I have at least one walk a [day] (not a day—no hope of that!). I mean one walk a week.

George and I argued occasionally but we were steadfastly united in loving and caring for our children. In July, we removed our sons from the one-teacher Woodglen School. Eight-year-old Shane had been crying in bed every night because his teacher was making fun of his flappy ears. Rohan, age seven, had come home in tears one day too, because the teacher had sat in front of him with a needle and thread, threatening to sew his mouth up, annoyed because he was talking and was slow with his reading. I was fed up with that one-teacher school. I didn't want my children going through traumas like those I experienced in Grade Six. I enrolled our sons at the larger Lindenow Primary School. This increased our isolation from our neighbours because, together with the Glenaladale Hall, the small Woodglen school was the hub of the community.

Perhaps we lived too close to the birthplace of my illness. The upsets over our children's schooling left me feeling black. I gorged on sugary foods, which made me dopey and unable to think. I had to go to bed early, leaving my children to look after themselves. One evening my sleep was so deep I did not want to waken the next morning. When I did, I wanted to leave Woodglen. Without George's support, I didn't know what I would do.

My psychologist, who had prescribed the Dr Atkins Diet as an alternative to the hypoglycaemic diet during the past few months, decided this was not the answer either. (If a psychologist suggested today that I follow such a diet, I would terminate consultations immediately—because the food regimentation would feed my illness, not me.)

'Your metabolism is most strange,' he said, 'but I'll work on sorting it out.' I was to record my weight every 48 hours, and see him in four weeks. Also, I was to eat at least three oranges a day, no salt, and take a stronger Vitamin B tablet. I had too much sodium in my body—oranges contained potassium and my psychologist said they 'antagonised' the sodium. I hoped my problem would be overcome before George and I went to Missouri, a trip we were planning next year.

Our farm was more productive, and planning this trip provided incentive for me to keep working. My editorial skills were increasing and sometimes I had the responsibility of editor—writing and laying out most of the paper. The front page and page three were my regular main works. Writing for the newspaper brought me in contact with many people and involved me with local issues. This enabled me to feel at least a little normal. I enjoyed working with other members of staff too—putting the paper out was a team effort.

An unexpected boost to my self-esteem came in a phone call from Sydney from June Barton, who hosted the ABC Radio program *Morning Extra*, about a feature article I had written on cell therapy treatment for children with Down's syndrome. After publishing the article in the *Advertiser*, I re-wrote it and sold it to *The Age* newspaper in Melbourne. Now June was following the article up for her program.

Her 15-minute call left me feeling elated and helped me realise I enjoyed researching articles, particularly about social and health issues. I thrived on personal-interest stories and issues that concerned people. But this acknowledgement of how much my writing meant to my wellbeing added to my confusion. I vacillated between wanting to stay home, and help George, and pursuing my writing career. 'I'll try to manage both,' I decided, and added a new goal—that of improving my qualifications by enrolling for external studies in journalism at the Royal Melbourne Institute of Technology. I wondered why I hadn't done this study earlier but I'd been busy helping George establish our farm and caring for the children. With Amanda about to start school, I would have time to concentrate on improving my career.

At home, though, eruptions continued. A new summer tennis season had started, and one Saturday morning George announced he would be playing at Paynesville, 40km away. With only one court he wouldn't be home until dark. Before he left home we had a great argument. 'You have the stereo up too high,' he said. I said: 'No, I don't.' He turned it down and I started to get mad, so he turned it up full volume. Enraged, I threw what I had in my hand—cheese and tomato to make sandwiches for him to eat on his way—on the floor. He re-acted by swiping two cupfuls of milk from the bench over the floor. Blackness swooped in and I threw the electric frying pan, breaking its handle. George stomped out and went to tennis. I bawled my eyes out, cleaned up the mess and ate myself sick.

My psychologist decided I ate because I was deprived and felt unloved, and emphasised that George and I must spend more time together, like going to a show, or out to dinner. He encouraged me to both pursue my journalism career and plan our trip to the USA. 'Stay on the hypoglycaemia diet and ask someone for a hug every time you feel tempted to eat out of normal eating times,' he said. He thought the basic problem lay in my relationship with George but I didn't agree.

We continued with our plans to visit the USA for three months, staying for most of the time in Missouri with the Edwards family who had hosted me as an exchange student 14 years before. Mr Yeates was allowing me three months off work, and George was considering the break his long service leave entitlement after more than 15 years of farming. I saw my psychologist one more time before our departure. He now believed my over-eating was due to stress and said, 'You will see things more clearly after three months away.'

On my 31st birthday, I tried to take stock:

December 27: My birthday. 31. Sounds 'old', but then I guess it will seem young as the years continue to come. I hope this 31st year of mine will be a very fulfilling one personally—finding the right pattern for my life. What I'm doing now is not right I don't think. We may alter a few things. I may stop work. We may shift house. Go around Australia. Why not.

I had returned home to the valley with my husband and children, but times had changed. The popular old-time dances that George and I had attended in the Glenaladale Hall when we started dating had ceased. The Young Farmers' Club had folded. Fundraiser barbecues were held at the hall for the cricket club, tennis club and school, with the men standing in a huddle around a keg of beer while the women prepared the food.

I didn't approve of alcohol at fundraisers where children were running about, so we didn't attend.

George and I had changed, too. We had moved house more times than we cared to count and, like many of our generation, our lives revolved around working and caring for our children. Overriding all this, my illness would not allow me to rest. It denied me peace in my mind, my home, my family and the community in which I lived.

My father said something about 'cutting the cloth to fit the pattern' when we bought the Woodglen farm. But what cloth and whose pattern? I had yet to find those answers. For now, my illness was calling the shots. I wanted to feel settled; it wanted to isolate and destroy.

12. CHILDHOOD SECRET REVEALED

My return to the Lindenow Valley was turning into a minefield from my past. George and I had brought our rundown farm back to top production and built a lovely four-bedroom home with verandah on all sides, but I felt haunted; I could not relax. I felt driven to move away from my parents and sister. Joy's dependency on Mum and Dad appeared to leave no room for me, and this would irk less if I were not there to see her car passing by my home several times a week on her way to the family farm. I was glad I had my newspaper work to keep me occupied and hoped it would eventually take me many miles from the valley.

As if in answer to my prayers, the RMIT sent a letter offering a place as an external student in its Diploma of Journalism course. Suddenly I had a pathway to follow in the small part of my life unaffected by illness. Acceptance into the course was an affirmation that George, our children and journalism were genuine passions that belonged to the real me.

In the 12 years since starting journalism as a career I'd felt confused in my roles as George's wife and farming partner and mother of four children. We'd have our trip to the United States and then go elsewhere: where, I didn't know, but we wanted to give our children a good education. George was emphatic about this because he regretting leaving school at 16. He'd done so because his dad needed his help and he had wanted to be a dairy farmer. Dairying in the 1960s was a promising lifetime career.

George's ties to his family's land were broken but mine remained. Farming and the land were in my blood, and contemplation of opting for a softer and easier city life by writing for a living incited guilt of betrayal and weakness. Being of the land meant grinning and bearing the hard times: there was always next season, next year. Hardship, resilience and resourcefulness characterised farm life and farm people but right now my battle for self left no energy for coping with farming's uncertainties.

There were too many unanswered questions for me to stay in the valley. Besides, my experience of farming was that it left little time for family. There were no family holidays in my childhood. 'I'll take you fishing,' my father said to me once. His intention was good but we didn't go. Although weary from his day's work, he did take my sister and me out at night, to the pictures and the dances, and I loved him for this, but we never did more than daytrips as a family. The farm was my dad's domain. It was his world. 'I don't want to travel or go anywhere else,' he said. 'Everything I want in the world is here.' The only way to have time with him was to work with him, and I'd enjoyed this from a young age, following his footsteps so closely through the pastures that I adopted the limp he had from an injury in one foot. Dad's life and identity were entwined with his farm, but I wanted my children to experience their parents in play as well as work. Our three months in the United States provided opportunity for this, each of us returning home with a spectrum of experiences to cherish.

Returning to work after this long break was a challenge but I loved it, and besides, George was too grumpy to be with at home. He carried on 'like a Mallee bull' at times, saying the neighbours' crops were better than his or they had got a bigger contract with the vegetable processor.

I told him to 'Smile!' because when he grumped, I could not focus on my study and then I binged. Several years had passed and the psychologist wasn't solving my problem, but I made another appointment, as I didn't know whom else to turn to for help.

The psychologist now visited Bairnsdale once a month, but on the date I was to see him, I misplaced my appointment card. After phoning the Bairnsdale hospital four times to no avail, I drove to the hospital in my lunch break to find the consulting room vacant. Deciding that this was an omen, I asked the hospital receptionist to tell the psychologist that I would not see him again. I became convinced I could manage myself—I had organised our family trip to the United States, therefore surely I could organise my eating.

Five-year-old Missy, my Amanda, provided light relief. One morning she asked me to phone Santa and order a horse for her for Christmas, so that I wouldn't need to spend my money on one. What a kind thought from my little girl. She was my best girl friend.

The following Saturday, Amanda was sitting with her doll Linda on our wide verandah in the morning sun, having a picnic. I could see her through the window from where I was sitting in the lounge, studying, when a swallow flew into the window. Bang, the swallow fell beside Missy. She calmly looked down and picked up the stunned bird, fed it some bread, provided water, and nestled it in her doll cradle, rocking it gently, until it suddenly recovered and flew away. She was sad at losing her feathered friend but happy when I said that without her rescue, the cat might have eaten it. In the afternoon, while George and I were having a cuppa, Amanda ran to the kitchen to tell us she had found a mouse in the hen house; George went to look and found a big fat rat, so Amanda fetched a stick and George killed it. Later on she called out, 'Look Daddy, I'm riding my horse!' And there she was, with some hay string for reins and a bread bag filled with loose straw from the haystack for a saddle, astride the post railing next to our machinery shed. George had to hop on behind her and have a ride, and so did I! Such moments inspired me to persist in fighting my pain within.

Sometimes I thought we were unfair on our children, what with me working and studying so much; but all in all, we accomplished a lot in 1982. We had our trip to the US; I'd been promoted to an 'A' grade journalist at the newspaper office and had passed the first year of what had become a Bachelor of Arts in Journalism degree with distinctions. But food continued to plague my mind.

I felt sad at disappointing my parents, but my internal battle had become one of life or death. For me to have a chance, we had to leave Woodglen.

If not for my children, I would gladly die, and free George to be with a woman not troubled like me. I could not escape the blackness in my head.

We bought an old weatherboard house in Bairnsdale and moved into it, leasing our farmhouse to Joy and Ray. After living in town for almost a week, I believed we had made the right move. Our house needed renovating, but was livable.

With little farm income, George was working as labourer for Ray on building sites, and our children changed schools again, moving from Lindenow to Bairnsdale Primary. They seemed to settle in well, and our house was opposite the school, so they could walk there and back each day. They had lost the freedom of running free in the paddocks, but we enrolled them in tennis coaching and swimming classes and Shane and Rohan became Cub Scouts.

I completed my final essay for the second year of my BA Journalism studies. I thought I would pass, but there was a lot of pressure, especially with my heavy workload at the *Advertiser*, and George was unsettled without a steady income. Completing the picture was our small house with little hot water, worn carpet and torn linoleum, drab curtains, cracked tiles in the bathroom, the washing machine playing up, broken dishwasher, and children busy with after-school activities. Sometimes I wondered why I tried to study but resolved to persevere in hope of getting a good job.

My woes were small compared with those of Joy and Ray. Returning to the Lindenow Valley to live seemed to have opened Joy's Pandora's box as well as mine. She phoned early one Saturday morning in distress. Ray was having financial problems because clients had exploited his generous and easygoing nature and had not paid him for his work. Joy needed assurance that things would work out and I urged her to seek help in finding solutions. She scoffed at my suggestion and said she found all the answers she needed in the Bible.

George's and my marriage continued to have rocky moments. I asked him if he resented me for leaving the farm and although he said 'No', I believed he did.

In September I pushed such thoughts aside when Lyle Tucker, in charge of Journalism at RMIT, called for a chat and, on hearing of events in my workplace, said flatly: 'June, you are being exploited.' He encouraged me to apply for a vacancy with Leader Newspapers, based at Blackburn, an eastern suburb of Melbourne. 'Act promptly,' he said, giving me a number to call. I spoke with the editor-in-chief, who requested a letter of introduction and copies of my work in the next day's post. He assured me he'd be in touch. George, on learning of this when he came home from work in the evening, dampened my enthusiasm. He said: 'What will I do in the city?' Well, I thought, if he could get manual work in the country, he could get it in the city too. George had many skills—animal husbandry, irrigation, fencing, welding, pasture management, building construction and machinery—but, like many farmers, he had no certificates of proficiency. His options therefore were limited to manual work.

Meanwhile, being caught up with job, study, supervising homework and running the house, I didn't realise Rohan was sick. His constant coughing one night finally alerted me. A visit to the doctor revealed he had been suffering pneumonia on his left lung for two weeks, and I felt like throwing my job in.

My unhappiness grew when George, who had intended to train as a Cub master so he could participate in our sons' scouting interests, missed the first training night because it clashed with his tennis club's annual meeting. Shane had been looking forward to his dad's presence at cubs and I told George he was inconsiderate. That incident topped off a great line of events and it was well after midnight when I fell into an exhausted sleep. Despite his denial, I steadfastly believed that George begrudged me for leaving the farm. Lately he rarely showed affection and was hardly a friend. I felt like buying a single bed for myself, but supposed that would be the beginning of the end and I didn't want us to separate. I needed his friendship and love, and our children needed us both. Apart from my torment, I believed much of our trouble stemmed from the lack of security in George's employment. He'd yet to find a replacement for the loss of his dairying career.

I wanted to learn more about Leader Newspapers because the *Advertiser* was stressful for me right then and home wasn't much different. I tried talking to George once more, but he wanted to see a way ahead for him as well.

However, he adopted a fresh attitude when Leader Newspapers called again. I was shortlisted for a position as sub-editor at the Blackburn office and was invited to an interview the following Wednesday. This time George said: 'Yes, we'll go. I think I'll find a job in Melbourne as easily as in Bairnsdale and our children will adapt. We can all do with a change.' My interview went well and the job was mine if I wanted it, starting after Christmas. 'You will never be happy at the *Advertiser*,' George said. 'We should go to Blackburn.' His parents agreed this was a good opportunity. I hoped my parents would think likewise.

While we considered our options, Joy and Ray bravely worked through their crisis, which led Joy to shedding light on our past. In another Saturday morning call, without preamble, she asked, 'Do you remember when our relations and family friends stayed at our farm during the school holidays?'

I certainly did. They slept in what we called the top bedroom—the room our grandparents had occupied, a little further along the passage from our bedroom.

But one visitor did not stay in the top room. He came into our bedroom in the middle of the night.

Perhaps current events in Joy's life had built up pressure to the point where she could release this terrible secret that she had suppressed for decades.

'He came into our room more than once,' she said.

She was about eight years old, and I was four or five.

He not only entered our room, he got under the bedclothes too.

My stomach churned as my sister proceeded to describe what happened.

My head was swirling—her account was providing clues to many of my childhood mysteries. Missing pieces of my life jigsaw were slotting into place.

My sister hadn't told Mum or Dad. She'd told nobody until a few days before her wedding, when anxiety led her to confide in a girlfriend. My heart went out to her. Now I understood why she was tearful prior to her big day. She and Ray surely did deserve some good luck.

Joy's disclosure reverberated in my brain. I had no memory of the assaults but like her, had always felt an aversion to this man. With no locks on our bedroom or bathroom doors, we were wary, dressing and undressing, when he was in the house.

Taking a bath was a heightened time of anxiety because the bath was a long way from the door and faced it. If anyone opened the door there was no way to cover up. Feeling vulnerable, I had resorted to placing a chair under the door handle before undressing.

Here I was, in my 30s, and childhood experiences were starting to make sense. Now I knew why, when we went to bed at night, Joy often said, 'I can see a light outside our window.' I would say there was no light outside, but she would insist there was. Before getting into bed she looked under our beds, in the wardrobe and behind the thin curtain that hung over the old fireplace behind the head of her bed. Every night, these places were checked before climbing into bed. Sometimes she was so insistent I called to our parents to come from the kitchen and convince her that nobody was there.

Now I understood why Joy was vigilant. Perhaps the abuser was looking through our window, hiding in our room, or waiting to sneak in, in the dark of the night.

'When he came to stay I slept with one eye open and one eye shut, like our chooks in the henhouse looking out for the fox,' Joy said.

I suggested we to talk to our parents, and seek justice, but Joy was adamant we remain silent, as the shock of knowing what this man had done would be painful for them—and our mother already had a weak heart. Joy was obviously suffering however, and I encouraged her to seek counselling. Not for the first time she refused, stoically saying: 'If you are keen on counselling, get some for yourself.'

This childhood revelation added urgency to my desire to leave Bairnsdale and Lindenow Valley. I loved my childhood district but, unable to talk with my family about things that really mattered, the past was choking me.

I drove out to the family farm to see Dad. I found him down the paddock and proceeded described my need to go away—that is, as well as I could without mentioning the real reasons.

I had a good talk, cuddle, and cry with Dad about going away. And feel much better. I hope poor Dad understands. I think he does. He is very dear to me. And always will be; George and I will go to Blackburn and make a new life for ourselves, and I'll be able to leave here, knowing I've at last put my ghost in the cupboard. Never any more eating problems. Never, from tomorrow on.

Dad's blessing for my move to Blackburn meant a lot. He said: 'The main thing is that you are happy'.

George remained positive and by now both of our families supported our plan to move to the city. But doubts overwhelmed me. Mr Yeates offered me superannuation and a promotion to newspaper editor if I stayed at Bairnsdale. In a moment of clarity, I wondered if working on another newspaper would bring happiness, and if moving away from my childhood district would solve my inner problems. I told Mr Yeates that going to the city, at the very least, would provide some answers. 'Your problem,' he said, 'is that you cannot see the woods for the trees.' He added: 'But there will always be a job for you at the *Advertiser*.'

George and I arranged to auction our Bairnsdale house but the thought of packing and unpacking, of finding another house to live in and settling the children into new schools, weighed heavily on me. Confident everything would turn out well, George said: 'You must shake yourself and be positive too.' I tried to clear my doubts by staying on the hypoglycaemia diet, but confusion reigned. On my 33rd birthday I was feeling '*completely lazy, disorganised and mixed up*'.

My anguish over the Blackburn job offer mounted until the first week in January 1984, when I sent a letter declining the job. For me, the scales had tipped in favour of staying in the country. My rural roots ran deep and I baulked at the responsibility of taking not only myself, but also George and our children, to a new life in the city.

Luckily, our house hadn't sold at auction and I hoped that Leader Newspapers would not contact me, or I'd become confused again. After three tense months of negotiation I announced to Mr Yeats that I would stay at the *Advertiser*. Pleased, he appointed me chief-of-staff. I was determined nobody and no situation would upset me. I would allow nothing to trigger bingeing or starving because that was sure to bring me undone. Supreme calorie control would make everything manageable. Mr Yeates provided a new office to match my new role.

Within a week, my efforts to settle came undone. Blackness swooped in one Friday night and, drugging myself with food, I became suicidal, punching my head, slapping my face, pinching my neck and breasts, trying to stop the pain within. Such behaviour was no good for me, but worse for my children who saw me frothing at my mouth and writhing in distress on the kitchen floor. My blackness continued next morning and, trapped in the prison of my mind, I did not know how to escape. George took the children to the farm with him at lunchtime. After they left I cried, slept for an hour and awoke vowing not to fall so deep into depression again. Perhaps I should drop my studies—they made me yearn for what I couldn't have.

Two days later my depression was back. Crying myself to sleep and crying when I awoke, I became certain George was turning away when I needed a cuddle and a kiss. Perhaps my unhappiness was due to him, or to my work environment, or to a more minor matter, our house. I was unaware that illness, embedded in my mind, was the cause. I decided to continue with study because it gave me something else to think about, something that indicated I was sane.

Within a month, I was ready to resign from the *Advertiser* office— nothing had changed there. This time my notice would be short and permanent. I'd had another crazy night.

All but stabbed myself with a knife. Instead I've bruising—self-inflicted— on my breasts and abdomen. The strain ... is proving too much—any peace of mind is almost non-existent. I KNOW I must escape (this situation) before I go insane. It's just a matter of whether I can stick it out until I've somewhere else to work. My strategy is this —tomorrow morn I will make an appointment with my Dr, and seek advice. I know it's no good for the children to see me crying so often.

Physical self-harm helped to ease the pain within. I wore high-collared shirts and polo-necked jumpers to work in the summer heat to hide cuts and bruises. High on anxiety, little things sent me over the edge. I was upset because George knew he'd be late home from night tennis but forgot to tell me or because he had decided to work late, he missed the first meeting of a Cub leader course—it could be that simple. My negative thoughts intensified the anxiety in any situation to a point where I felt I was on a high tightrope, wavering, about to fall. Unreasonably at such times I almost hated George, and hated the *Advertiser* more.

I was going insane. The fine line was beckoning. Next morning, before losing my resolve, I called the Main Street medical centre. My doctor was on leave, so I was referred to another, younger male doctor and could see him at 5.30pm that day. The date was February 13.

After struggling through my day's work, I went straight to the clinic. I had waited more than an hour and was worrying about my children being home alone when the new doctor called my name. Through tears, I begged for help. Desperate, at the end of my tether, I didn't care if this doctor thought I was mad. I wanted HELP: 'Please help me.' The GP listened as I described my crying spells, awful eating habits and fear of making a decision on anything such as another job. If I could get myself in order then maybe I could make decisions in other areas. I particularly wanted to be cured of the past for the sake of my children. The doctor prescribed medication in the short term. Something, he said, that helped people who fluctuated greatly between moods—and I was to take the pills twice daily.

'But we need to get you more help for the long term. Have you heard of Melbourne psychiatrist Professor Graham Burrows?' the doctor asked.

'No,' I sobbed.

The doctor said, 'Professor Burrows is the one man I know who can help you.'

He suggested, like my usual GP, that I had a chemical problem. He gave me a glimmer of hope. I thought how wonderful it would be to cope confidently and ably, in control of my inner self. Then I could make a decision regarding my job, and George's and my life together. I was to phone the clinic the next day to check for an appointment date. Meanwhile, I'd try to do as the doctor said and stay on the hypoglycaemia diet.

The clinic called for an appointment with Professor Burrows but he was in high demand and my name was added to a waiting list that was 'several months' long. Every day, my pressures were magnified: my job, George's job insecurity, my study and the children's many activities. I did not think I could survive another month, but relief came from an unexpected source. Our wee house that had remained on the market, after not attracting one bid at auction, suddenly attracted a buyer. The agent dropped in to say we had 24 hours in which to accept the offer. George and I went to bed, wondering what to do.

Events the next day provided the answer. Lyle Tucker rang from RMIT and said bluntly: 'You are too soft, June. That's why you are still at the *Advertiser*.' Lyle said the editor-in-chief at *The Leader* would retire soon and 'if you want a job there, you need to hurry'. George said to call immediately, so I did, and was told: 'There's a job here for you!' A sub-editor had left and I could take his place, starting 'as soon as possible'.

George said we should go, and I agreed. This time we really would get to Blackburn. Perhaps this was where I would find peace. I gave notice at the *Advertiser*, and contracts were signed for the sale of our Bairnsdale house. We would move to Melbourne until our children completed their secondary education—for at least 10 years—and would look for a house with this in mind.

A week later, Mum phoned me at work, and to my relief she was bright. She asked about my new job and starting date, inquired if accommodation was organised, and offered to help with the children until we were settled. I hoped she stayed pleasant. I treasured George and our children and would be glad when we were in Melbourne and putting our health and happiness first.

We found a house to buy in Blackburn. It was a 10-minute walk from my workplace, Leader Associated Newspapers, in Whitehorse Road, and near the railway station, primary and secondary schools; also near the library, parks, church and tennis courts. George applied for jobs listed in the employment section of *The Age* newspaper and quickly obtained a full-time job—at the RMIT in the city. He was elated. He would be a cleaner, starting work a week before me. My only disappointment was in another call to the clinic: due to some slip up, my appointment to see Professor Burrows had not come through.

13. MOVE TO THE CITY

George and I moved to Melbourne in April 1984. We stayed with friends, and our children remained with family in East Gippsland, until moving into our 'new' home in leafy Blackburn eight weeks later. The house was old and ready for a facelift but in a great location, we had two jobs and we were going to lead a normal life. George was almost 36, I was 33, Shane 11, Rohan nine, Ben eight, and Amanda, seven.

We each faced challenges in adjusting to city life. For me, driving the family car was nerve-wracking. With my neck movement limited due to the log truck accident, I panicked if driving down a road with more than two lanes of traffic. Single-lane country roads had been manageable, but driving along busy city roads with three lanes of traffic was terrifying. I hugged the kerb like a frightened rabbit, too scared to venture into the centre lane. My fear hampered our lifestyle, as the children often required transport and had to depend on George's availability. Luckily I was a 10-minute walk from my workplace.

George adapted to urban living with surprising speed. He didn't need the car to get to work either: he had a five-minute walk to catch the train for the half-hour ride to the city. He treated this new chapter as an adventure and enjoyed exploring the city in his lunch breaks. I liked my new job as part of a large sub-editing team. Our children settled in at Blackburn Primary School, across the road from the newspaper office.

I was making a huge effort for this new start but months were slipping by and I had yet to receive an appointment with Professor Burrows. In June, in desperation I joined the local Weight Watchers club, vowing to stick like glue to the program until I weighed 50kg. *Otherwise, I might as well die.*

That's how I feel. I'm crying out for help, but who can help? It's so long since I ate like a normal person.

Weight Watchers was not the answer. A few days later, I was eating handfuls of peanuts.

Weak! Better than smoking or drinking alcohol, or taking drugs, but not as good as not eating.

At least my workplace was happy and I had good workmates. We had some laughs.

Home life was not much fun. George and I were rearranging our finances because I felt an urgency to renovate our Blackburn home; I wanted everything to be finished. Now. I was desperate to clear our debts and stresses, thinking that by reducing possible causes of anxiety, I would have more chance of overcoming my eating disorder. We paid for the house and the improvements by subdividing, then selling, our house and five acres from our farm at Woodglen. Income from the remaining land, which was leased to a local farmer, would provide for our children's education.

Explosive moments continued. I loved George but felt confused, asking myself, *'Am I having difficulty coping because of my stupid eating habits or because we are becoming incompatible?'* The following week I phoned Professor Burrows' office to ask about my appointment and was told the waiting list was two months. I had waited four months already.

I'd like to think the problem is one I can handle myself—I've tried for so long to do just that, but each time I fail I feel such a mess and am crying out for someone to help me. The thought of going on like this for the rest of my life makes me want to die. So I must try for some help. I need to alter my eating behaviour, to be disciplined, and oh, I'm sure I'll feel so free.

Desperate, I contacted a local clinic and arranged a check up. Perhaps my warped mind problem was physical, but if only psychological, surely I could exercise mind power and conquer it myself. I liked to think I could but so far had failed miserably. The thought of continuing to live in this struggle made me want to die. For my children's sakes, I had to persist in seeking help.

The local GP scoffed at the Traralgon psychologist's low-blood-sugar solution to my problems—the hypoglycaemic diet had been useless—and scoffed equally at the delay in seeing Professor Burrows. He referred me to another psychiatrist, saying the first appointment would be within six weeks, but warned that recovery would take a long time. I didn't mind, I just wanted HELP. But 42 days was a long time to wait when I was sliding further into a deepening well of depression.

A few days later, unable to find a foot-hold to escape from my darkness, I returned to the same local clinic. This time a female GP was understanding and helpful. After asking more about my anorexic history she phoned for an appointment with yet another psychiatrist in the inner Melbourne suburb of Richmond, in 28 days.

'He's a colleague of Professor Burrows,' the GP said. If I could hang on until my appointment, surely one of these men could help me. The doctor asked me to let her know how I got on. She said, 'You have been through a lot. There must have been a lot of friction in your family during your childhood.' Her observation caused me to stop and think. My childhood world had been my only world and I had not thought about my family in that way.

With 27 days until the Richmond appointment I tried to pace myself—my next attempt at seeking help had to succeed or my marriage, and maybe my life, would end. My illness had all but devoured my sense of self. I felt sure George was finding it hard to love me. Walking along Blackburn's lovely tree-lined streets helped me connect a little with myself and buying a plant now and then nurtured my soul, despite George and the children protesting that I was creating a forest in our house yard.

I sent in a 13-page, hand-written letter to George's parents and extended family, for the first time telling them of my 22-year struggle with eating disorders. I was inspired to write after George's mum visited and told our children that I didn't know how to be a parent. I decided to explain myself in hope of being understood. Until now, George had been the only person, other than doctors, in whom I had confided about my illness.

I think it's time my past was made public. I've always felt ashamed of it. I suppose, though, I realise now that I shouldn't feel this way. I haven't done anything wrong; I've just had an illness.

After writing to George's parents, I opened my heart in a letter to my parents, describing my depression, and my impending visit to the Richmond psychiatrist. Mum wrote back, ignoring my outpouring, instead stating that our act in selling our Woodglen house had caused them a terrible time, forcing my sister and her family to move to other rented accommodation and 'now your father's hands are all shaky'.

She wrote, 'We wanted to keep the house in the family, but at that price it couldn't be done.' Initially George and I had been criticised for building the house, suggesting it was an extravagance; now, too late, my parents were revealing they had wanted to buy the house for Joy and Ray. Unaware, we had sought the best price on the open market to pay for our Blackburn property. As for my health problems, Mum dismissed them, saying, 'The past is gone—forget it.' But I had to live with my past. I was haunted by it and needed help to free myself.

Four months after moving to Melbourne, my parents were due to visit. The day before they arrived I felt ill:

They don't understand me and can't accept me. I don't fit their image of June with short hair working on the farm.

My parents called in on a Friday. I made a cuppa and sat at one end of the table and my father sat at the other end and looked away. Mum sat between us. Neither parent commented on our house or garden or asked about my work. They were out of their comfort zone, the valley. They shared news of my sister's family but didn't stay to see my children, who were due home from school at any minute. Within an hour of arriving they departed to stay with my Aunty Carlie in a nearby suburb for the night. They could have stayed with us. I was burning inside.

After they went, I threw a self-harming fit. My appointment with the psychiatrist could not come soon enough. I was in a vacuum when I went berserk, and that was no good for George, the children, or myself. I was starting to blame my upbringing. The farm had always come first. I felt deeply sad and wished my parents had not called in. Their visit had unsettled me, big time.

The following week, Joy phoned and I confided to her that I would see a psychiatrist in a few days.

She tells me I've Satan in me and I must ask God to help me. Well, I've been trying that for a long time. I think God must think I need other help as well! She probably thinks I am weak not being able to cope with my past, but then I've never cured the eating habits. The only time I've eaten sensibly since I was 11 was when in hospital, and meals were prepared for me. Joy spoke of the sexual abuse by '...' when she was seven or eight. She says she's accepted that. She might have, but it certainly made her difficult growing up. And her behaviour had awful effects on me.

Joy could not understand why I wanted to talk about the past, but that was when my life had been sabotaged by first anorexia, and then bulimia. She was saying she had healed, and I knew I had not—this made me feel worse. As far as I knew, our parents remained unaware of the abuse. They must have been unaware, because they continued to welcome '...' into their home. The creep.

George and I, in an effort to become part of the community in Blackburn, joined the congregation at The Avenue Uniting Church. I began to develop a sense of connection, especially when a speaker at a social group meeting spoke about the importance of love; how it was at the root of many personal problems. He had worked at The Ark outreach ministry in Amsterdam. Much of what he said was relevant to my life and I felt strengthened. I'd felt wanted at times, but often rejected. I felt freshly inspired to persist in finding a way to recover from my illness. I would go to the psychiatrist, return to the nice woman doctor and also see the church minister. My problem was complicated, I thought, and I would need constant supervision, free of pressures and upsets, to have any hope of success.

Two days before my appointment with the Richmond psychiatrist, my mind was as helpless as tumbleweed being buffeted about by a gale force wind. I felt my soul was somersaulting down a country lane; sometimes grabbing hold of the barbs on the wire fence, then a fresh gust hurtling me off again; afraid to stop, not knowing what to hang on to, terrified of another failure. I hoped and prayed this psychiatrist could help end my turmoil.

If tension was unavoidable, I thought, there must be a way of managing it without losing control. Perhaps George was a little to blame for my state. His temper didn't help, and his poorly paid job had become a strain. This was not his fault, because it hadn't been easy for him, changing from farmer to cleaner. He felt looked down on by men who walked by him, dressed in their suits and ties, as he cleaned the floors in the corridors of the big tertiary institution. He was developing an empathy with the blue-collar class and planned to break with family tradition and vote Labor at the next State and Federal elections.

From my work in the Department of Social Security, I knew that if I stopped work and George stopped work, we would receive more in welfare payments than George received in his wage, but we had been raised in a culture of work, no matter what the pay.

My visit to the psychiatrist coincided with Ben's ninth birthday and I hoped for good news. I travelled alone, by train and tram, to the consulting rooms in Richmond. The psychiatrist could not fathom me out. He seemed disappointed when I said I didn't have many moments of panic or great anxiety—not until many years later would I realise my life had been a string of anxious moments. Before this psychiatrist could help me he said I would need two visits with a clinical psychologist and then I was to return to him.

I departed his consulting room feeling dejected. I was going from one health professional to another and wondered if my mind could stay afloat until I found the right lifeline. One night I loved George and the next night I didn't. A male colleague in the newspaper office had upset me, second time in eight days. This guy was saying I should do work that was not my responsibility and if he harassed me again I told George I would resign rather than be exploited again. 'You get things out of context,' he said.

My mind was like a hand grenade with a loose pin and after tea one night it exploded. George had begun to sand the window ledge in our kitchen with a noisy machine that spread fine dust everywhere. I tried to tell him over the noise that I'd washed the floors at lunchtime and he said: 'I'm ashamed to face our neighbours because of your yelling.'

My mind snapped, I banged my head on the wall and threw things, anything that was near: the jar of Vegemite (I was about to make school lunches), a jar of cookies (the glass jar smashed beautifully), a ceramic plate (also smashed), margarine and bread. Then I tipped the cutlery and crockery on top of it all, got a large packet of potato crisps (George by this time, had left the house), went to bed, read and ate and promptly fell asleep. George returned some time later and slept in Shane's bed, a wise move.

I'd bruised myself again and next morning my colleagues expressed concern at my 'terrible' battered appearance. The left side of my head was sore and fragile and I wanted to rest it on a pillow but I had a job to do. I cheered up as I focused on my work and began to feel useful. At lunchtime I walked home and sat in the sun on the backdoor step for five minutes of solitude. Doctors had always told me to keep working but the job at *Leader* was not my answer. When he returned from work that day, George phoned Professor Burrow's office to ask if my appointment could be brought forward. Six months had passed and we were still waiting for an appointment date.

The following week I returned to the woman doctor. She contacted Professor Burrow's office too and completed her call with a smile. A date had been fixed—August 24. 'Forget your other appointments and focus on seeing the professor,' she said. She assured me that George and I had made the right decision, leaving Woodglen and encouraged me to keep working.

Having waited a long time to see the professor, I worried he would conclude there was nothing wrong with me, thus confirming I'd been an incredibly inadequete person for 22 years. However, within minutes of meeting him I knew he would help me.

'Prof' (as I came to call Professor Burrows) said the recovery rate of people with my illness was usually 85 per cent. I wanted to be in that 85 per cent. 'You have never been helped since age 11,' he said, giving me a long life history questionnaire to fill in, and asking me to keep a diary of everything I ate and my moods each day. He suggested my diaries might help in sorting out my problems. My next appointment, in four weeks, seemed a long way off. I was trying to cope with my work situation until I could see my path more clearly. Right now, I was not sure of anything.

Sunday was my favourite day of the week as, after church and Sunday School, I had time with my children, especially Amanda. Blessed with a sunny nature, she lifted my spirit and I felt ashamed of my many faults. She made me laugh. I was crying when chopping onions for a casserole and she expressed concern at my tears. I said: 'It's only the onions. Really, I'm happy and the doctor I'm seeing now will help make me so happy that I'll hardly cry any more at all.' She returned a little later and asked seriously: 'Will this doctor take all the water out of you, Mummy?' and I said: 'Good heavens, no!' She explained she thought that must be the case if I was to stop crying! We did lots of baking that day.

I liked baking, but cakes and cookies were not good to have around when my binge trigger went off. At least 15kg overweight, I was sick of being FAT and was counting the days until my next appointment. I'd do my best to get better, knowing that THIS TIME I had the RIGHT HELP. There was one big fight left in me, and I'd start it under Prof's guidance.

I wanted to be stable to help my children feel secure and confident.

The children need me, and I'm not as stable as I should be for them to feel secure. And it is so important for them to feel good within themselves. Don't I know it. I remembered tonight, how Joy always looked in cupboards, under beds etc., before getting into bed at night, and then saying she could see someone out the window. I would try to reassure her. She made me so irate. Of course, no wonder she did this after being abused by that Monster Man. But of course I didn't know that then. Oh, what a mess. Why did this have to happen?

Besides looking in cupboards and under beds at night, during the day Joy would walk past an object, such as a flower in the garden, and touch it, walk a few steps, then return and touch it again. I understood the reasons for that behaviour now—she had felt insecure—but this repetitive behaviour had bewildered me then.

Meanwhile, back in today's world, and following a colleague's tip-off, I inquired about a job at Melbourne's major afternoon newspaper, *The Herald*, and was invited for an interview the following week. Striving to be positive, I caught a train to Flinders Street in the city centre and walked several blocks to *The Herald* and *Weekly Times*' office for an interview with the editor. He painted a harsh picture of being under pressure and meeting deadlines but that did not deter me. He said I'd hear from him soon and introduced me to the deputy editor who said likewise. Feeling happy, I walked up Swanston Street to RMIT and asked for Lyle Tucker, and met him face to face at last! We chatted for an hour. Lyle was a mentor and a comfort because he believed in me. Then I took the train to Box Hill for X-rays on my neck. I was home by 3.30pm to greet the children after school, and help Shane make some toffee for a school fund-raiser. A productive day had kept my tormentor at bay.

The next day, a doctor called about my X-rays. Worried by the results, he was referring me to an orthopaedic surgeon. He said degenerative damage was evident and I needed a new neck.

I often felt like I did. A new head, too.

Less than a week after my interview with *The Herald*, the newspaper offered me a job as a 'B' grade sub-editor. I thought this was the best path to follow. I'd talk to Prof when I saw him in another two days and then resign at *Leader*.

My second visit to Prof provided the first real diagnosis of the illness that had been plaguing me since childhood. He confirmed I had developed anorexia nervosa and now bulimia nervosa and described my condition as 'fair.' He said, 'Your life has been full of anxiety and depression.' Before he could start trying to control my eating he had to control the anorexia/bulimia. He prescribed Parnate, which I was to start taking the next day. Prof said the tablets might give me a severe headache and if so, to contact him. (Parnate is also known as tranylcypromine and belongs to a group of medicines called monoamine oxidase inhibitor—MAOI—antidepressants.) Chocolate, cheese, avocado, bananas, dried fruit, yoghurt and red wine, all of which I liked, were banned and the tablets would take three or four weeks to have an impact. 'You should feel livelier,' Prof said.

My next visit to Prof would be in October. I was in the preliminary bout of fighting my illness and there was a long, hard haul in front. The enormity of my struggle hit me as I left his consulting room and I wondered not for the first time if problems in my mind could be altered after 22 years. Prof. seemed to feel sorry for me. This was worrying. Regarding my job situation, he suggested that I stay at *Leader*; seeing as my boss there wanted me to remain on his staff—the less stress the better—but I thought *The Herald* might be the answer.

Into my second day on the pills I had a dry mouth, one of the many side effects I'd been warned about, so was drinking many cups of tea. My job remained in the balance. A formal job offer arrived in the mail from *The Herald*. Some friends said to take this job and others said stay at *Leader*. Besides myself, I'd my family to consider but the decision was made when Lyle Tucker from the RMIT called and, on hearing of my new job offer, said, 'You've hit the big time! Take the job at *The Herald*.'

Lyle said this career opportunity might not come again for a long while. So I became 99 per cent sure I'd take *The Herald* job. My only misgiving was the need to find someone to mind the children for one-and-a-half hours each morning. Also, I'd have to learn to use the new visual display units—computers—and adapt to another new work environment but these challenges could be overcome. In the long term I imagined *The Herald* was by far the best career proposition. I gave notice at *Leader* and sent a letter of acceptance to *The Herald*. I also saw the orthopaedic surgeon who said several discs and bones in my upper spine had fused and he suggested physiotherapy might help. I was too busy for that, so would have to put up with the grating, grinding, pressure and headaches: the legacy from hitting the log truck.

After finishing at *Leader*, I had four days as a full-time mum before starting at *The Herald*. A caring young secretary from Leader Newspapers took on our child-minding role which would include walking with the children to school.

My very first day with Melbourne's major broadsheet afternoon newspaper passed happily, though nervously. The introductory two-week visual display unit course was intimidating. I was comfortable with words but, at 33, knew nothing about computers. After my first day, I knew a little more than nothing. My mind was not in the best state to be absorbing new technology.

However, apart from the technological challenge, I felt pleased with myself for getting a job with *The Herald*. I was one of few women in the sub-editors' room. I started work at 7am and finished at 2.30pm, enabling me to catch a train and arrive home in time to welcome the children after their day at school. One afternoon I accompanied Amanda to her induction as a Brownie, and she greatly enjoyed having me along. I joined in and played Winkie and Fruit Salad. Amanda knew her Promise well and I felt sure she would enjoy being involved in the Guide movement. With three brothers, she enjoyed the company of other girls her age at Brownies.

By the end of October I had completed my third year of journalism studies. I hoped to be well into the recovery phase of my illness when studies resumed in February. For now, though, repetitive sounds continued to make me want to scream and, as Shane said one afternoon, 'You are so sensitive, Mum.'

Shane had worked hard at his Grade Six studies since we moved to Melbourne and was accepted at one of the city's top private schools, Scotch College, for his secondary education. We'd be penny-pinching but Shane, who had attended five different State primary schools, deserved this opportunity. His State primary school principal said he was bright, and would benefit from the structure, support and discipline of the private school system.

In November, Prof affirmed I'd made the right choice in going to *The Herald*. My urge to binge had seemed to ease, so maybe the tablets were working. Prof explained the drug was compensating for a deficiency of a chemical associated with messages to my brain.

In December, I was worrying about arrangements for Christmas. Prof said I must take responsibility for myself first, then George, the children and my parents. As for Christmas at my parents' farm, he said to say we wouldn't be there and focus on having a merry time at home. I sent the letter that night.

The following night I was tired and binged. I had baked a big batch of shortbread—and had just placed it on the cake cooler when bang, crash, the ceiling fan protector fell down, landing, yes, on my shortbread. I cried. Many pieces were smashed. George kindly said he would eat them. He was banging and drilling at the time, installing a new door.

All went well until December 22, Amanda's eighth birthday. The sub editors organised a lunchtime office Christmas party of festive treats including meats, cheeses, bread, crackers, wine and beer. I consumed no alcohol, but in my desire to behave like my colleagues I forgot my medication restrictions and ate some cheese. Within 30 minutes my head was thumping. At first I couldn't make out what was happening —then I remembered cheese was on the Parnate banned food list.

My heart was heaving and surging like it wanted to jump out of my mouth and waves pounded through my head. The shocks were so powerful I couldn't see the words on my computer screen and we had an afternoon press deadline to meet.

Today I thought I would die, and all because I ate some cheese! The sub editors at work had a lunchtime party of meats, cheeses, bread, crackers, wine and beer. I drank no alcohol, but without thinking I did eat some cheese. It began reacting on me within 30 to 45 minutes after eating it—a most thumping headache. At first I couldn't make out what was happening—then I realised: the cheese. A banned food while taking the Parnate drug. I began to really worry when my heart began to heave and surge and waves were pounding through my head.

I phoned George, who rang the Austin Hospital who said to go there and have my blood pressure checked, but I didn't have enough money for a taxi and I didn't want to tell anyone at work, so I just concentrated on staying conscious until we could leave about 4pm, and managed to get home on the train 4.30pm, and flaked it on our bed. George and children were glad to see me home and I sure was glad to be there. I got up later, ok except for my sore neck and head.

Amanda's eighth birthday. I was so worried I wouldn't see her. My beautiful girl.

I was too scared to tell anyone at work that I was on medication and needed help; I feared that if my employer knew about my mental illness, I would lose my job.

On Christmas morning, the children were up early and excitedly searched the Santa bags at the foot of their beds. Ben, who enjoyed pulling things apart and putting them together, had spent Christmas Eve inventing a burglar alarm to catch Santa, and it had worked. I set it off when entering his bedroom with an armful of ironed clothes about 10.30pm. He awoke and was disappointed to see he had snared Mum rather than Santa.

We went to church on Christmas morning but three-quarters of the way through the service the shock waves surged through my head again. Amanda comforted me with her Cabbage Patch Doll Anastasia, a birthday gift that she was taking to church for the first time. As the congregation stood to sing a hymn, the beautiful sounds touched my soul and tears streamed down my face. I sat and buried my face in Anastasia, trying to regain control. At home I lay down and George phoned the doctor, who said to keep taking the tablets. I improved enough to sit in the lounge while Shane played Santa and distributed our gifts. George helped me to prepare lunch. We enjoyed our day— just the six of us.

On New Year's Eve I felt like throwing my domestic chores to the wind and having a free night—but supposed I'd do the ironing. George was scraping away at the kitchen ceiling, creating another unavoidable mess in our kitchen renovation. He was doing a good job, and was ready to start painting the walls and ceiling. He wanted to finish the painting before taking the children to the farm to visit our families for a week or so in January. Being ineligible for holiday leave for 12 months, I'd stay home and go to work. I'd miss the family, and Amanda didn't want to leave me, but I would have Shane's puppy, Sam, now two months old, for company.

George and I reflected on an eventful year: we were glad we had come to Blackburn. We were both happy in our work and I was receiving treatment for my eating disorders.

When Prof saw me in the first week of January 1985, he said my headaches had been a reaction to the cheese, but he didn't know why my neck was painful. I saw him again at the end of the month and on hearing that I tended to binge in the evening and therefore my mood swings worsened, he said to take one less tablet a day for a week. My dose was either too little or too much.

At work I made a stupid mistake, luckily spotted by the chief sub before the newspaper was printed. Now, I thought, probably 100 years would pass before I was entrusted to edit a major story and I had only myself to blame. I had quoted the wrong person. I was not getting enough sleep, being up at 5am and in bed at 11.30pm.

Shane began his secondary education at Scotch College in February, travelling by train and tram to Hawthorn, while Rohan, Ben and Amanda began a new year of primary school. George was continuing to adjust well to city life and, after almost a year acquiring skills at RMIT, was offered the job of head cleaner at Haileybury College, a private secondary college. He was elated. The college campus was at Keysborough, a 20-minute drive from home. His hours generally would be noon to 8.30pm, so he would be with the children in the mornings, and I'd be with them in the afternoons. He gave a week's notice to RMIT, which had provided a pathway to this better job.

I was settling in at *The Herald*, working on the finance desk while a sub-editor was on leave. The finance chief sub was friendly but said, 'You will have to be twice as good as a guy to get ahead at *The Herald*.' This, I assumed, was due to the attitude of chauvinistic males. Also, he said, 'Your advancement will be hampered because you don't go to the news bar after work, don't bet on the horses and don't go to bed with the boss!'

I wanted to get ahead on my skill as a journalist, and blow those obstacles. I was doing what I loved and being paid for it—I just wasn't sure what to do about my studies, with so much else on. The children needed help with their homework in the evenings and George's job left little time to help with domestic chores. My journalist studies were almost complete but, with our altered circumstances, I thought I would be selfish to continue.

In April, Prof indicated my recovery would 'hopefully be slow and sure'. Eventually I'd be able to stop taking the Parnate drug that, although a chemical, was not addictive. Unfortunately, while the drugs might have been helping my brain in one way, they were not helping me in another. For the first time since I met George, almost 20 years ago, I began to feel attracted, with a magnet-like force, to other men.

It was like the power of my eating disorder, which until now had been confined within my mind, was suddenly externalising its manipulative domination and once it grabbed hold, it held on with an iron force.

I became fixated on a friendship with the chief sub, and began to feel alive. But at home my moods, due to bingeing one day and starving the next, continued to swing chaotically. One night while preparing dinner (now we were living in the city, 'tea' had become dinner) I became exasperated with Shane. I threw a raw egg and, being a good shot, it landed and broke on his head. The catalyst was Shane's stubborn refusal to change out of his good grey suit trousers when he arrived home from

Scotch College. My head felt as fragile as the egg.

On my next visit with Prof I dejectedly said I was getting nowhere. I cried, afraid I would not recover from my horrid eating disorder. Now, when I binged, sweat poured off me during the night. This happened regularly and I didn't know why.

One cold June day I spent a happy hour with my finance friend. We wandered along the paths through the pretty Fitzroy Gardens near the HWT building and afterwards ate toasted cheese sandwiches and drank cappuccinos in Collins Place. I had eaten no breakfast but the sandwiches were still a challenge. Determined to appear normal, I counted the calories to suppress my fear of losing control for the day. Later I strolled with my friend to the railway station to go our separate ways home. I wasn't attracted to him physically so didn't feel I was committing a moral sin and Prof said a friendship with a person of the opposite sex was perfectly acceptable: 'You're allowed to window-shop, so long as you don't touch the merchandise' was about what he said. But Prof was nonplussed as to my night sweating, and was concerned about my headaches and vomiting, and asked me to let him know of any recurrence.

I thought I had worked out what was making me 'go to pieces' and overeat, in the evenings—George's late work hours. My 'after work' jobs began with organising my children's attendance at ballet, swimming, Brownies, Cubs and Scouts and tennis coaching. This was followed by grocery shopping, cooking a meal for eight (as we had two lodgers as well as our children) helping with homework, listening to how everyone's day went, attending to the laundry, cleaning up after the evening meal, making tomorrow's lunches and attending to the ironing pile. George generally arrived home at 10pm while I was ironing.

My coping skills declined further when I overate; I loathed myself for being weak and undisciplined. I began waking about 3am, sopping from head to foot, my bed saturated as well. Mum said the reason was 'menopause', but I was only 34 and was not convinced. I wasn't sure of anything and hoped my brain would stay well enough to keep my job because it helped me feel sane, at least sometimes. Written words were my friends, but doubt-filled clouds forever hovered on my shoulders. Fearing I might appear too needy in my friendship with the finance chief sub, I began avoiding him.

Collecting the day's mail and seeing my mother's hand-writing on an envelope is enough to spark anxiety. I am afraid to open her letters, fearing something will upset me; will compound feelings of worthlessness. Thankfully her latest letter is extra bright: 'Thank you, Mum. Your brightness has saved me from falling in a deep hole.'

But the next night I was a glutton. I yearned for my next appointment with Prof. I needed his help. The drug seemed to be losing its effect. I hoped I wasn't in the 15 per cent that didn't recover. If I got through one day without bingeing, I felt a little stronger in coping with the next day. I prayed to the Lord, to help me find the resolve, the discipline, not to stuff myself. Perhaps there was something wrong with George's and my relationship that set me off, though George said he needed loving, just as I did; he suffered when my chemicals played up.

Prof decided my night sweats were due to the drug, but said to stay on it and see him in six weeks.

George had settled into his new job but said mine left no time for our family. I had one weekend in seven off, otherwise Sunday and one week day, but everything I did, I thought, was for the family. He seemed to want more than I could give. Writing in my diary and taking Sam Dog for walks were about my only breaks from work, and I usually wrote my diary in transit on the train. I was lucky to have 20 minutes a day for my self. I liked a little outing on my day off, if only to a local Opportunity Shop, to save money on clothes, especially for our children.

I hoped George and I would rediscover our passion during a holiday in the New Year, as our children were sensing the tension.

Prof prescribed a tranquilliser so I would feel less uptight when arriving home after work. He assured me that one day I would eat like a normal person, but right now many strange things were happening and I often felt unwell. At night I continued to waken, sopping, water running off me almost in torrents. George was comforting and continued to push me off to work the next morning, which was the right thing to do, and arranged some domestic help.

The moment I started to feel good about my marriage, my internal tormentor found fresh doubt. If George came to bed late I would feel an urge to be more independent because his comfort was not always there when I needed it. Without his constant presence, I felt like bingeing.

Prof seemed concerned when I saw him next and asked me to return the following week. I hoped George would go with me. My illness was hard on him, because I demanded and needed much love. I feared he would think I was weak for lacking self-control and overeating. I didn't want to do it.

On Prof's suggestion I increased my Parnate medication to four tablets daily, and took care to get enough sleep, but continued to slip—bingeing continuously and feeling angry and frustrated. I hated me. Day after day.

George accompanied me to see Prof in late October. Fourteen months had passed since my first visit and Prof was concerned about my regression. He told George to be firmer and stronger with me and to not let my stubbornness—my illness—beat him. When it raged I could be horribly inflexible, insistent and unreasonable. George and I spent an hour with a social worker as well, and I went home feeling desperate to be happy with myself so I could be happy with others. Overeating made me feel horrid and act horrid.

Increasingly weary, I made several more mistakes at work. I feared my powers of concentration were slipping. Maybe the medication was making my brain sluggish. I vowed to make a fresh effort to eat, sleep and exercise in a sensible routine. Then I'd have no more bad days and maybe my editor would take me off the 'get rid of' list that, by November, I suspected I must be on. Some journalists were being pressed, in humiliating ways, to resign during a company 'restructure'.

Some days I saw George for no more than five minutes. He would be snoring when I left for work at 615am and he didn't get home before 9pm. Our relationship was reducing to a means of communication for the care of our children and house.

By the end of November, Prof decided my eating habits were askew due to stress between George and me, and suggested the three of us have more talks. 'Eat no more than 1000 calories a day, record everything in a book and bring it on your next visit,' he said.

At least if nothing else is going right I can tell myself I'm getting slim.
(Counting calories is known today as an enabler of eating disorders

—the sense of control in counting calories is based on a false premise and provides a false sense of security. It is doomed to fail every time. With every failure, comes more anxiety, more self-loathing.)

Counting calories was not going to solve my problems.

More change was on the way with the editor calling me to his office in the first week of December and saying 'Editorial 2' required a sub-editor to work on the company's country newspaper, *The Weekly Times*. The position involved writing as well as subbing and, with my rural background, I was 'ideal'. Apart from missing my friends on the main subbing desk, I was pleased because I couldn't see myself advancing on *The Herald* with its male dominance in the office and a falling circulation in the marketplace. On the other hand, *The Weekly Times'* sales were healthy and my opportunity of advancement there would at least equal that on *The Herald*. I would start the following Monday.

I had the weekend to get my mind around my new job while catching up on household chores, but Sunday became a day best forgotten. George was invited to take his family to a Christmas barbecue at Haileybury College. I didn't want to go. My mind was already overloaded, overtired and finely strung. But George insisted. To try and fit the event into my already crowded weekend, I didn't attend church and began my week's baking while the children attended their Sunday School break-up.

We departed home about midday for the half-hour drive to Haileybury. The braking and accelerating at the many traffic lights agitated my head and stomach as if in a washing machine. On arrival at the college I sat in the car to recover from the nausea. I didn't eat lunch and didn't feel sociable. To avoid small talk I wandered around the college grounds, soaking up the sunshine, trying to quell my inner turmoil. George was networking with his new colleagues and our children were playing in the college gym and in the college pool.

We returned home about 6pm and, thinking of lunches to cut, shirts to iron, new job to start the next day, and how many calories I had eaten for the day, my fragile control snapped. My mind entered its black vacuum. Screaming, I threw the new kitchen drawers on the floor, the cutlery clanging loudly as it hit the ceramic tiles, the crockery smashing. Berserk, I turned to attacking myself to numb the pain within. My children ran to bed without a sound.

I saw Prof a week later, on my 35th birthday. 'You're not to give up hope,' he said. 'You've had the illness more than 20 years and it will take time to get well.' I was too tired to think clearly, but thought 35 would be a good age to start LIVING. I told Prof about my madness episodes and that I was barely floating along. He hoped, like me, that my holiday would work wonders. For the first time in 20 months I had a two-week break from work coming up. George and I were taking our four children to Merimbula, a seaside town in southern New South Wales.

We did not know this would be our last family holiday.

14.ILLNESS ISOLATES AND CONQUERS

The summer of 1986 was our first free of farm jobs like milking cows, making hay and irrigation. We could be like most other families and take a holiday. I had never had a holiday with my parents and sister —the farm always came first. But George and I were striving to be 'normal'. We packed our four excited children in the car and set off on the five-hour journey to Merimbula. The back of our station wagon was bulging with clothing, beach towels, body boards and the children's Christmas present—an orange and blue inflatable rubber dinghy. This holiday was part of my New Year's resolution to 'get normal', so I wouldn't need prescription drugs and could enjoy being a mum and wife.

I was determined to address problems rather than suppress them and to avoid doing 'too much'. The urge to binge, I decided, was like an amber light, warning me to relax. My challenge was to recognise and arrest the urge before its trigger went off.

My defence was a calorie and fibre diet plan, which I began the first day of our holiday. I weighed 64.5kg and aimed to be 50kg by April 10, when George and I would celebrate our 15th wedding anniversary. My allowance was 1000 calories, with 30gm of fibre daily. After the first week I felt confident and determined this would be a marvellous year when I would kick anorexia and bulimia out of my head forever. By the time we returned home at the end of the second week I'd lost 4.5kg.

I know what you are thinking—this effort to be normal was doomed to fail. But at this time in my life, calorie-counting was engrained as a gear stick for getting through each day. I did not know any other way. My life was black or white, in control or out of control, no grey.

All went well until I returned to work and my stress trigger went off. It was St Valentine's Day, February 14, and I felt anything but romantic. The temperature was 37 degrees Celsius and coming home from work I binged on ice-cream, bread, watermelon and oranges. I wanted the temperature to drop, wanted my role at work straightened out, wanted to know if I would be resuming my studies; wanted time to relax and ride the bicycle that George had given me for Christmas; and wanted to be more involved with the children and local community.

Regarding my studies, Prof said to continue only if my boss allowed time for them. There was no way the editor would agree to this, but giving up my studies was not easy. I didn't like starting a project and not finishing it, and believed I'd need a Bachelor of Arts to get ahead, to get a position a man might get without a degree. George convinced me I could manage both study and work, but after another month of uncertainty and anxiety I agreed Prof was right: I couldn't work fulltime, look after four children and study as well. One of the three had to go. My children were top priority, work was essential as my income helped to support our family; the study had to cease. I felt dejected at this sacrifice though because that very week George was appointed captain of a winter tennis team. He would play almost every Saturday, including the following Saturday, which was our wedding anniversary. And Saturday was our only full day of the week together.

Cracks forged easily in my fragile sense of self. Instead of being happy for George, I thought, 'George likes his tennis more than me.' His work hours meant he was not home during the week until the children were in bed and now would be away most of Saturday as well.

I saw Prof Burrows. Told him I'm still adding weight and feel fed up with myself—feel as if a cloud is sitting upon me—if only I could lift it off, life would become carefree, easy, light and springy. The opposite of my present feelings. The aggravating part is that I don't know why I feel this way. I'm to see Prof B in another six weeks and by then I'll have seen a neurologist, and then, depending on those results, Prof B says he'll try a new approach.

Prof arranged for me to see a neurologist about my headaches. After

listening to my account, the neurologist concluded the injury from the log truck accident was causing the headaches and I would have to learn to live within that framework and do only what I could, without discomfort. I mentioned my difficulty in relaxing because of entrenched guilt and he said,
Remember your parents have the right and freedom to make choices for themselves, and likewise, you have the right and freedom to make choices for you.'

I felt a burden had been lifted—and tried to tell myself not to feel guilty for the choices I had made.

Meanwhile, George came home from work with the good news that he had been appointed assistant curator at Haileybury College. His knowledge of soil and irrigation had been noticed and he would be outdoors, working 'the land' again, albeit on parks and sports ovals instead of cow and vegetable paddocks. Moreover, his daytime work hours would allow us more time as a family.

George was doing well, but by mid-year I feared another relapse would send me over the edge.

I am determined to keep going one way only; henceforth, and that's forward. I am keeping a devout pledge with myself—I don't think I could take another relapse without going totally to pieces and that is unthinkable. Prof Burrows can't fathom me out. I am determined to show myself, and Prof, that I can be fathomed, that I can cure myself—with help.

It didn't help that my role as sub-editor on the *The Weekly Times* was unfulfilling. The editor said on starting the job that my role would be chief sub or editor of a new lift-out magazine but six months later, neither position had come to fruition. While weighing my options, a new editor, Kevin Boyle, was appointed. He seemed friendly and I hoped for a chance to improve myself.

At the same time, however, my illness began leading me down a new path of isolation and destruction. I became drawn to men who personified its traits of instability and insecurity. With my sense of self in tatters, I did not understand what was happening.

I had met Noel while working on *The Herald*. We travelled on the same train to work and chatted on the way. One morning, we entered the Flinders Street foyer of the newspaper office and were riding the lift to the editorial section on the second floor, when he grabbed and kissed me. I was stunned. He let me go as the lift doors opened. I'd admired Noel's wordsmith skills on the subs desk but had never felt attracted to him. George had been the only man to kiss or hold me for more than 20 years. If not for my illness, I would have slapped Noel's face and said, 'How dare you?' I'd have phoned George immediately and reported the incident to Human Resources.

But I had no strength to react.

Noel's kiss symbolised a new stage in the loss of my self. My deluded thought was: 'Noel must be good for me, because I'm not thinking about eating'. The time shared on the train was sufficient to convince my duped mind that he was the key to defeating my illness.

The force of this thought was magnetic. No matter what Prof said, I knew Noel was good for me. In his presence my illness disappeared. He filled my every need, so I thought. I had to believe this because I could not bear the thought of my eating disorder coming back. Noel had become my life raft and I clung like my life depended on it.

The chance to escape the horrid eating disorder that had plagued me since childhood outweighed any concern over the destruction of my marriage. This was my one big chance to escape a torment of more than 20 years.

In fleeting moments of clarity I knew I should feel guilty, but my eating disorder was a master manipulator. I believed my illness had gone. I was healed. Noel was my panacea.

Work pressures didn't bother me now.

A very hectic day at work. Noel helped me overcome what I know, without him, would have been an insatiable urge to eat and eat when I arrived home. Instead, thinking of him, I simply made a cuppa for the children and myself and took Sam Dog on a walk.

My effusive state initially misled Prof. I'd not binged since Noel had made his attentions known and that was three weeks ago now. He was my strength, my salvation.

Two nights later, when George came to bed, he asked what was on my mind, and why I was so 'cold'. I told him the truth. He was upset and angry. This continued next morning, which was a Saturday, and not until we had taken Amanda to her pony lesson, Shane and Rohan to hockey and Ben to a friend's home, did George express his feelings.

I broke down and cried. I didn't want to hurt him or the children. All I wanted was for us all to be happy, but in my desperate state I believed only Noel had the strength to cure my anorexic bulimic habit.

I still cared for George and continued to love him as father of our children. I cried and he cried and said awful things, including that I would have to take him to court to have custody of any of our children. The thought of having to fight for my children shook me to my core. But later George put the pain of his love aside and asked for a chance to talk to Prof, saying: 'If Prof believes being with Noel will help you, then I will help you go.' The situation was hard for both of us.

George's attitude fluctuated widely, wanting me to get well yet not wanting to lose me. Sadly he was no contest for my powerful illness. For almost five weeks, I had not binged. This was my longest period without a binge in 24 years. My headaches disappeared too. I believed my horrid 'food plague' was behind me, forever.

After discussing my intentions with a mate at his workplace, George said he would support me in finding a place to live and defend me against the expected flak from my family. 'If things don't work out, I want you to return home,' he said. Alternatively, he would sell our farm the following year if I wanted money for a house. He was being very brave and kind.

A week later I almost weakened—George was hoping I would change my mind and, not wishing to hurt him, I buttered a thick slice of bread and was about to eat it when I stopped. Putting the bread back on the kitchen bench, I phoned Prof and managed to grab hold, diffusing the urge to binge. I wanted George as a friend and companion and loved him as father of our children, but was convinced I needed Noel to get well.

August began with George 'letting fly', tormenting me in front of our children and telling them that I was in love with another man. Shane agreed with George that I was 'disgusting', telling me flatly: 'Mum, you are breaking one of the Ten Commandments.' George threw his wallet, saying: 'Get out and find a flat.'

George was hurting and I was too overtaken by my illness to respond rationally. He ranted and ranted and all I wanted to do was get well and achieve peace in my mind.

In 37 days I lost 8kg, and weighed 54kg. Concerned at my rapid weight loss, George said I shouldn't lose any more but, as always, 50kg was my goal.

Counting calories and exercising were the only ways I knew to reduce my anxiety, and I was doing both. I think I misled Prof with my progress. He said to cease taking the Frisium medication (Clobazam) and drop one Parnate tablet, taking three instead of four. Suspecting that Noel may back off, he said: 'I have told George he should be pleasant whether you decide to go or stay with him, because if you do go, the two of you will continue to have the children to care for as parents.'

I said, 'I fear without Noel I'll relapse and fall into my old bulimic ways and I would rather die than do that.' But I needed George too, as a friend and as father to our children.

The next night, in tears in bed, I told George I had shared my situation with our children, and he said, 'I suppose you've turned them against me.' No, I had praised him in glowing terms for living with me, and my illness. He was not the reason I was leaving our marriage; the reason was I had to beat the anorexia and bulimia that was scrambling my mind and eating holes in my soul.

George is not the prime issue—my first issue is to beat anorexia bulimia and all else that 'screws' my mind.

One night early in September, George's incessant efforts to reason with me sparked an explosion in my brain. In my irrational state, I felt that to give in to him would be to give into my illness. I might as well be dead.

George was at me and at me until I broke down and went berserk and punched my head hard and also my face and really knocked myself around, head bleeding. I cried and cried when George kept on; he cried too, later...

Prof was not convinced my food problems were over, but I would not listen to him either. On the weekend, George took me to look at a few flats and units, thinking a touch of reality might help me think more clearly, but driving around the suburban streets sent my head berserk and agitated my stomach. Too sick to look at anything, we returned home and I went back to bed. Curled in a foetal position, I rocked back and forward, my will broken, calling on God to take me and wishing to die. I felt terrible for dragging George into dark pits with me and wanted to free him to be happy. Then I thought of our children, and pleaded with God, bargained with Him, offering to give the rest of my life in return for two torment-free years with my children. George rubbed my back in an effort to ease my nausea and distress. He said I could have our bedroom until I left home. I felt sorry for hurting him and said he deserved a woman who did not have my illness.

I was exhausted from fighting my eating disorder. I hated it and hated me. I couldn't get away from it. I could see no way out.

I arranged to see Reverend Robin Prior at the Uniting Church Manse in The Avenue, Blackburn, to discuss my feelings. I'd always been moral-minded but now my beliefs and values were flying out the window.

During a three-hour session, in which I emptied a tissue box, I poured out my guilt. I described how I had used the terms of my pregnancies to try and gain control over my tormentor. I feared I'd had my children for the wrong reasons. Rev. Prior said there was no right or wrong reason to have a child. 'Each one is special,' he said, putting my mind at rest. 'You love your children, and that is the most important thing.'

After listening to me unravel the complexity of my life, Rev. Prior gently suggested I might find committing fully to God the safest option for healing my soul, but I couldn't contemplate that thought. My thinking process was totally inflexible. It was black and white. All or nothing. To contemplate anything between was too scary, way too scary. My anxiety was sky-high. I believed in God but needed Noel 100 per cent or I'd die. I felt ill thinking about it. My hold on reality was exceedingly fragile.

In the third week of September, Prof questioned why Noel avoided me. Noel had seen me only once, for two hours, in 10 days. Strange, when he professed to love me. Each day seemed like a year. I could have suspected I was being 'used' but that would have meant contemplating a grey area, so I trusted him, even when his procrastination and avoidance

On my wedding day, April 10, 1971. (I had fainted that morning).

Home on the farm at Sarsfield, 1972.

George and me with Shane, our firstborn, Christmas 1972.

Age 29, with children Amanda, Ben, Rohan and Shane, ages three to seven.

Living in Bairnsdale, 1984. Not a happy time for the children, due to my illness.

As Miranda in the 1990s at my desk on *The Weekly Times* newspaper.

Miranda

issues from the country
with June Alexander

Farm planning can save pain

Love plays a part in farming probably more than any other business.

While it gives strength when adversity strikes, it also causes pain when deciding who will carry on the family farm.

Solicitor Richard Dwyer, a former farm boy from Swan Hill and Bendigo, has led many seminars in Victoria and NSW on the handing on of the family farm.

"Probably the most difficult situation I deal with is with someone who no longer lives on the land, but still has strong affinity with it," Richard says.

Richard urges parents to arrange succession planning "while you are fit and well".

"Don't put it off," Richard says.

"Unfortunately, people like me can't help until parents or the next generation are prepared to talk.

"Thank goodness the problem is nowhere as big as it was a few years ago as rural counsellors have helped to break down the barriers.

"There is a greater awareness of the need to talk. Everyone knows one horror story of what can happen when families don't talk."

Accountants, who see their clients more often these days, also jog the farmers along by gently reminding them they are not getting any younger.

How the situation is handled may unite or divide a family.

Richard says superannuation and family trusts are the key to succession planning. These items, he says, are outside the will. Only assets left in the will can be challenged.

Families should assess their situation, share their aims, seek professional advice and act. It is sad when the farm goes to one person and ends up in the hands of creditors, but there are strategies to avoid this.

"I'm known as the 'three D man'," Richard says.

"Protection to deal with divorce, death and departure from the farm needs to be built in at the time the land is transferred from the parents."

To safeguard their lifetime work, should things not pan out as planned, parents can retain an option to lease back their property for 25 years or so at a peppercorn rental. They can also place restraints on the mortgaging of the land, he says.

Rather than risk the transfer of land to a young person not well established with his family life, a family trust offers protection for all concerned.

"Unfortunately many issues are not addressed until circumstances such as illness or divorce suddenly confront the farming family," Richard says.

"To prevent potential financial or property loss, parents should seek advice and take action while all is well in the family unit."

● Family trusts, superannuation and age pensions are among the topics to be covered by Richard Dwyer in a seminar at Inverleigh on August 22. For details, phone Richard on (03) 5273-5246.

June

As Miranda, I raised social issues and enjoyed interaction with people on the land. 'Farm planning can save pain' was one of many weekly columns written from the heart.

I was Miranda on *The Weekly Times* newspaper from 1993-2004. Work provided a much-needed sense of self-worth.

George and I after 15 years marriage, 1986. I had recently started treatment.

Beside the dam that 'leaked' the family secret.

Shane and Angeli's wedding, May 2008. From left: George's partner Roselyn, George, June, Rohan, Angeli, Ben, Shane, Amanda, Lachlan, Nick and Anke.

With my parents, Lindsay and Anne, on the farmhouse verandah, 2008.

With grandson Ashton Cherubim Coster, five months, and Olivia Rose Snart, three months, 2010.

Olivia Rose and me, early 2010.

was increasing my anxiety. I was about to crumble when, in the first week of October, he saw me for an entire 90 minutes. That was sufficient time to inspire me to hunt for accommodation. I found a three-bedroom unit, four kilometres from home, and applied for it. George looked at it too, and liked it. We paid the bond and I signed a six-month lease.

In tears, I saw Rev. Prior again. A great comfort, he helped me sort out my options. He said the most important thing was my own relationship with God, and if I felt God meant for me to be with another man then God would not act harshly, that it would be part of His plan in helping me to do my best in my life. Rev. Prior again suggested a safer option would be to forget about other men for a while and seek refuge in a total relationship with God.

Sorry God, but right now the void in my soul is too frightening to confront.

My illness was at its worst. George had not changed. He was the same man I had married 15 years before. He was solid and reliable: he was the antithesis of my illness that thrived on chaos and manipulation. I was the same woman too, except my illness was occupying about 95 per cent of my mind. It drove me to live on the edge, dangerously so.

I was trying to hang on to my sanity until my lease started. My parents, informed of my impending move out of the family home, made a weekend visit, which was most unusual, but I supposed the circumstances were unusual. Both tried to understand, but were disappointed about the breakdown of my marriage. 'You are placing scars on your children's lives forever,' my father said, but both he and my mother said: 'Look ahead, not back.'

I wonder if Dad knows about the childhood scars on my life and that of my sister.

My unit became available a few days later. While I was collecting Amanda from Brownies and cooking tea, George tossed my clothing into the car, tied my bed on the roof rack and drove to the unit. He threw everything on the lounge room floor, returned home and filled the car again. I managed to grab a few baking utensils and small items like vases and photographs of the children before George drove me to the unit, unloaded and left. I pushed the queen-size double-base bed from lounge to bedroom, made my bed and hung my clothes in the walk-in robe. By now it was after midnight. I was up at 5.05am and felt strange boarding the train at a different railway station to go to work. After work I went to the local shops, a kilometre from the unit, to buy an iron, ironing board, rubbish bin, clothes' basket, broom, mop and bucket and other items. With no car, I struggled carrying them to my unit, but didn't mind, believing every painful step was a step towards recovery.

A week later, I went to our family home and prepared afternoon tea for Ben and Amanda while George was at work. Amanda was condemning of me but Ben kept telling her to 'ease off'. Amanda appeared to be absorbing much of George's woe. She said, 'Dad's angry and says he'll shoot you if you take me from him.'

I said, 'I hope he'll use a pop gun,' and she gradually thawed. By the time I escorted her to her ballet class, a 10-minute walk from home, she was chatting like her usual bubbly self. Ben wanted to live with me, so I decided to suggest to George that Rohan and Ben live with me and Shane and Amanda with him, with access both ways.

Noel continued to postpone his arrival and saw me for maybe an hour every three or four days. I struggled to concentrate at work. I was sliding into my old quagmire. Joy and Mum wrote to assure me of their love, support and acceptance of Noel, though, as Mum wrote, I must allow them time to absorb the shock. George's mum wrote, imploring me to come to my senses and get home to George. I ate myself numb almost every night.

Such a wreck. If only Noel could be with me. I am anxious; that's why I eat. Well, I ate myself to 'knockout' stage last night and am doing so again tonight. I will set out a 24-day food diary tomorrow, and stick to it, strictly, until Nov. 15 comes as Noel assures me he will join me that night. If he doesn't, I'll be well on the way to death. I am anxious he won't come—I suppose because already he has deferred the date twice.
I went to see Prof, and am going again on Monday, 'cos I am slipping.

By now I was seeing Prof twice a week, to try to halt my slipping.

Acting on Prof's advice that 'action beats anxiety', I arranged to see a Family Law solicitor. Relating George's and my business and property transactions during the past 16 years, took several hours. Reflecting on our many moves helped me put my life in perspective and understand why I was so tense. 'How wonderful I feel to be off that spinning top,' I thought.

I arranged valuations of our house and farm and visited my children as often as possible, telling them I loved them every time I spoke to them. Rohan moved in with me but Ben remained with George.

My illness encouraged me to distrust George—I decided he wanted me to be in a mental hospital because he seemed most supportive when I was regressing and not coping. To a normal person, George's behaviour would be considered very caring, but I was not thinking normally.

In reality, George wanted me to go home. 'The door is open,' he said. I wanted to go home but feared my illness would torture me.

George says I only want to do what I want to do. (He said to write that.) All the drama. I cracked last night—George refused to take some pavlova home—the children had been for a visit and Amanda wanted a slice for him. I handed the plate to him, asked him to take it for the children's sake—still he refused and walked away, so I dropped it where I stood, on the pavement at my back door, and ran inside, too upset to farewell the children. And poor Rohan picked the 'smashed' pav up, later. I ate until I felt sick. Stupid. Stupid. This morn at work I had tears rolling down my face. I phoned George—horrid in his attitude. I suggested he see Prof, and wow, he did—obviously hasn't liked what he heard, even though Prof has offered George counselling help and said that he'd have more hope of a reconciliation if he would be more like 'sugar than vinegar', and that while I feel less tense with Noel than George, only time will tell if it is the answer 'cos it's 'my head' that counts. I wish George would accept some of the help offered to him.

As for Noel, he continued to fail to turn up. Prof said there were two possible reasons: either I was a game for him; or he was unable to make decisions for himself. I didn't like either of these possibilities. My intense distress eased, however, when Noel said he would be with me on

December 23.

I counted the hours to this new deadline while knocking myself out with more food. While I slept, sweat from panic attacks poured through the pores of my skin and soaked my bedding. December 21 was a Sunday and my happiest day since leaving the family home because all four children came for a visit. Shane was 14 that day, and Amanda would be 10 the next day. My children were my best medicine, but my negative voice, the tormentor, clung to Noel. On December 23, he announced yet another postponement—to Christmas Eve. I clung to this latest promise. George was taking our children to Merimbula for a holiday and I'd be alone for Christmas if not for Noel. My life was on hold for him.

On Christmas Eve, Noel wasn't with me but I wasn't alone. I was in a psychiatric hospital.

I had 'snapped'.

15. FIRST STEP TO RESTORATION

December 24: I'm in hospital. At least it is better than being in my unit 'prison'. I don't know what to think—I don't like thinking—I am devastated emotionally...

Lying on a bed in the Melbourne Clinic, a private psychiatric hospital, on Christmas Day, I thought wistfully of George and our children. They would be enjoying lunch and exchanging gifts on the family farm before driving further east for their holiday at Merimbula. Events that led me to the clinic in Richmond were too painful to think about.

Noel had reneged one more time. I held out until 2pm on Christmas Eve, completing my newspaper work, before insisting on seeing him to seek assurance he would be with me that night.

He would go no further than the street pavement outside the office to talk and said, 'I can't be with you tonight, but will visit you tomorrow.' Not even I would believe this. Walking beside him as he returned to *The Herald* newsroom, I collapsed in the corridor on the polished linoleum floor, thumping my head on it until my world went black. I had not seen or heard from Noel since. The HWT medical staff cared for me until a taxi was arranged to take my close friend and colleague, Bernadette, and me to the Austin Hospital, where Prof arranged my admission to the clinic.

December 25 1986 ranked as my unhappiest and dopiest Christmas Day. Groggy due to prescription drugs, I managed to give George a quick call at the farm to let him know where I was, and gave the clinic phone number, 'in case the children call'. My 36th birthday two days later was best forgotten, except for a visit 'out of the blue' from Joy and her little daughter Anne-Louise. A phone call from my children would have cheered me more than any of the medication, which helped me sleep at night but dulled my mind during the day. Despite my grogginess I did something positive on December 29 and went to work for the first time since my calamity on Christmas Eve. I worked for half a day and my mind was clear enough to accomplish a few editorial tasks.

The next day I returned to work full time. My colleagues brightened me and one, Julie, presented a lovely bunch of roses for my birthday. Several of my colleagues who had experienced a broken marriage, assured me I would get through this difficult time.

The editor was compassionate when I explained my marriage break-up and the cause of my blackout the previous week. We agreed that I would keep working for now and take a holiday later. Prof had suggested that keeping to a routine was important and I enjoyed my work and the company in the newsroom.

Mum did not suggest I should return to George but knew I cared for him as a friend and that we both cared for and loved our four children. Both sides of the family now knew of our marriage break-up. Prof said I could discharge myself from the clinic when I felt strong enough but to return if afraid of not coping.

I celebrated New Year's Day by going home. The husband of another patient kindly dropped me off at my unit about 8.30pm.

Alone, with the radio on and bleary eyes, and a thick head and sleepy head. Very weary. Gee, no trouble falling asleepy [sic]. George will be back tis [sic.] time next week. Well, I took the 'bull by the horns', friends giving me advice, telling me not to contact Noel. This is hopeless. I keep falling asleep. Noel I did not see; seems he is out of my life. I'm falling asleep and must go to bed.

Several drugs, including Tranxene (clorazepate dipotassium), sedated and kept me calm and mostly happy. In a clear moment I thought the New Year was a good time to start making up for the months I'd 'lost' while attracted to Noel.

My children returned from their Merimbula holiday suntanned and happy. Their dad returned with a fresh resolve, 'I refuse to do anything more about our divorce until you are better.' George was taking a wise and firm stand, but my illness was a formidable opponent. Neither of us knew how to fight it. I continued to block my feelings with food. One Saturday afternoon, feeling bereft, I binged and was 'knocked out' from 7pm until 10am. Fifteen hours of oblivion. Barely 'hanging on', each day was a new mountain to climb. Often a full day was too scary to contemplate, so I divided it into quarters to make it more manageable. Survive until 10.30am, and then focus on 1pm, 4pm and evening. Evenings were the toughest. I frequently went all day without food and then stuffed myself at night.

Once I started to eat, I could not stop until I dropped, so I delayed starting for as long as possible. I had no control and wondered how people knew instinctively to eat when hungry and to stop when full.

I tried to move on with my life. Between upsetting and knocking myself out with food every second day, I attended to arranging child access and completing the property settlement with George. There were anxious moments, especially when my solicitor suggested my admission to the Melbourne Clinic would hinder my chances of obtaining custody of my children. Not for the first time, I feared I'd be deemed an unfit mother. Such judgment would finish me off for sure. Without my children I could not live. They were my light.

The new school year was about to start and I longed to return home for one big reason: to be with all of my children.

I accomplished something positive for Rohan at least, enrolling him in Year Eight at Blackburn High. He had been at Scotch College for a year, but with my unexpected medical expenses—I did not have private health insurance—and the purchase of a house to consider, I could not afford private school fees. Blackburn High, a government school, was a bicycle ride from home, and Rohan was happy about this.

I arranged a loan from my workplace Credit Union to pay the private clinic bill and obtained extra work, as a sub-editor on the *Sunday Press* newspaper on Saturday nights, to meet the repayments. This meant I was working six days a week, but I did not mind. Focusing on writing, editing and layouts and joking with colleagues, helped me to live in the moment and supress illness thoughts for a while.

Nothing, however, could overcome or divert the pain of being separated from my children. I suggested to George that if I lived in the flat at the rear of our house I could mind our children when he was out and when he was home he would see little if anything of me. He was getting on with his social life, playing tennis and going to dances. He said he would think about it. Later he said he didn't want me in the flat because: 'I don't want you on the property when I'm bringing friends home.'

George blamed Prof for our marriage breakup and Mum and Joy suggested I was wasting my time seeing him. 'Why are you still seeing that doctor?' Joy asked. 'If he hasn't cured you yet, he can't be any good.' But Prof was one of few people in whom I had trust and faith. He understood my illness.

Feeling powerless and misunderstood by my family, the tiniest achievements became very important. My potplants provided a precious sense of purpose. I carried them inside and outside my rented unit, depending on the weather, and a new shoot, leaf or bud was enough to brighten my day. Another positive was that I was walking for an hour each evening. Exercise helped me feel strong and connected with the world.

Gradually George became more friendly and willing to help me move on. He said he would start negotiations to sell our farm the next week, and, 'Ben boy will definitely be with you; we just need to decide access arrangements.' Touched by his compassion, my tears ran like rivers.

Prof said, 'You are improving but should stay on the Tranxene medication.' He suggested that when my anxiety and stress levels subsided, so would my urge to eat. Rather than eat only at night, Prof said to spread my food intake into three or four meals a day, consuming up to 2000 calories, and yes, it was okay to count them.

(Today we know the importance of three meals and three snacks a day—regular meals and snacks are vital in overcoming an eating disorder and maintaining recovery—but forget the calorie counting. Calorie counting, remember, gives a false sense of security.)

Getting well was a slip, slide, slog. George let our four children stay overnight with me while he went to a dance. I was glad to have the children but did not like the thought of George dancing with another woman. We had always danced as one. We had been inseparable. I had to try and divert such thoughts because they were painful and debilitating.

I will not make headway thinking like this.

My lease on the unit had ended and, not wanting to renew it, I needed somewhere to go. One evening after work, George and our children accompanied me to look at a unit nearer his home, but it was too small.

We had returned to George's home for a moment when my blackness swooped in. A myriad of pain and pressure burst in my mind with one mighty bang. I hit my head repeatedly against the plaster wall in his lounge room. My head was bleeding. George and Shane restrained me on the carpeted floor. One held my ankles, the other my shoulders, but I continued to bang my head, frothing at my mouth, wishing the wall and floor were concrete and brick, wanting to hit my head harder and stay in my blackness. My tormentor had all but taken me and I wanted to go with it. George asked Shane to call Rev. Prior, who came to the house quickly, and I cried as his great big arms enveloped me. He offered to drive me back to my unit but I declined; the 50-minute walk would help calm me. George drove Rohan home in the car later. My head was sore and throbbing, my heart broken.

The following week George helped Rohan and me move out of my unit and let us stay at his house. Rohan slept in his old room with Ben, I slept in a single bed in a small back room and George was in the main bedroom at the front.

Six months had passed since our separation, and we went to the Family Law Court. Terrified my illness would be raised and I would lose my children, I was relieved to learn that Ben would join Rohan in my custody and care within a month, and assets would be shared 50–50. Neither George nor I would pay maintenance because we had two children each. No mention was made of my mental or emotional state. Everyone was respectful and I sensed compassion in the judge's address, as though he knew about my illness and appreciated how vital the children were for my wellbeing.

George also surprised me by now agreeing to attend marriage counselling. He said, 'If it doesn't work, at least we will have tried and the preparations for divorce will have been completed.'

This positive news eased my emotional and mental agony, but medication was keeping me in a zombie-like state. Despite the medication, I was constantly anxious, scared to make a decision, big or small.

George and I travelled together to see the marriage counsellor, who was a retired minister and clinical psychologist. I encouraged George to see Prof with me regularly as well, so we could work on our relationship and my illness together, but George indicated we had little chance of reconciliation. I didn't blame him. He was starting to get on with his life, free of my illness. I wanted us to be together for our children's sake and financial security, but we also needed love and my illness right now had robbed us of that. 'Whatever you decide,' I told George, 'I will understand, and care for your welfare always.' He replied, 'I can't be bothered with more hassles. The best solution might be to live apart and be friends.'

I clung to simple joys, such as my pot plants and the warmth of a sunny autumn day. Meanwhile, George was attending more dances for Parents Without Partners and was playing tennis—I was glad he was connecting with others, was happy and moving forward, but as for me, I was very unsure about which way was forward, and panic attacks were intensifying.

My lawyer, concerned about my health, phoned Prof. I was bingeing, my confidence was zero and I had gained 7kg in six weeks. My lawyer and Prof said I was 'attractive and intelligent' and must focus on getting healthy. Slight steps forward came with the news our farm had sold, and George arranged a loan from his parents so I could buy a property and vacate his house. I was to pay 10 per cent interest and repay the full amount within six months.

I found my 'dream home' in *The Age* property guide. George accompanied me on an inspection and we agreed it would be a good buy. I paid a deposit and procured a 30-day settlement. The three-bedroom brick-veneer house was a 15-minute walk from George's house and a 20-minute walk from the train station. The walk times were important as I remained too anxious to drive a car. I began counting the days until June 5, when Rohan, Ben and I could move into our new home.

Having cleared my Credit Union loan for the clinic fees, I arranged a housing loan at 16 per cent interest. Meanwhile, George was taking a new woman out on Friday night. He said he wouldn't be coming home. So he was getting into serious dating. 'No point dwelling on this, I must get out of my shell, take a leaf out of George's book and start socialising,' I told myself. Perhaps I would join Parents Without Partners too.

On May 11, Rohan celebrated his 13th birthday. He was a quiet boy, solitary, insightful and supportive. I tried to be strong, but two days after his birthday:

I hit the pits last night. Soaked, absolutely soaked. Ate myself to sleep by 5.30pm. Children waiting for their tea. So unfair on them. I have decided that I can go no lower than this—I can go only one way: up. Have eaten five litres ice cream in two or three days. Also a loaf of bread. Awful. And of course saturated all my bedding. Robin, like my lawyer, suggests I'm not ready for Parents Without Partners, so I'll wait and ask Prof on Friday.

Rev Prior, like my lawyer, suggested I repair my soul before turning to Parents Without Partners. But looking into my soul was too painful a thought, too confronting and scary for the little bit left of me.

Prof agreed I was not ready for socialising because my anxiety was extreme. He advised that I return to the Melbourne Clinic for more intensive support until I could move into my house. 'You can go to work from there, and the cost will be nothing compared with the worth of your sanity, your life,' he said.

I went home, ate myself numb and fell asleep. I moved into the clinic the next day, missing my children enormously, but I was no good to them while sick. Recovery had to be my priority. I had upgraded my health insurance, but on my third day discovered it did not cover the full fees. To avoid another big bill, I discharged myself and became 'homeless', carting my clothes to the newspaper office in a few garbage bags like a gypsy. A workmate told me of a motel near the clinic. The rooms were cheap but clean and comfortable, and I could get to work easily, via tram and foot.

With temporary accommodation organised, I focused on living again. Prof said to avoid clubs for singles and concentrate on my children, the church, craftwork, my house, work and friends. Next day my children called to say George's date had jilted him; they thought this funny, but I suggested they not let their dad see them smile.

After a week in the motel, I moved back to George's house because in nine days I could move into my new home and I needed to pack. Life was appearing brighter, with fresh possibilities:

I have moved back to George's house. Only nine more days. Hurry up and go. I thank God I have seen Prof today ... he said George was not the answer, and neither was Noel—there would be someone else. He is right. His advice for surviving the next nine days is:

1) Avoid George as much as possible

2) Give attention to the children

3) Concentrate on success at work and planning my future

4) Think about my house

5) Control my eating. He set a 1200 calorie limit; so this I will do—for Prof, for me.

I ate myself silly last night but have eaten nothing so far today -- so will keep record from today.

I HAVE TO FIGHT AND WIN THIS TIME.

I attended to the settlement regarding my house, arranged phone, electricity, gas and water connections and received comfort and strength from a prayer and healing meeting at Church. I enrolled Ben at a primary school at the end of our street.

On the eve of moving house, Prof gave me 10 out of 10 for being positive. I was to stick with 1200 calories daily for the next week, and could join a singles' group. I made calls from the *Yellow Pages* that night and selected one with more than 400 members and a large social calendar, including bushwalking. The next 'get-to-know-you' meeting would be in a privatae home in a neighbouring suburb the very next evening. Seizing the moment I said: 'I'll be there.'

Little did I know when I went out that next night, after a day of making beds and unpacking boxes, that my journey of recovery and restoration would continue for another two decades.

There would be many tumultuous times as I struggled to weave together the threads of my identity, and separate them from the thoughts and feelings that belonged to my eating disorder. There was a big mountain to climb, with avalanches and ravines along the way. I would have painful lessons as I gingerly put one foot in front of the other, unsure if I was on the right track for me or on the track developed by my devious eating disorder.

At the age of 38, I wrote:

... for years I have been searching, seeking my identity, my purpose, my meaning, in life. Years. I've concluded that I am a prisoner to myself. And if I don't set myself free, if I don't take a stand, I will live the rest of my life feeling frustrated, and unfulfilled; I will not know the joy of inner peace, or the achievements I can enjoy if my energies are set free in a positive way. I can see that, for many years, since I fell prey to anorexia nervosa, much of my creative energy has been wasted in a negative way, for I have turned it on myself; my own private obsession with food has robbed me of my true self.

I have had some hard lessons. I know I can live with myself only if I accept that my mistakes, my bad experiences, can be the catalyst, the seed, for new beginnings and fulfilment.

I find great difficulty in understanding myself, my behaviour, but I must try to understand myself, my fears, my needs, if I am to correct myself and live out the rest of my life free from the nasty inhibitions that have plagued my inner self for so long.

At the time, my medication comprised four Parnate and three Tranzene pills daily. The type of medication would change as new drugs came on the market or Prof decided another would be more appropriate. Sometimes I felt very uncertain, not knowing if my feelings were due to my illness, the medication or the 'real' me.

Several of the drugs have since been banned.

Aside from medication and psychotherapy, I continued to find strength in my Christian faith. George—who met a new partner, Roselyn, soon after our divorce—remained a rock of support, and our children were my constant inspiration.

I read extensively and slowly gained self-awareness.

At the age of 39, I welcomed 1990 with a revelation, acknowledging the futility of calorie counting:

Happy new resolve, happy new me. Farewell to bulimia. Farewell to counting calories, farewell to bingeing, farewell to starving. Hello to counting portions for this year as I rid myself of all bulimic behaviour. This year is the year I GROW. No more wasted energy on bulimic torment. Positive growth. No more dwelling on things I cannot change—therefore no more wasted energy. I will, with God's guidance, concentrate on those things I can change. This is the year, the decade, I make a move on establishing myself as a writer, apart from a journalist. This is my mission. This, and to enjoy and guide my children. Forward, forward. Life is too short to waste on things/people which/who cannot/don't want to change.

At least I was on the right track now, but retraining thought patterns and finding a replacement for the calorie-counting behaviour was a challenge. Whenever a stressful moment occurred, which was often, I went on automatic pilot, resorting to calorie counting as a coping mechanism.

Only two weeks later:

This day is the LAST, the very LAST, terrible day I will ever have due to bingeing. I made myself feel absolutely terrible and unable to think straight.

My first priority is to reduce to 52–53kg and stay there. Nothing else matters. An average 1200 calories daily. Keeping to this goal is all-important. I am fighting this thing inside me unto its death; this is the transition of me, afflicted by anorexia nervosa at age 11 and then bulimia wreaking havoc on my thoughts and behaviour, me, setting me FREE from all this to enjoy life, to give, to grow. This is what I am doing; 28 years is ENOUGH. The rest of my life I shall be FREE of the horrid torment.

My relationship with my parents and sister became more estranged:

May 1990: I have started a lot of new lives. I expect I have one more to start, because I have mucked up so far. I will start as soon as I get a hold on things. I suppose starting by dieting will be better than not starting at all.

I am feeling quite out of kilter. I phoned Mum this morning. I told her I felt unhappy and hurt when she did not visit me yesterday (she came to Melbourne to visit George but not me). I feel I come somewhere near last in her list of priorities. It is not a nice feeling. She said something about 'sometimes you do things you don't really want to do'. But that is really no excuse. I don't think I will visit her next Sunday (Mother's Day); rather

be with my four children. I am just not ready to cope with this rejection
stuff, which hits at my very core and has left me such a confused person,
unable to fully appreciate my own children, because I have felt unwanted
for so long—since 11 years old, at least. The most horrible thing is to feel
unwanted, rejected, by one's parents. After all, they are the reason one is
here.

The perceived rejection from my family made me vulnerable with the opposite sex, and for years I lived life 'on the edge' while struggling to overcome the gulf of darkness within my soul.

I married another two times—within days of divorcing George, in the late 1980s, and again in the mid-1990s. Both relationships were highly charged and chaotic like my illness. They could not last. However, I remain friends with each partner and am grateful to them and others who have shared my journey. Some men commented that I had more than one 'voice' and they did not know which was the real me. Other men replicated my illness characteristics with dominating and manipulative behaviours. Such romances were inevitably exciting but in a state of continual unrest. Extracting myself from unstable, insecure rollercoaster relationships that fed my illness was a difficult and tedious process.

I remained in these unhealthy relationships, which Prof called 'mistakes' for years, too scared to let go. It was small comfort to know that a 'mistake' would become a 'lesson' if I learnt from it. The genuine me could see that such a relationship was maintaining my illness and allowing it to keep me a prisoner. The problem was that attachment to the relationship was as strong as the attachment of my illness to me. In my quest to be me, I had to develop sufficient strength and self-belief to confront and overcome the illness behaviours. Only then would I be free—free to be safe, secure and stable.

Along the way, I met caring, loyal and stable men who could identify my illness behaviours and were drawn to the real me. George and my friends would approve and say encouragingly, 'He's a good man,' but I would feel I did not deserve such men; their compassion made me feel suffocated and on edge, so I would push them away. Deep down I knew I had to overcome the fear of being alone, and learn to withstand my illness, and trust and respect myself.

I had to learn skills to manage my anxiety. I had to learn to eat three meals and three snacks daily, without fail. Only then would I have the best foundation for a healthy relationship with my self, and be open to a healthy relationship with others.

16. FILLING IN THE GAPS

Forward steps came slowly. There was no quick fix. More like drops of water, one after the other, on my head, slowly penetrating and eroding my illness. My friend Helen from school bus days could not understand my struggle but remained a steadfast support. She often expressed a wish for a large acorn to fall and land strategically on my head with sufficient force to spark rational thinking. Gradually the combination of therapy, medication, and love of family and friends instilled me with sufficient courage and trust to step out and regain more of me. At the end of the day, if it was to be, it was up to me. I had to believe in my SELF and ignore my illness.

April 8, 1991: I have been reading a relaxation book suggested by Prof and today I'm starting the rest of my life, my new life, and the focus of it is: be kind to myself. I really believe I have found the key to my cure of anorexia bulimia—and the answer is simple: respect myself in every way, including my energy intake (food, drink). I am looking after my total health—having enough sleep, enough of the right foods, enough exercise and so on. And I am learning to manage my time. I am now putting myself first.

Sometimes I needed time out—for me.

January 2, 1992: Here I am, in a lovely room in the Melbourne Clinic. I was ambivalent about coming, right up to the clinic's doorstep, but at last I am doing something for myself and therefore for others. I yearn to be 'free' in my mind of the wretched obsessive thoughts about FOOD. Prof explained that the two Adifax tablets I'm taking daily contain a drug or chemical that he believes may balance the deficiency of this drug in my body (it's in

everyone but tends to be less in anorexics/bulimics). But a check on my
blood pressure shows it is quite low (unusual for me) and Prof says this
could be due to Adifax, so I'm to have blood tests tomorrow and will be
able to go home 'in a few days'. At least I've private health cover now to
help meet my expenses.

(Adifax was a serotoninergic anorectic drug approved in the mid-1990s by the United States Food and Drug Administration for the purposes of weight loss. However, following multiple concerns about cardiovascular side effects of the drug, such approval was withdrawn. I took this medication for about two years, with unpleasant side effects, including loss of libido.)

April 1, 1992: I am a guinea pig again, on a new drug called Prozac20,
which has 'serotonin' in more potent form. Prof says trials show this drug
is helping many anorexics and bulimics; he says it has many side effects;
so many he won't give me the details except to say I could feel nauseous,
have diarrhoea and feel jittery. I will start the pills tomorrow. Prof said I
won't feel the effects for three to four weeks.

I would build up to taking 80mg of Prozac daily.

May 24, 1992: I have run four kilometres without stopping and feel pleased
with my effort. I have got myself worked out now: I am NOT counting
calories again. I am setting myself free. Silly, isn't it? I've taken 30 years to
let go of this form of control and as recent as last week I was being tempted.
But I can see the folly of that now. No more will I stuff myself silly, thinking
that I'll gorge myself today and diet (starve) myself 'tomorrow'. I mean,
after 30 years of trying, and failing, I can see this line of control is simply
doomed to fail. I realise I might take the rest of this year to stabilise, while
I convince myself that there is no need to binge or overeat today as it's
okay, I can eat when I feel hungry tomorrow.

By September, 1992:

I want to go off Prozac and take nothing. My head feels so strange. I want to be 'me' and I'll cope, however I can, living with limitations brought on by chemical imbalances. This is because every drug I take has side effects; it might help me in one way but bothers me in another, and life becomes very confusing.

My biggest problem is I don't know who I am. I know I'm a mother to my four children but feel incapable as a parent and don't know how I feel in a relationship with a man. Sexually I am in limbo and am 14kg overweight. My top priority must be to find my centre, to identify who I am, and work from this base.

A dietician assured me:

... anorexia is completely environmental—cannot be inherited—and therefore treatment should include the entire family (especially parents and child) for treatment to be successful. This is good news regarding my concerns for Amanda, but disheartening news regarding my relationship with my parents, my mother especially, and my sister.

(Today, evidence-based research is yet to provide a specific answer but suggests anorexia is a brain disorder, influenced by genetics, environment, personality, biological makeup and life events.)

A family event in 1993 led to a big step forward in regaining me:

George's dad is celebrating his 90th birthday with a party this weekend and I'm experiencing a deep pain of rejection because I am not invited. When I spoke with George today, he had no apology for me being snubbed and not being invited. My children, my parents and my sister and all of her family are invited, and attending. I feel painfully alone and am having great difficulty restraining my tears.

This was one of those times when I hit rock bottom, grabbed hold of the thread that was me, and amazingly found new strength. Strength came with the realisation that no matter how much my family ignored me, the bottom line was they could not take away my right to be born. They could take my life and hurt me only if I let them. By snubbing me they helped me to find the motivation to live my own life.

The very next week I started the process of adopting my birth name: June Alexander.

This is my name; this is me.

First I went the motor registration office and arranged for a name change on my driver's licence. Immediately I felt 'more me'.

I've faith that as June Alexander I will rebuild my identity and set myself free. Even if I meet another man with whom I'd like to share my life, I will remain June Alexander.

I notified the *Herald* and *Weekly Times'* human resources department of my 'new' name.

My new ID card has JUNE ALEXANDER on it. I told Nick (newspaper editor) of my name change and he was understanding, saying: 'Is this to help you establish your identity?' and I said: 'Yes, to help me know who I am.'

Other big steps forward occurred within weeks. Encouraged by my children, I purchased a small car, took refresher driving lessons and gained the courage to drive on suburban streets. Now I could drive to the supermarket and I could collect Amanda from George's house to go shopping and swimming together. For the first time since my divorce eight years earlier, Amanda and I began having mother-daughter time. One memorable day I pushed aside my fears, gripped the wheel and drove across the city to watch Amanda row for her school in a championship event. My sense of self was gradually being rebuilt. Each time I stepped out bravely in faith, a reward seemed to follow.

Shortly after, the newspaper editor offered me my dream job—that of Country Living editor and columnist as Miranda, on *The Weekly Times*. I would hold the Country Living editor position for the next seven years, and that of Miranda for the next 11 years—until I departed the newspaper in 2004.

My illness was being pushed to the sidelines, but sometimes it hit back. In 1996:

I'm in the depths of despair. I must take hold of myself. I feel I need four to eight weeks off work, to nurture myself back to health. I have regressed about three years in the past six months and especially since I sold my house. The way J (the new man in my life) has been behaving isn't helping. I'm eating erratically, almost non-stop. I need to make decisions and stick to them. But I make them and go to pieces anyway, so can only presume I've been making the wrong decisions so far and I really must make the right one and look after my diet.

I'm wafting along, out of control. Sinking, sinking, silently screaming inside. Help me! I am losing my identity. I thought I would not get like this again. I am scaring myself.

I will seek help this week. I feel dreadful but will be courageous and see my dietician, and also see Prof and, if need be, I'll have to accept medication. I'm eating nearly non-stop, eating so I don't feel my feelings through.

Having said this, I don't know why, but seems like I will move in with J. I've counted up and this will be my 14th house move in 26 years. That's an average of more than one move every two years.

Prof says it is no wonder my bulimia is the worst it has been in four years: I've sold my house, met a man, am thinking about buying another house and am in a new family situation.

In 1998, at age 47, I met therapist Belinda Dalton. I was referred to her initially for a dietician appointment. Instead of talking about food, however, Belinda talked about feelings. Her empathy and compassion quickly won my trust. She was the first therapist I met who suggested that separating my thoughts and behaviours from those of my illness would assist in regaining my identity. Slowly I began to recognise the thoughts and feelings that did not belong to me; then came the hard part of catching those thought triggers and diffusing them before they went off. There were slips and slides but over the next eight years, under Belinda's gentle guidance and encouragement, I practised and eventually mastered this mindfulness and self-awareness skill. It became a major tool in not only regaining, but also protecting and maintaining my soul and sense of self. As I gained trust in my self, my illness lost its power. Food became just that—food—and I was no longer drawn into relationships that fed my illness. Belinda remains part of my ongoing support team.

At the same time, depression over the pain in my neck led my long-time supportive GP, Yael Bodian, to refer me to Mr Graeme Brazenor, a neurosurgeon at the Epworth Hospital in Melbourne. Twenty-seven years had passed since I drove under the log truck. Mr Brazenor gave my efforts to create a 'new me' a real boost, taking out the four damaged vertebrae and three discs at the top of my spine, and inserting 6cm of titanium rod. Technological advances had made this operation possible. At my first consultation with Mr Brazenor, he was impressed with my determination to maintain quality of life despite my spinal injury. He promised to take away 90 per cent of my pain. And he did.

Two days after the operation:

I've had X-rays and it was eerie to see the results of my operation —the titanium rod standing out like a vertical dumbbell in my neck. Everyone is amazed at how well I am doing for a major operation. I've eaten all my meals and I've walked a lot around the wards and made new friends. Details of my rod: 6cm long; buttressed each end from C4 toT1, four discs and three vertebrae taken out. My neurosurgeon said: 'I'm very pleased. Within three months you can expect a pain-free neck'.

For months I marvelled at the 'eerie' silence in my head and neck, after 27 years of grating, grinding and clicking. It took some adjusting. I felt Mr Brazenor had gifted me with a new life and I wanted to make the most of it.

A month later:

I've received a very good report from my neurosurgeon, which has been a big shot of sunshine in an otherwise stressful day. I learnt that I am about 15mm taller than before my operation, I am the 36th person in the WORLD to have the operation and I am the FIRST such person to be without a brace.

I asked 'why me?' and Mr Brazenor replied: 'because you're sane'. 'You're sensible'. Coming from a neurosurgeon that is music to my ears!

For several months I tried living without prescription drugs for my eating disorder and co-morbidity, but soon fell into a 'black pit', lacking the strength to make decisions that were in my best interest. A counsellor at my church encouraged me to take the medication that Prof was persistently prescribing.

Prof is pleased that I've resumed taking medication. I feel more calm, less bothered and have been able to detach myself emotionally from (the man in my life) in the past week. Prof has increased my medication (Lumin) by one tablet to three each night. He said the medication will make me 'less depressed, less anxious and less obsessive' and he is right; so I am happy to stay on this medication until I am in a safe and happy and secure environment with my home.

(Lumin is an antidepressant, containing the active ingredient mianserin—hydrochloride—and I built up to 60mg daily.)

In the year 2000 my sister's husband, Ray, died suddenly as a result of a heart attack on his way to work; I attended the funeral in Bairnsdale and stayed overnight at the farm. In shock, I was completely unprepared for what happened next morning:

I entered the kitchen at about 7.45am. Dad was sitting in his usual place at the head of the table and Mum was doing some ironing. I thought this was a chance to talk over the events of the funeral, before heading home but I hadn't time to make a cuppa before my parents began talking about the farm. They had considered subdividing a small portion of land on the hill opposite the homestead for me to build a house, but until now each time I had inquired about progress the answer had been the process was costly and time consuming. Now, Mum confirmed several titles were being put into one, for Timothy, and Joy would have the homestead and some land.

But my 'house block' remained a dream—I'd not seen any plans and concluded by the delays and inferences that I was being a nuisance, so said not to bother with the block if it was troublesome. My parents seemed relieved and Dad said he would provide 'something else' for me 'in place of the land'. I asked if Timothy would pay for his land. Dad would not answer: Joy would own and live in the house and Timothy would live a few miles away in another house he owned. I expressed concern that this proposed division of our family's assets seemed unfair, and surely Timothy should live on the farm if he was going to farm it. Dad turned and sharply said: 'You won't fight this, will you?'

I said that my sons hadn't been consulted about the farm succession; only Joy's sons—the two eldest at least—had been asked.

Dad said: 'Your children will only want the money, they won't want to keep the farm'. As if to explain, Mum said Timothy was getting the farm 'because he loves it'. I felt deeply insulted and reminded my parents that I loved the farm and so did my children.

This conversation was not going well. I had lost a lot of what I loved because I'd not stood my ground in the face of conflict, and for once I tried assert myself.

I diverted the conversation to that of a teenage cousin mentioned in a newspaper court report that Mum had shown me the day before. I said he was not the only man in our family circle who should have been brought to justice, and Mum said, 'Are you talking about '...'?'

I said, 'You know?' My heart began to pound.

Mum said, 'Yes'.

Both she and Dad knew.

Suddenly I was in a flood of tears, saying over and over: 'I didn't know you knew, I didn't know you knew.'

The gates to my past burst open. Like a scared five-year-old, I wanted Mum and Dad to hold me and help me feel safe. But to them the childhood sexual abuse seemed no big deal, like it was something to be swept under the doormat, and definitely not to be aired in the community. I went to Mum and tried to hug her. She did not respond, so I retreated to the kitchen doorway and stood there alone, tears streaming down my face, sobbing, 'I didn't know you knew, I didn't know you knew.' For almost two decades I had refrained from telling my parents of this terrible 'secret' of abuse, because I didn't want to upset or hurt them. But they had known, and had done nothing about it.

They still welcome '...' into their home! I feel nothing more than a piece of meat. My soul, the part not yet devoured by my eating disorders, is shredded.

I left the farmhouse in tears and cried all the way home (a three-hour trip). When I arrived I phoned George, my rock, my anchor. He can't understand my parents' behaviour: why have they raised the issues of the farm and the Will at such a deep time of mourning? Why did my mother produce that newspaper cutting at this time? George has helped me think a little straighter. He urges me not to call my parents; after all, they could see I was upset. Why don't they care? 'Let them call you,' he said. He arranged for Amanda to come over to my home and go walking with me. Amanda arrived within minutes and we walked and talked; gradually my tears eased, and by the time we returned to my house, I was feeling stronger. I called Rohan and, when I said I felt my heart had been ripped out and thrown away, he encouraged me to see beyond my pain, reminding me that life can be beautiful and that 'Mum, remember you want to walk on the Great Wall of China'.

Monday dawned and I went to work but remained in a state of shock and despair. Incredible. I felt like I had lost my parents, that I must mean little to them. Mum had made light of the sexual abuse, saying: 'It happens to others, what's so special about you?'

That really hurt. I was not special, but sexual abuse was a criminal offence. I cried and cried some more. Action could have been taken against '...' 18 years ago. By adhering to my sister's wishes to keep silent, I had not saved my parents from pain; but had added to my own.

Shortly after this revelation, I wrote to my children:

August 25, 2000

Dear Shane, Rohan, Ben and Amanda,

I am writing to you to help you understand me, your mum.

I feel now is the right time to write to you because, since your Uncle Ray's death, the final missing piece of my childhood seems to have fallen into place.

I wish I could have had my childhood 'sorted out' before any of you entered this world, so that you and your dad and I could have enjoyed our family life together, forever.

I was 32 when the missing pieces of my childhood began to fall in place, and by then you were seven to 11 years old. I have cried many tears.

I still have a way to go in my healing journey, as I am terrified of being

ALONE. This is a FEAR I know I have to face, so that I can heal the hole in my soul. I am receiving support from friends, from my work colleagues and the medical profession.

They tell me I am strong and brave, and to keep working as I do.

Your dad tells me to focus on the four of you as my family, as our family. Your dad tells me to stay away from the farm and not to contact my parents, 'because they know where you are if they decide they want a daughter'.

I know your dad does not want me to be hurt any more, and I know I cannot cope with any more hurt, so I'm doing as he suggests.

This is hard for me, as I love my parents and the farm, but I have to accept what is, and I cherish the support that your dad and you give me.

I am receiving advice from the Centre Against Sexual Assault and others, and they suggest that the man who scarred my childhood and that of my sister be confronted—they say this will be stressful but is necessary for my life to have meaning now that I know the truth.

I would cope much better if my parents showed some interest in me, but that is how it is. One phone call would have meant a lot.

As your dad says, you are my family now.

I love your dad—he has been part of my life since I was 16, and my one big regret is that we are not still together, that this sexual abuse, combined with my mother wanting me to be a boy, proved too big a struggle for me, for us. I cherish the knowledge that forever, your dad and I remain friends. He is THERE for me when I need him and we are UNITED in our love for each of you.

Please share with us your fears, your confusions, your hopes, your uncertainties, your joys and your dreams.

I apologise from the bottom of my heart for the pain I have caused in your own childhoods, while struggling to sort out mine.

Knowing that my problems have affected your happiness is my second big regret.

I hope you will feel free to call me any time, about anything. I am always happiest when any of you, when you all, are with me, or contact me.

I hope that knowing my story will help each of you know more who you are, and enable you to be free to enjoy your life in all its fullness,

With love,

Mum

Shortly after, I was admitted to the Epworth Hospital, unable to walk due to pain in my spine. At the same time as the stressful situation with my family in East Gippsland, I became submerged in a relationship that reflected and fed my illness. Mr Brazenor, on learning of my home situation, expressed concern beyond that of his neurosurgeon role. He confined me to a hospital bed, with strict instructions to lie on my back for two weeks.

When Mr Brazenor next came on his rounds he said: 'Something has to be done about your home situation, because you can't have stresses of any kind.' He asked to speak with Rohan. So I phoned Rohan, who called Mr Brazenor and then called me, saying, in his slow, deliberate way: 'Mum, I don't think returning to (the-man-in-my-life's) house is an option.' Mr Brazenor arranged for the hospital chaplain to offer comfort and strengthen my battered sense of self, and Amanda also visited.

The day I was able to walk again, Mr Brazenor said he wanted a consulting psychiatrist, George Wahr, to see me. I said, 'Okay' and a small, bespectacled man with a neatly trimmed grey beard came to see me that same day. He said he was keen to help and would return 'tomorrow'. I tried to focus my energy on Mr Wahr. He wore a bow tie, so I called him 'Bow Tie George' or 'BT George' for short. On his next visit he said: 'You have an internal inhibitor, a saboteur, which causes your life to be in constant turmoil. Very early life experiences have left you with a hole you have been unable to fill, but that can be filled with therapy.'

BT George said, 'You do not need medication, you just need love, the right kind of love, and maybe you don't even know what the right kind of love is right now.'

He said the-current-man-in-my-life and I were a mix that would not work, 'He won't change and you must change, because you are caught in a very dangerous pattern—dangerous to yourself and your health and worrying your children, family and friends.'

BT George said, 'You must think about your internal saboteur.' I didn't know what this saboteur was, but I hoped to overcome it and replace it with a peaceful life. I would do whatever I had to do to achieve this.

I called Rohan to tell him of BT George's visit and said I would fill my void and we would have good times. My problems had affected him and Shane, Ben and Amanda. Every time I talked with my children, I continued to tell them I loved them; they were my biggest inspiration. I was grateful that George was from a stable family, for he was a fine father and role model. Meanwhile, my doctors were drumming into me:

I DESERVE TO BE TREATED WITH RESPECT.

They insisted I repeat this over and over, to counter my negative thoughts.

The day before I left hospital, Mr Brazenor said flatly: 'You must cut the cord with (the-man-in-my-life); don't return to his house.' BT George backed him. But against the advice of everyone who knew and cared about me, I did return to the house, armed only with the affirmation 'I deserve to be treated with respect'. To be told I had a saboteur had given me hope. I'd find the saboteur and conquer it. But right now, I didn't know how to recognise or be aware of it.

Three more years would pass before I developed sufficient self-love, and became sufficiently self-aware, to catch the thoughts that belonged to my saboteur or illness and disable them before they took hold.

I was nearing the summit of my restorative climb in 2002 when fresh revelations from the family farm in the Lindenow Valley ambushed my progress. During a visit accompanied by a friend, I took my usual walk along the Mitchell River track to the log cabin at Lambert's Flat. Dusk was falling and we had hardly entered the flat when I stopped suddenly, staring at a huge mound of earth in the top corner of the paddock. The realisation that it was a freshly built dam sparked alarm in my mind. My mother had not mentioned this major project in my weekly phone calls to her, and both parents denied having anything to do with it when asked about it over dinner that night. It just did not make sense.

On my next visit to Prof Burrows, he encouraged me to make inquiries to avoid anxiety build-up. I arranged for a title search and learnt that 18 months before, prior to my father's 80th birthday, my parents had gifted all five titles of their property to my sister's eldest son, Timothy. I looked in disbelief at the signatures of my parents and Timothy, and the word 'GIFTED', stamped on each of the five titles. I called Mum to let her know I knew; she had always said she would inform me when decisions on the farm succession were complete. She was angry that I knew and confirmed that Timothy had the five titles. The farmhouse and six acres, including the stable, hen houses, car shed, cottage and orchard, would go to my sister.

'And you will get some money one day, and I hope it is a long time coming,' Mum said.

I did not know who to turn to, to help convince my parents that I loved the farm and that this was my family heritage, too. I spent many tearful hours talking on the phone with a government-funded rural counsellor, based at Bairnsdale, who revealed that he had 'mediated' between my father and Timothy in arranging the family farm succession, but had been refused permission to share any details with me.

Several months passed before I summoned the courage to visit my parents with a friend, to seek a discussion around the kitchen table. I waited until we sat down to afternoon tea before mentioning that I would like to discuss what was happening with our farm. My parents stood up from their chairs and Dad scolded me, saying, 'How dare you come here to upset your mother like this.' One clarification I sought was that if one day Timothy no longer wanted the land, that other family members would have first option to buy. Timothy, who had come in and sat down, looked into his teacup and said, 'If Aunty June hadn't gone digging around, none of this would be happening now.'

Slowly it dawned on me that I was not supposed to know about the gifting of the farm while my parents were alive. George, our children and my medical support team helped me come to terms with feelings of loss and alienation. I felt I had failed my mother as 'Tim' the girl, but she had found what she wanted in 'Tim' the boy. To quell deep anxiety, I sought again to be included, to be given details, but Mum flatly stated, 'You won't know anything until we are dead.'

The sense of rejection from my family became extreme. I could not think of my parents, especially my father, without thinking of the farm. They were entwined. Desperate for healing, I became filled with an urge to return to Gippsland, find my own patch and immerse myself in the layers of a rural community. The opportunity came in 2005, not in East Gippsland, but in South Gippsland where I accepted the position of editor of *The Great Southern Star* newspaper in the dairying town of Leongatha.

I knew nobody in this country town, population about 5000 nestled among green rolling hills 90 minutes southeast of Melbourne, and two hours southwest of the family farm; yet everyone made me feel welcome. Initially I felt nervous, and repeatedly recited affirmations to allay panic. At times the Earth seemed a thin saucer and I was on the edge, about to drop off and plunge into darkness, but deep in my soul I knew Leongatha was where I was meant to be, that there was no other way. This was the way to regaining me. I gradually confronted my fears. Belonging and acceptance began to replace each one. I sold my two properties in Melbourne to purchase a sheltered farmlet. Just out of Leongatha on several acres, the property came complete with creek, pond, geese, koalas and a brick homestead with a wooden verandah right around. I added some chooks and felt like a cicada emerging from its shell into the brightness and warmth, connecting with life.

My children boosted my happiness. Ben had wed the girl of his dreams, Anke, in South Africa, in March 2004, and now I was looking forward to the upcoming wedding in September of Amanda to her fiancé, Nick.

17. WEDDINGS, A BIRD AND ME

Amanda and Nick had set their wedding date for September 17, 2005. But during May, a black cloud gathered overhead.

My sister's daughter Anne-Louise announced she would marry one week before Amanda and Nick's wedding.

'What strange timing,' I said, when Amanda phoned to tell me. 'If the weddings were four weeks apart, instead of one, we could more easily anticipate and savour each one.' Amanda's date had been set well in advance, and the news about my niece's wedding was unsettling—I wondered why Mum, who loved family weddings, had not shared the good news about her granddaughter Anne-Louise in my weekly call, or perhaps even called me especially.

The silence was ominous.

Amanda and my sons received invitations to my niece's wedding, now eight weeks hence, but I did not. My anxiety was mounting. Amanda sent a text message to my mobile telephone: *'Mum, don't worry. We got the invite on Friday. If u don't get one, I'll reassess my wedding list! Don't stress yet. You're a Champ, Mum!'*

Amanda's SMS buoyed my flagging spirits. Four months had passed since I'd moved to Leongatha and I had overcome my long-time fear of living alone. If I felt a little panicky in bed I said the Lord's Prayer —it always helped me feel safe and I would quickly fall asleep. I had company during the day at the newspaper office, and was enjoying Monday-night dinner meetings at the local Rotary Club, where I'd become a member. At home I had my pets and cosy log fire. A foundation of stability and security was forming to take on my saboteur, but the wedding saga was testing me. Two weeks after my children received their invitations, I began to think about organising entertainment for the weekend of my niece's wedding to keep me detached, smiling and dignified.

Amanda was more proactive and phoned Anne-Louise, who confirmed I was NOT invited to her wedding. Now Amanda became uncertain about her own wedding list.

The pain of rejection was sharp, but I said: 'We must invite my sister and niece to your wedding; they are family, it is the right thing to do.'

Rohan put the wedding drama into a perspective with which I could cope, saying: 'Mum, you have done well. You seem happy and Leongatha is your home now and we're your family (Shane, Rohan, Ben and Amanda) in Melbourne. Go for a walk along the South Gippsland beach and focus on these things, and forget those people in East Gippsland.'

Nonetheless, I felt greatly distressed that the family rift was infiltrating the next generation.

Rohan gave more good advice: 'Mum, Amanda's only distress will be over her concern for you, if she sees you are distressed.'

His wise words penetrated and I resolved not to allow the behaviour of others to sap my happiness or that of my children. I tried to be strong in front of Amanda, but tears flowed when discussing her wedding arrangements with George. We agreed that Joy should be invited to our daughter's wedding, though George, together with my new South Gippsland friend Jane, suggested my sister would be hypocritical to accept. But I said: 'She will accept the invitation because she considers me at fault. I am the one with the problem.' Feeling bereft, alone at home, I ate lollies, chocolate, anything, to numb my feelings. The sugar was poor comfort. I prayed:

'Dear God above, please give me the strength to cope, please, dear Father. I must take control—nurture myself.'

Prof said to focus on putting my best interests first: choose not to allow Joy's behaviour to upset me; and meet with my parents to discuss the farm, which was an ongoing source of distress, preferably with a mediator and prior to the two weddings. Both were difficult challenges.

Four weeks prior to Amanda's wedding, in my weekly call to Mum, she mentioned she planned to give each granddaughter money as a gift as each had 'everything'. I said, 'Are you aware I am not invited to Anne-

Louise's wedding?'

Mum was dismissive: 'I had nothing to do with the invitations. Don't blame me.' I exchanged six emails with my friend Helen, who emphasised: 'You must send a letter to your parents and tell them of your distress.'

Leongatha
Sunday, August 17, 2005
Dear Mum and Dad,

I hope that you are both well. I think of you every day and want to share my dismay at being excluded from Anne-Louise's wedding.

I hope you and Joy can see that my exclusion from this important event will widen the rift in our small family. To heal the rift, we must respect each other and share thoughts and feelings, we must communicate and provide explanations when sought. I want to be included in our family and to be treated equally, to know as much as Joy (and Timothy) about our farm. Right now I have nothing to say to them because none of my questions have been answered and I must avoid pain.

Like the decision on the farm, nobody told me what was going on with Anne-Louise's wedding. I'd have appreciated one of you telling me I was not to be invited, to save Amanda being caught in my distress.

(Believe me, not knowing what is happening, is far worse than knowing. When you know, you may not like what you are told, but you can start to deal with it and accept it.)

My deepest hurt has been caused, not by you gifting all of your property to Timothy, but by not being told about it. Joy and Timothy obviously know details, but I do not.

I hope you will respond to this letter so that Anne-Louise's wedding can be a happy occasion for all of us.

Life is too beautiful to be bogged down in sadness, so I am trying to make my own way, build my own life and create my own patch. I'm having a little hiccup in my progress, coping with this wedding disappointment. It has knocked me flat and feelings of rejection have re-surfaced.

I hope to hear from you.
Your loving daughter,
June

Mum replied immediately, which was a breakthrough, but ignored my pleas for information and asked me again not to blame her for being excluded from Anne-Louise's wedding.

Two days later, collecting my mail from the post office during my lunchbreak, I saw an envelope addressed in Joy's handwriting. My heart leapt, hoping for a belated invitation to her daughter's wedding; instead it contained Joy's acceptance to Amanda's wedding. Every day I checked the mail for a late invitation.

'You don't deserve one, you're worthless,' my illness thoughts raged every time I turned the key to my mailbox. Working long hours in the newspaper office helped to repel the rejection pain, which hit hardest at home in the evenings. *'You're a nothing,'* my illness thoughts said.

My children, friends and George helped to disperse my blackness and maintain my dignity, assuring me: 'You are a worthy person.' They encouraged me to focus on Amanda and Nick's wedding rehearsal, scheduled the day after my niece's wedding. This was a happy place for my mind to be. I prepared to be mother of the bride by practising my favourite imagery—that of being a beautiful, colourful bird, soaring high into the sky.

For decades my illness—anorexia, bulimia, anxiety and depression —had pervaded my mind. Now, exclusion from my niece's wedding was culminating in an almighty last stand, with my illness unleashing an onslaught of debilitating self-doubt and rejection. But only momentarily: I was rapidly picking up the threads of my identity, severed when anorexia nervosa developed in my mind more than 40 years before. Every day I became more June and less illness.

The evening before my niece's wedding I was home alone. I hadn't heard from my parents or sister, though I had sent several more letters. Only months ago I would have numbed my feelings by bingeing. But now, now I called on my colourful bird imagery, flying above all sources of pain.

I must hold on to this image and my dignity. I must love myself; be true to myself and not allow the behaviour of others to make me feel rejected or sad.

I counted my blessings: two cats, one dog, four lovely children, a beautiful home and a job I enjoyed in a country town filled with friendly, community-minded people.

The day of my niece's wedding, a Friday, dawned. My early-morning walk along the country lane to the railway line with my dog Titan left a trail of teardrops, there and back, but at the newspaper office, my small team of journalists provided cheery support. After work, a friend accompanied me to the movies to see *Charlie and the Chocolate Factory*, followed by dinner at the Leongatha Returned Services League club. My friends helped me through a difficult day.

My children had felt torn, being invited to a family wedding knowing I had been excluded.

The next day I drove to Studley Park Boat House, beside the Yarra River in the Melbourne suburb of Kew, for Amanda and Nick's wedding rehearsal. I almost fell over in surprise when George greeted me with a kiss me on my cheek—his first kiss in more than 20 years. I felt he was saying, 'You're doing well, keep it up.'

George hoped my parents, sister, nephews and newly married niece wouldn't attend Amanda's wedding. 'They probably won't come,' he said. But I said, 'They will come.' I knew they would come. I had received no response to my letters. The thought of facing family members who had rejected me only one week before made me very anxious.

Rain fell and wind blew on September 17, but Amanda was radiant. The marriage ceremony was about to start when my parents and sister, her four children and their partners arrived. To settle my churning stomach I focused on my bird imagery, its wide and powerful wings carrying me skywards. My children were my bodyguards and George and his long-time partner Roselyn my support. During the reception, which took the form of a cocktail party, the small and crowded dance floor was my haven. Dancing to the beat of the music, I focused on my brilliantly coloured bird and on the happiness of the newlywed couple. This was Amanda and Nick's big day, and soon we were waving farewell as they departed on their honeymoon. At midnight, as we said goodbye to final guests, George said:

'I'm proud of you for rising above your family's behaviour. You have maintained your dignity and coped very well.'

His words meant a lot and I clung to them as I drove home to Leongatha the next day.

Four weeks after Amanda's wedding, I'd received no word from my parents or Joy. Gathering courage, I phoned, and Mum said: 'I'll send a letter.' Her letter arrived three days later and a fresh challenge unfolded.

Her 80th birthday was two months away. 'My wish is for my family to be together, the way it once was,' she wrote. Ever hopeful and believing this was a chance to clear up family secrets and unite as one, I wrote to Timothy, now in his mid-30s, inviting him to Leongatha to discuss family matters in a bid to give Mum her birthday wish. I hoped he would care enough to come. Every time I seemed to make headway in my recovery, the behaviour of my family in East Gippsland sorely tested the triggers of my illness.

Timothy's response to my request to discuss and resolve our family's rift came in a condescending note. He was 'too busy' to make the two-hour trip to Leongatha to talk about a problem that was of my own making. No one was stopping me from being part of the family, he said. I was 'the only one not talking', I was the sole cause and reason a family rift existed.

Refusing to give up, I phoned and left a message for him to call, but no call came. Rohan said: 'Mum, stop bruising yourself.' I should have known by now to take notice of Rohan but wanting to please my mother, I pushed on.

Focusing on her 80th birthday wish, I offered to host a party at my home. I had been at Leongatha for almost two years and Mum had yet to visit. She agreed to come but did not want the celebration on her birth date of December 23, saying, 'It's too near Christmas,' and instead suggested December 18. With four weeks until this date, I mailed invitations to Joy, nephews, niece, aunts and uncles, as well as my children and George and Roselyn.

Rohan said flatly, 'Your sister and her family won't come. Why do you persist in trying to bring your family together? You are setting yourself up for more rejection and bruising.' However, despite Timothy's disparaging response, I dared to hope the party would mark the start of happier family times. I invited George to mediate a family discussion in the lead-up to the party, but he declined, saying, 'I remain disgusted at how your family is treating you.' Perhaps Rohan was right. *At the age of almost 55, maybe*

I should stop trying to win my mother's love and acceptance.

Encouragingly, lovely Aunty Gwen, my mother's oldest sister who lived in Melbourne, accepted my party invitation. I loved Aunty Gwen, and she loved me. Every time we talked she said: 'I love you, June dear, right up to the sky,' and I would say: 'And I love you too, Aunty Gwen, to the moon.' I told Mum I loved her, too, but she could not respond.

Five nights before her party, I phoned the farm to discuss arrangements. Mum's wish was doomed—Joy and her four children had each declined the party invitation—but I was determined to do my best to give her a happy day. Joy answered the phone. She said Mum was out, and we exchanged small talk before my long-suppressed thoughts and feelings exploded. 'I am disappointed that you and your children are not coming to Mum's celebration,' I said. Joy said she was arranging her own celebration at the farmhouse on the 23rd—the date Mum had said was unsuitable. This was news. So she was having two parties. I asked Joy why I was excluded from our family. She refused to explain and said, 'June, there is something wrong with your head.'

My sister was definitely a trigger I had to avoid. I took a deep breath and called again the next morning and this time Mum answered. I said I had tried but was failing to provide her wish of uniting her family, adding: 'But since Amanda's wedding I have realised I am not the only one with a problem in our family.'

'Who is, then?' Mum snapped.

'Look around you,' I said.

The 80th birthday party passed happily despite the absence of Joy and her children. George and Roselyn, my children and friends came in support; several aunts and uncles came, and a long-time family friend, Lorna, brought my parents.

That evening, as dusk gave way to night, I sat on my verandah and watched the geese gather on my dam; a kookaburra laughed in the nearby gum trees; Titan Dog and Ginger and Dora Cats sat at my feet. Gazing upwards, to the full moon and Milky Way in the gloriously clear, star-studded southern sky, I suddenly felt an intense moment of great elation. YES! The little girl inside me had escaped her eating disorder prison. The clarity of this moment matched that of 44 years before, when my anorexia first budded. I was healing; I had crossed the half-way mark in the journey of regaining me.

My next challenge was to become medication-free. In the three months since Amanda's wedding, by attending to emotions instead of numbing them with food binges and starvation, I had lost more than seven kilograms. I was the most 'me' I had been for decades. Amanda's wedding had marked a major turning point in my healing, and organising the celebration for Mum's 80th birthday had been 'the icing on the cake'.

Ben, living in London with his wife Anke, wrote an email with encouragement not to dwell on the loss of heritage: *'Make your own mark in life, Mum. Make your own goals; your rewards will be greater.'*

My thoughts turned to a long-held dream of writing my memoir; this would require the reliving of decades I would rather forget; it would be my literary 'Everest'. But I was ready for the climb. I felt safe and secure now. My illness would continue to throw up a few obstacles, but none would tear my soul.

The biggest jubilation in reclaiming my personality was the opportunity to build a relationship with myself, loving and being with me and myself, without the intrusive and tormenting eating disorder. My spinal operation had provided a physical peace and now I achieved mental and emotional peace as well. It took some getting used to. I was gloriously happy being alone. I wanted to hug myself over and over and over. Of equal elation was time shared with my children. Every moment was cherished; every day I counted many blessings.

The year 2006 was the first in more than four decades not dominated by my eating disorder. As a first step, under Prof Burrow's guidance, over a seven-month period, I eased off the Lumin medication (60mg) that I had been prescribed for nine years.

Prof understands my desire and need to be totally me. He has warned that even a small reduction of 10mg one month at a time may cause me to feel depressed, so I'll be very careful and do all I can to ensure I am feeling happy and bright. Progressively, I am determined to reduce my dosage to zero. I feel I need to be medication-free to write my book. Prof is also encouraging me to write my book.

The week I eased off the last 10mg of anti-depressant medication, my first grandchild, Lachlan, was born. This little baby immediately became an important part of my health support team. His arrival boosted resolve to prepare for the task ahead.

In early 2007 I resigned as newspaper editor at Leongatha. It was a big step after 38 years in journalism to say 'Goodbye' to the friendly staff at *The Star* and to the career that had provided a sense of self worth and means of financial support when everything else in my life was crumbling. Next, encouraged by Steve, a long-time colleague and friend from *The Weekly Times*, I bought a property at Clifton Springs on the Bellarine Peninsula, 90-minutes southwest of Melbourne. I felt sad departing Gippsland, but happy too, for by now I knew that wherever I lived, everything I needed to feel safe and secure was always with me—within me.

On the peninsula, nurtured by early-morning walks by the seashore with Titan, a new journey began. This journey was different to any other. I didn't know where it would take me. All that mattered was that I was true to myself. Slowly but surely I began turning the power of my long-term illness on itself.

My story of hope and renewal began to unfold in amazing ways.

18. SOARING

Fast forward to 2011. Four years have raced by. Four years of freedom. Four years of learning astounding facts about the illness, anorexia nervosa, that developed within my brain half a century ago. Four years of catching up with me.

At age 56, I set out to confront and expose my anorexic-bulimic tormentor in the only way I knew how, with words. I wanted to share my experience, to ease the suffering of others. On settling into my seaside home in May 2007, I began to contact eating disorder support groups and met Claire Vickery, founder and executive chairperson of the Butterfly Foundation, Australia's largest charity supporting people with eating disorders and negative body image.

On finding that I was interested in the effects of anorexia on family relationships, Claire said: 'You must meet Daniel Le Grange.' Daniel, a Professor of Psychiatry and Director of the Eating Disorders Program at the University of Chicago, specialised in researching the treatment of adolescent eating disorders. In particular he was a pioneer in the Maudsley Approach, also known as Family-Based Treatment, introduced in Australia at The Children's Hospital at Westmead, Sydney, in 2002. I was planning a trip to Missouri to visit my student exchange host family in October 2007 and with Chicago close by in the neighbouring state of Illinois, I sent an email to Professor Le Grange, outlining a book concept. I thought this important academic would not have time for me, a long-time eating disorder sufferer and grandmother from the south-eastern corner of Australia, but Professor Le Grange responded immediately to say he would be pleased to catch up.

Our meeting resulted in my memoirs going on hold while Professor Le Grange and I collaborated in writing *My Kid Is Back—Empowering*

Parents to Beat Anorexia Nervosa. Along the way, a steady stream of revelations shed light and understanding on my own journey.

This knowledge fuelled an urge to inform parents about Family-Based Treatment without delay. My dominant thought was that if such treatment had existed when I was a child, it could have saved my family, as well as me, much suffering. Tragically, here we were in 2007 and many families and clinicians remained unaware of this treatment that had originated at London's Maudsley Hospital in the 1980s. The illness was continuing to tear families apart. I didn't want children who developed anorexia nervosa today to become alienated from their families because of their illness. I didn't want their illness to tag along when they left home, entered relationships and embarked on careers. I wanted today's parents and clinicians to know about Family-Based Treatment.

My Kid Is Back was published in Australia in 2009 and in the United Kingdom in 2010. Through the voices of 10 families, the book explains that anorexia is NOT an illness of choice and parents are NOT to blame. Professor Le Grange brings reassurance and empowerment to parents by explaining the evidence-based research behind Family Based Treatment, and the phases of treatment leading to recovery.

Parents are integral to the treatment, which comprises three main steps. First, parents play an active and positive role in helping to restore their child's weight to normal levels; second, they hand the control over eating back to the adolescent; and third, they step back and encourage normal adolescent development.

Throughout my illness I yearned for my family's understanding, believing recovery would occur more quickly if my parents and sister understood my inner battle. I wanted them to know the real me was trapped inside the illness. Family-Based Treatment helps parents and siblings understand anorexia. It teaches them first and foremost that food is medicine and helps them to recognise and separate the behaviours of the illness from those of their child.

Looking back, with the benefit of latest research outcomes, I can see that my biological and genetic makeup, together with my environment, made me a 'sitting duck' for developing anorexia. My nature was such that I liked to please; I was conscientious and worried when things 'weren't right'; I liked people to be happy and didn't like missing a day of school; I was a perfectionist. By age 11, I felt uncomfortable with my sexuality. All up, the school doctor's impending visit intensified my anxiety level to such a height it triggered my illness.

My anorexia and subsequent bulimia had nothing to do with the glossy magazines and slim string-bean models wrongfully cited as causes of eating disorders. When my eating disorder developed, the family home was not even connected with electricity. There was no media influence. I realise now that my mother, who was always doing good deeds for others, was an anxious person. She coped by being constantly busy, and I grew up feeling guilty whenever I sat down—for instance, to read a book. I learnt to hide, if I wanted to do so during the day, because Mum would give a stern reminder that 'there are jobs to be done and you know that your father is tired'. Mum obviously had her own problems, but would not discuss them with me. Her solution was to keep active at home and in the community.

Evidence-based research continues but for now, swift diagnosis and intervention with Family-Based Treatment achieves the best outcome for children and adolescents who develop anorexia nervosa. For those who miss the chance of early intervention, and who do not have family support and understanding, the road to recovery is harder but at any age and stage, there must be hope and belief that improvement in quality of life is possible.

Every step of faith taken in reclaiming my sense of self has resulted in an outcome that seems to say: 'Well done, maintain your conviction, believe in yourself, you are on the right track.' The more I challenge my fears, the more I am able to conquer them, trust myself and withstand the devious urges of my illness.

Tiny threads of my eating disorder remain—around five per cent. I disable them by eating three meals and three snacks a day without fail and, in susceptible moments, by trusting my support team. This team comprises my psychiatrist, my dietician, my children and George, my friends and my pets (my faithful companion of 10 years, Titan, passed away in 2008. Harley, a Staffordshire Terrier, has taken his place, alongside Ginger and Dora Cats). My children, now in their mid-thirties, are my main 'minders'—they know by the sound of my voice, if I am experiencing a vulnerable moment and know what to say to defuse and deflect triggers.

Sometimes my children need to be firm and authoritive—like they are the parent and I am the child. At such times I accept their guidance as I trust them and know they have my best interest at heart.

Four months after *My Kid Is Back* was released in Australia my mother, Anne Alice Alexander, died. The date was July 28, 2009. I had hoped *My Kid is Back* would help her understand my struggle and bring us closer. I sent a signed copy, with a message to that effect, but Mum never commented on the book. I doubt she read it. Decisions had been made and perhaps, for my parents, it was all too late. My parents' neighbour, Aunty Mil, who has known me all my life, read the book after hearing about it on ABC radio, and phoned to say, 'June, I did not know about your illness.' Now, she was sharing the book with her extended family. When I appeared on national television to speak about my experience with eating disorders, my parents did not watch. However a family friend had recorded one segment and, on learning that they had not seen it, invited them to watch it. An external process was beginning to encourage family awareness.

Family secrets remained, however.

My mother died at home. She had gone to bed that evening, suffered a massive heart attack and apparently died almost instantly. She was 83 years old and on the day she died, had driven to Bairnsdale and back, prepared Dad's evening meal, living busily until the last minute.

More than 400 people attended Mum's funeral. More mourners stood outside than were seated inside the small Uniting Church at Lindenow. The minister and the funeral director ushered me to the front row, where I sat on the right side of my father, my sister on his left. I clutched the arm of Rohan, sitting on my right. This was the moment I had dreaded for years: looking at my mother's oak coffin, with beautiful red roses on top, wondering what the 'secret' was, that she said I would not know until both parents were dead.

Overwhelmingly, I felt relief—that my mother was at rest, and that I could no longer seek answers from her that would not be given. I had never given up trying to talk to her, trying to establish communication. As little as one month before her death, Mum shared that she remembered one night 'when we were at the Glenaladale Hall, you were so weak, we had to take you home early'. For her to acknowledge this much of my childhood illness, was as good as it would get. I asked if she had photographs of the 'anorexia, emaciated' me. 'No', Mum said. 'I burnt all of those photographs; I hated looking at them and put them in the fire.' So that was that.

When the long line of cars followed the hearse to the Lindenow South cemetery, I was in about the 24th car. *'It does not matter,'* I told myself, *'I am here to say goodbye to my mother, and I will focus on this. The behaviour of others does not matter.'*

At home, several nights after the funeral, I phoned George and he was comforting—he had told our children that I was brave, adding: 'You coped well, as it could not have been easy.' George said my family had not done the right thing by me for years. His words provided solace, as my illness triggers were forever ready to shoot into my soul the message that I was my family's one and only problem.

My five per cent dark hole within was painfully tested, but I minimised anxiety by eating three nutritious meals a day even when my stomach felt full of knots. I was tearful, but supposed this was a normal way to be when one loses a 'loved one'. Actually I was happy that Mum was resting. She had consumed every ounce of her life. It was all the other stupid stuff, the family secrets about the farm, and feeling alienated and rejected, that dragged me down.

I told myself to look forward to bright and positive events coming up soon in August and September, including the Australian and New Zealand Academy of Eating Disorders conference in Brisbane, the National Eating Disorders Association (NEDA) conference in Minneapolis, USA, and a trip to London to see Ben and Anke, who had lived there for some years, and the eating disorder research team at Guy's Hospital and King's College.

There was joy on my home front, too with the birth of two more grandchildren. In November, Ashton Cherubim became the first child of Shane and his wife Angeli, who had married in 2008. In December, Lachlan became a brother to Olivia Rose, born on my mother's birthday.

This new generation helped me stay afloat mentally and emotionally while writing my memoirs, for reading my diaries, kept for almost 50 years, was gruelling. At the same time the process was cathartic and I could see that my devotion to diary writing had helped me stay alive. Writing was therapeutic. It helped me to hold on to sanity, reflect, analyse and try to make sense of my often confused and tormented world. It's hard to equate the person I am now with the person whose mind was manipulated by illness and affected by prescription drugs for four decades. The years dominated by my eating disorder stand stark and desolate like a burnt, blackened forest. Luckily the small amount of the real me that survived has re-generated into the fullness of my identity. Writing continues to be important—essential in my recovery maintenance and in efforts to raise awareness of mental health.

In June 2010, 11 months after my mother's death, I flew to Salzburg, Austria to receive an international award for my writing in the field of eating disorders. The patient carer scholarship, awarded by the Academy of Eating Disorders, provided recognition and acknowledgment from the world's top eating disorder organisation that my life has purpose. For me, this was priceless.

I had not long returned to Australia when Dad died, at home, on August 7, 2010. He had lived all of his 88 years in the one house on Weeroona, the property he loved. He had been lonely without Mum and now, after one year and 11 days, they were reunited. They had never explained why they excluded me from their inner circle but I loved them both.

In my final chat with Dad, he said he wanted the farm to be for all. Too late, perhaps, he could see that the real me had never left—that an illness had dominated for decades, but now I was back. He was proud of my award in Salzburg and that I was helping others who suffer my illness. His final words were for Weeroona—he wanted the property to be shared and enjoyed by both his daughters and their families. Although Weeroona was now in the hands of others, I felt Dad needed to believe this was how the future would be, for him to let go and die peacefully.

August 12, 2010:
Right now a tearful me is sitting in George's car on the roadside outside the Lindenow South cemetery. Inside the cemetery which is surrounded by green, grassy paddocks, my father's coffin is being lowered into the ground to rest with that of my mother.

I am not by the graveside.
Hundreds are standing there, but not me.

I was overcome with burning chest pain during the funeral service in the Bairnsdale Uniting Church. I was sitting with my girlfriend Helen on my left, George and our family on my right, and seven-month-old grand daughter Olivia Rose on my lap.

With this loving support, sitting three pews back from the coffin, I thought I could cope with this final 'farewell' and I was doing okay. Olivia Rose smiled and cooed as the eulogy was read.

Then a slide show began of photographs I had never seen, despite my request two years earlier for photographs of my father's early life —which was also part of mine.

I had one childhood portrait of my father in a kilt, but that was all.

I watched in disbelief as images of him as a toddler, young boy, teenager and young man appeared on the screen.

To see him in these phases of his life for the first time in the presence of hundreds of others seared my soul. I could bear no more. I arose and left the church.

Helen followed. 'I want to go home,' I wailed. I had a desperate need to feel safe and secure. George came and we drove to the cemetery where we are waiting for Shane, who is travelling with us back to Melbourne. None of my family will attend the wake.

Writing right now is helping me to relieve my distress and defuse old triggers of rejection. I keep telling myself, I don't have to bruise myself again. George said as we departed Bairnsdale for Lindenow South: 'Now you are free.'

Free to be me. I must keep saying this. Free to be me.

I had longed to feel close to my parents, to be accepted by them, but that hope was buried with them. For years they excluded me from family matters and said: 'You will know nothing until we are dead'. They kept their word.

Several months after my father's death, I continued to know nothing. Dad's last Will and Testament contained no mention of the family farm called Weeroona. My parents' decision to deny me an explanation of decisions on the property, and to deny me the pleasure of selecting even one small keepsake from the family home, was an overwhelming disappointment. The little Vegemite jar of coins that my Grandma

Alexander left with the words *'This is June's'*, 50 years before, would remain my most meaningful treasure. I felt sad for my children and grandchildren, as my loss of heritage was their loss, too.

However, as George and my children quickly reminded me: 'Look ahead to the sunshine, for NOW YOU ARE FREE.'

Much better that I turn from the sundown of my parents' lives and focus on the light that is my children and grandchildren. While my children are my carers, my grandchildren are my very special 'medicine'. When I feel a little down, I call Amanda, who lives 90 minutes away, and say, 'I need a Lachie fix' and we arrange a visit. 'Come on Grandma, let's play,' four-year-old Lachie says, and we do. Lachlan chats like a warbling magpie and insists on inclusiveness, whether we are piecing a jigsaw together, playing golf, exploring the adventure playground, watching *Thomas the Tank Engine* on my laptop or reading a book. My spirit soars when I call Amanda, and Lachie answers the phone and says, 'Grandma, I want to come for a sleepover at your home.' Ashton and Olivia Rose are babies yet but are always ready for a hug. The trusting acceptance of this new generation of young and lively treasures encourages me to live in the moment and look forward to many bright tomorrows. A testament to the power of love of my growing family is that I have required no antidepressants since the day my first grandchild was born.

When I departed full-time journalism I did not know that 'being brave and stepping out in faith' would lead to Salzburg, and to having new friends ranging from eating disorder sufferers to top academic researchers around the world; that following my attendance at the AED Conference in Salzburg I would be invited to join the AED's Patient Carer Task Force; or that I would travel to the United States in October 2010, to share my story with parents and friends at the annual NEDA Conference in New York City. Or that I would address researchers in the eating disorder teams led by Professor Daniel Le Grange at the University of Chicago, and Dr Walter Kaye at the University of California in San Diego.

Exciting progress is starting to occur in Australia, where I am involved in a project aimed at improving treatment and outcomes of eating disorders. In 2010 I began a three-year term as a co-chair on the Consumers and Carers Reference Group of the National Eating Disorders Collaboration (NEDC). This federally funded body aims to develop a nationally consistent approach to the prevention and management of eating disorders.

Stepping out in faith has opened up a world of understanding and hope. There is great comfort in knowing I am not alone. Largely through the Internet, since 2007, I have become part of a global community comprising researchers, clinicians, parents, sufferers and support groups—raising awareness of eating disorders. My children encourage this participation. Ben, in London, established my website (www.junealexander.com) and Rohan, in Melbourne, helps to maintains it.

Every forward step leads to another. The process of interviewing families for *My Kid Is Back* provided insight into the helplessness and frustration my parents must have felt when an eating disorder hijacked my mind and led me to behave out of character, causing them great embarrassment and shame over several decades. They did not know why I behaved as I did, and they did not know that when an eating disorder develops, every member of the family is affected in some way. They did not know that almost without exception, the family's inclusion is integral to the success of any treatment plan. They did not know that apart from assisting in the crucial re-feeding to a healthy weight, parents, siblings and partners can acquire skills to confront and defuse the illness behaviours, and along the way, gain a better understanding of themselves. I began to think my next book would provide support and guidance for families and carers of people with eating disorders.

However, on contacting international researchers to invite input, their overwhelmingly enthusiastic and strong response revealed a greater need: that of closing the gap between research and practice. Even today, many clinicians are unaware of the importance of family involvement and teamwork in treating eating disorders.

Thus the concept developed for *A Collaborative Approach to Eating Disorders*—to educate general practitioners and other frontline health professionals. My co-author for this international textbook is Professor Janet Treasure, an academic and consultant psychiatrist at Maudsley Hospital, South London and Maudsley National Health Service Trust, and Professor at the Institute of Psychiatry, King's College, London. This book emphasises and explains the importance of family involvement as part of a unified approach towards treatment and recovery.

Living in a culture where 'thin is good' and 'fat is bad', I frequently come across a misconception that only young people have eating disorders. Adults suffer, too—often since childhood and often in silence, feeling too ashamed, too filled with self-loathing, to share their dark secret and seek help. There is Jennifer, aged 38, who, until she heard my story, thought she was the only adult with an eating disorder. Her greatest sadness is that some members of her family of origin do not understand her illness and have alienated her from their life.

And there is Lorraine, age 48, who wrote:

Listening to your talk was the first time I have felt that someone knows what I'm going through. Until now I have never really told anyone the truth about my anorexia and bulimia which began to develop at age 10. I'd been treated for anxiety and depression but now I'm in treatment for my anorexia. I think my new doctor will help me get better.

I am glad I did not give up. I am grateful to doctors who said to 'walk tall' and to repeat over and over 'I deserve to be treated with respect'. I am glad I found the courage to reach out and accept the guidance of people who understood and believed not in my illness, but in me.

I feel content and rich in all that matters.

APPENDIX A: AN EATING DISORDER IN YOUR FAMILY

Eating disorders are serious, sometimes fatal, mental illnesses that usually develop in childhood or adolescence but affect people of all ages. Prompt intervention is crucial for the best hope of a full recovery.

Families can help! If worried about your child, educate yourself, especially on Family-Based Treatment, (sometimes called the Maudsley Approach), which is currently the most effective evidence-based treatment for children and adolescents with eating disorders. In this treatment, the family consults with a therapist who helps parents take an active and positive role in restoring their child's health. The later stages of treatment centre on re-establishing independent eating and addressing concerns that interfere with resumption of healthy life and development. With good treatment and family support, there is every reason to be hopeful. If you are a parent or partner and feel concerned, make an appointment with a doctor, preferably one with experience in treating eating disorders. Above all, trust your gut instinct and seek help immediately.

Signs of an Eating Disorder

You do not need to be thin to have an eating disorder. The manipulative illness comes in many shapes and forms. Anorexia nervosa is not the most common but is the most serious, with the highest death rate of any mental illness. It is usually very visible while bulimia nervosa and binge eating disorder are easier to hide. All three illnesses—together with variations under the umbrella of Eating Disorders Not Otherwise Specified (EDNOS)—are isolating for not only the sufferer but also the family.

Anorexia nervosa: This illness is characterised by self-starvation and excessive weight loss, or failure to make expected weight gains in children or younger adolescents. Worry signs: limiting food portions, cutting out groups of foods, avoiding family meals, exercising excessively, and becoming secretive. There may be anxiety or uneasiness about eating, or preoccupation with food, calories, or exercise.

Bulimia nervosa: This can be even more secretive, and any signs of bingeing and purging should be taken seriously. This illness is characterised by a cycle of bingeing and compensatory behaviours such as self-induced vomiting designed to undo or compensate for the effects of binge eating.

Binge eating disorder (BED): This illness is characterised by recurrent binge eating without the regular use of compensatory measures to counter the binge eating.

Causes of eating disorders

Pinpointing the root cause of an eating disorder remains an enigma, although research into genetics and neurobiology is beginning to shed light in amazing ways. Several factors play a role. Certain temperament and personality traits, including childhood anxiety, are common in those who develop anorexia nervosa:

- A person who is more sensitive to punishment or threat. There may be many causes of this excess sensitivity including genetic or even indirect difficulties experienced while in the womb or during childhood.
- An enhanced ability to perceive and analyse detail. This may be associated with a tendency to be focused and somewhat rigid.
- Stress (minor or major) can trigger onset, especially if it occurs during adolescence.

Many questions remain and misunderstandings abound. What is becoming clear is that although reversing this causal chain may not be possible, treatment can be effective if it focuses on factors that cause the illness to persist, rather than those that have caused it.

A Message for Parents, Partners and Close Others

Banish any assumption that you are to blame for the eating disorder. Instead, empower yourself with knowledge for you are an important part of the solution.

Re-feeding is a vital first step. Our brain needs nourishment to think clearly and rationally, and our bodies function best at a healthy weight. Stand up to the illness on the sufferer's behalf until weight is restored, and eating disorder behaviours diminish, and then remain vigilant.

You can help to interrupt the vicious circles that maintain the illness. Breaking through these traps will not be easy but the more people that are involved in this process, the better. You can gain skills to assist with the re-feeding and to recognise and respond to behaviours which are traits of the illness and not of your loved one.

ANIMAL METAPHORS HELP RESPONSES:

Eating disorder symptoms and their consequences may lead family members to react in particular ways, and the sufferer may feel increasingly alienated and stigmatised, retreating further into eating disorder behaviour.

Animal metaphors have been devised by Professor Janet Treasure and her research team at King's College, London, to illustrate how these instinctive reactions can be unhelpful. Altering these responses is a challenge but with awareness and skills training, life-changing results can be achieved for all members of the family:

The jellyfish—too much emotion and too little control.

The ostrich—avoids emotion.

The kangaroo—tries to make everything right.

The rhinoceros—uses force to win the day.

The terrier—uses persistence (often criticism).

Inspirational animal metaphors include:

The dolphin—just enough caring and control.

The St Bernard—just enough compassion and consistency.

My family of origin resembles the ostrich. Living in a family of ostriches, where emotions were not discussed, was difficult and confusing for a child who was very anxious. To survive, I had to climb a mountain to escape the triggers that fed my illness. Only since reaching the summit of that Recovery Mountain at age 55 in 2007, did I start learning of evidence-based research, and begin to understand WHY I had to climb that mountain. I wish my family had climbed with me.

I am fortunate, however, for my family of choice comprises a great line up of dolphins and St Bernard dogs. And this, together with a supportive, progressive health team and loyal friends, has made all the difference.

What does your family comprise?

Changing your behaviour and response requires hard work but the reward—that of saving and uniting your family—is priceless. In challenging times remember the adage, *'every mistake is a treasure'*—this must mean that I have many treasures—and as Martin Luther King said:

'You don't have to see the whole staircase—just take the first step.'

Empower Yourself

Information in this chapter is drawn from my experience and resources listed here. Explore the following links for further information on treatments and support on caring for a loved one with an eating disorder, and in seeking help for yourself: Remember that what works for one person may not work for another and therefore it is vital to persist until you find the right treatment for you.

AUSTRALIAN AND NEW ZEALAND-BASED SUPPORT:

Eating Disorder Association of New Zealand (EDANZ) provides support and advice for families and whanau of people with eating disorders throughout NZ. Ph: (09) 5222 679. www.ed.org.nz/

The Butterfly Foundation offers support for sufferers of eating disorders, their family and friends. A confidential, supportive National Support Line staffed by professionally trained personnel is available on 1800 ED HOPE (1800 33 4673), and on the website: http://thebutterflyfoundation.org.au or at support@thebutterflyfoundation.org.au

The Victorian Centre of Excellence in Eating Disorders (CEED), provides consultation, training and education to health professionals treating people with eating disorders and their families. www.ceed.org.au/about-eating-disorders/w1/i1001230/

The Centre for Eating and Dieting Disorders (CEDD) is a professional service and support centre, providing information for sufferers, families and carers. www.ceed.org.au

The Eating Disorders Foundation of Victoria is a source of support, information and advocacy for people living with eating disorders and their families. Confidential support and information is available from the Eating Disorders Helpline, 1300 550 236, or e-mail help@eatingdisorders.org.au. www.eatingdisorders.org.au

National Eating Disorders Collaboration (NEDC): This body aims to develop a nationally consistent approach to the prevention and management of eating disorders. www.nedc.com.au

Depression and Anxiety

beyondblue provides information on depression, anxiety and related disorders, available treatments and where to get help. Visit www.beyondblue.org.au or call 1300 22 4636.

headspace provides mental and health wellbeing support to people aged 12 to 25 years, and their families, across Australia. headspace helps find solutions for depression, anxiety, alcohol, self-harm and psychosis. Funded by the Australian Government, headspace is the National Youth Mental Health Foundation. www.headspace.org.au

WORLDWIDE EATING DISORDER SUPPORT

Beat is the leading charity based in the UK providing information, help and support for people affected by eating disorders and, in particular, anorexia and bulimia nervosa. www.b-eat.co.uk

Families Empowered and Supporting Treatment of Eating Disorders F.E.A.S.T. is an organisation of and for parents and caregivers to help loved ones recover from eating disorders by providing information and mutual support, promoting evidence-based treatment, and advocating for research and education to reduce the suffering associated with eating disorders. www.feast-ed.org

Maudsley Parents has information on eating disorders and family-based treatment, family stories of recovery, supportive parent-to-parent advice, and information for families who opt for Family-Based Treatment (Maudsley Approach). Maudsley Parents holds an annual conference to bring together leading researchers, families and community clinicians. www.maudsleyparents.org

National Association of Anorexia Nervosa and Associated Disorders (ANAD) works for the prevention and alleviation of eating disorders. www.anad.org

MentorCONNECT: This online eating disorders mentoring community provides mentor matching services, monthly teleconferences, weekly support groups and recovery blogs. www.mentorconnect-ed.org

National Eating Disorders Association (NEDA) is dedicated to supporting individuals and families affected by eating disorders. The website serves as an entry point for people to find information on eating disorders. NEDA's information and referral helpline guides people toward treatment options. NEDA's programs include toolkits for educators, parents and coaches and athletic trainers; an annual conference for families and professionals; sponsorship of National Eating Disorders Awareness Week; Young Investigator Research Grants; Parent, Family and Friends Network; and state legislative advocacy on behalf of families. www.nationaleatingdisorders.org

Proud2Bme: This free, anonymous online community forum for teenagers and adolescents, launched in the Netherlands in 2009, offers easy, direct access and attracts input from young women with and without an eating disorder. www.Proud2Bme.nl (English version via Google).

The National Eating Disorder Information Centre (NEDIC) is a Canadian, non-profit organisation providing information and resources on eating disorders and weight preoccupation and aiming to promote healthy lifestyles that allow people to be fully engaged in their lives. www.nedic.ca/

The You Are Not Alone Support Letter is a monthly recovery email newsletter filled with pro-recovery information. www.youarenotalonebook.com/supportletter.php

EATING DISORDER RESEARCH

King's College, London: the Institute of Psychiatry's eating disorders research team, led by Professor Janet Treasure, works to understand the causes of anorexia nervosa, bulimia nervosa and other eating disorders, and to develop improved treatments and ways of supporting carers: www.eatingresearch.com

University of California, San Diego: The Eating Disorders Treatment and Research Program is led by Dr Walter Kaye: http://eatingdisorders. ucsd.edu

University of Chicago, Chicago: Eating Disorders Program, led by Professor Daniel Le Grange: www.eatingdisorders.uchicago.edu

MY FAVOURITE BOOK RESOURCES

Help your teenager beat an eating disorder (Lock, J., and D. Le Grange. 2005) New York: Guilford Press.

My Kid is Back -- Empowering parents to beat anorexia nervosa (Alexander, J., and Le Grange, D.) Melbourne: Melbourne University Press, 2009.

Skills-based learning for caring for a loved one with an eating disorder: The New Maudsley Method (Treasure, J. et al., 2007)

MY FAVOURITE BLOGS

Are you "Eating With Your Anorexic" at: http://eatingwithyouranorexic.blogspot.com
Recovering from anorexia, one bite at a time: http://ed-bites.blogspot.com
Last but not least, my website:
http://www.junealexander.com

APPENDIX B: KEY STRATEGIES

The following strategies have been helpful in regaining my self and maintaining recovery. Some are essential, others are a matter of choice. I'm sure you can add to this list:

- Without fail, eat three meals and three snacks daily. Food is medicine.
- No calorie counting
- No weighing.
- Employment can provide a sense of purpose and self-worth at a time when nothing else does.
- Be candid with understanding family members and friends, as they provide ongoing support.
- Keep a journal and list daily accomplishments like planting seedlings, baking a cake, phoning a friend.
- When anxious, divide the day into quarters. Make it to 10.30am, and record feelings, again at 1pm, and so on.
- Pets are loyal and trusting friends. Cats and dogs are always ready for a hug.
- Repeat affirmations, such as 'Action beats anxiety' and 'I deserve to be treated with respect', at times of stress.
- Take up a hobby to help live in the moment. I chose photography, gardening, needlepoint and tapestry.
- Accept that prescription drugs, while often causing side effects, are at times essential.
- Separate self from illness. This self-awareness tool helps in recognising and avoiding people and situations that feed the illness. Practise this mindfulness at all times.
- Imagery is helpful. Sometimes I picture a bird, sometimes I picture a

raw egg, with the yolk my soul, and the white the world around me. No matter what goes on in the white, I strive to protect my yolk. Don't let it scramble.

- Be my own best friend. Would I want to bruise my best friend? No, no, no!
- Ask: Does this thought belong with my illness, or with me? If with the illness, hit the delete button fast.
- When feeling vulnerable, anxious and confused, allow trusted others to provide a lifeline to safety.
- Attend to feelings to diminish food as an issue.
- Daily walks. Embracing the beauty of nature is food for the soul.
- Test boundaries -- facing a stressful situation or fear achieves personal growth. I learnt that fear is a wall of nothing through which I can pass.
- Participate in safe, supportive social groups to connect and strengthen oneself.
- Acknowledge the right to be born, to live and to be happy; feel empowered by this.
- Embrace every moment; choose fulfilment and fun!
- Acknowledge the right to be treated with respect at all times.
- Remember that 'action beats anxiety' every time.
- Focus on being true to self and everything else will work out.

EPILOGUE

December 27, 2009

Dear Olivia Rose,

(Born December 23, 2009)

Right now you are a sweet wee babe wrapped snug in a rug and bunny suit. By the time you are old enough to read this letter, I picture you as a happy, bubbly little girl hopping from one foot to the other without a care in the world.

Olivia Rose, I will be forever telling you that you are very special and very loved. This is not because you are my first grand daughter, or because you were born on your great-grandmother Anne's birthday, but because you are you.

I cuddled and kissed you when you were a few hours' old. You were sound asleep and yet already radiated serenity and self-assurance. Somehow you indicated you are aware of your role in life, and that as you grow up you will quietly and confidently go about fulfilling it. I am sure I felt this as I held you, Olivia Rose. I didn't only wish it. My heart was filled with gladness.

When I was a little girl, I felt confused and unsure of myself. I enjoyed going to school, and did my best to get top marks but felt upset and cross with myself when I made a mistake. Then, at age 11, an event occurred which made me feel very anxious. I felt alone and scared, Olivia Rose, and an illness called anorexia nervosa developed in my brain. Basically, I felt afraid to eat. My mum and dad did not know what to do because back then, there was no family-based treatment like there is today.

Untreated, my anorexia set in and took over my thoughts. When I was a teenager, it evolved into bulimia, which meant I sometimes ate a lot and other times ate nothing. I felt very mixed up. I worried about little things and often felt sad. All up, I took 45 years to get on top of this sneaky bunch of thoughts that were not really me, playing havoc in my brain. I'm sure you agree this is a very long time to be bossed around but the important thing is that now I am free, Olivia Rose.

With much help from doctors and loving support from your Grandpa George, your mum Amanda and Uncles Shane, Rohan and Ben, I have picked up the threads of my childhood, and am having great fun catching up on living my life. You will see!

I have been free for four years now and keep healthy by taking care of my feelings as they arise – reaching out for help if I need to—and eating three meals and three snacks a day.

I feel like a bird soaring and swooping with glee in the clear sunny sky—such is my joy on escaping the darkness that was my illness.

When I started my recovery journey, I had to work out what thoughts belonged to me, and what thoughts belonged to my illness. I had to be brave enough to trust the thoughts that belonged to me and push the other thoughts away. I liken this process to that of a small bird with weak wings, flying for the first time. I dropped to the ground more than a few times but amazingly, my thoughts got stronger as I persevered and gradually learnt to trust myself and others. Now that my wings and sense of self are strong I am devoted to giving hope to others. I am flying around the world with this message.

My wish is for you and other children to grow up feeling happy and confident, feeling free to achieve your dreams and live your life to the full.

Olivia Rose, I am glad I did not give up, that I reached out and found help to beat my illness, because I am here to enjoy you and our beautiful family.

If you ever feel a worry coming on, remember that we are here to listen and to help.

And you might as well get used to it now—as your grandma I will be forever reminding you that to soar like a bird, you must simply eat three meals and three snacks every day!

Love always,
Grandma June

ACKNOWLEDGEMENTS

I thank my health support team, especially the president of the Mental Health Foundation of Australia, Professor Graham Burrows, for believing in me, often when I did not believe in myself, and guiding my recovery. I also thank my eating disorder therapist, Belinda Dalton; my GP, Dr Yael Bodian; neurosurgeon, Mr Graeme Brazenor; consulting psychiatrist, Mr George Wahr; and Uniting Church minister, Rev. Robin Prior.

I thank my children—Shane, Rohan, Ben and Amanda for your support and encouragement in writing this book. I thank my children's dad, George Coster, who deserves a gold medal for loving me when my illness raged, and for remaining a lifelong friend and confidant. I thank Aunty Gwen, for loving me 'all the way to the moon'.

I thank my friends—Helen Hammer (nee Edwards), American 'sister' Pat Hardesty (nee Edwards), Jane Ross, Lonnie Shepard, Mary Salce, Maree Wallace and Richard Lester.

I thank author Hazel Edwards, for friendship, mentorship, guidance and constant encouragement; Jodie Allen (Cambridge University) for reading my draft and providing helpful insights; and writer and friend Steve Cooper, for ensuring I had safe 'anchorage' while writing this book. I thank my son Rohan, always a wise sounding board, for reading the manuscript and providing feedback on behalf of his siblings. I thank John and his team at Bellarine Photographics, Drysdale for assistance in preparing the photographs.

I thank friends in the field of eating disorders, including Jane Cawley (Maudsley Parents), Laura Collins (F.E.A.S.T.), eating disorder blogger Carrie Arnold, Claire Vickery (The Butterfly Foundation), Lynn Grefe (National Eating Disorders Association, USA), Susan Ringwood (Beat, UK) and Mary Tantillo (New York). To professors Daniel Le Grange (The

University of Chicago), Janet Treasure and Professor Ivan Eisler (King's College, London), Dr Walter Kaye (University of California, San Diego) and other researchers and clinicians, families and sufferers around the world, thank you for believing in me.

Last but by no means least, I thank my literary agent Margaret Gee, and New Holland Publishers, for giving my memoir 'wings'.

First published in Australia in 2011 by
New Holland Publishers (Australia) Pty Ltd
Sydney • Auckland • London • Cape Town

1/66 Gibbes Street Chatswood NSW 2067 Australia
218 Lake Road Northcote Auckland New Zealand
86 Edgware Road London W2 2EA United Kingdom
80 McKenzie Street Cape Town 8001 South Africa

National Library of Australia Cataloging-in-Publication data:
Alexander, June, 1950-
A girl called Tim : escape from an eating disorder hell / June Alexander.
1st ed.
ISBN: 9781742570792 (pbk.)
Alexander, June, 1950- Anorexia nervosa--Patients--Australia--Biography. Anorexia in children--Patients--Care.
362.1989285262

Publisher: Fiona Schultz
Publishing Manager: Lliane Clarke
Project Editor: Rochelle Fernandez
Designer: Celeste Vlok
Cover Design: Emma Gough
Production Manager: Olga Dementiev
Printer: Toppan Leefung Printing Ltd

10 9 8 7 6 5 4 3 2 1